CASHING IN ON PAY EQUITY?
Supermarket Restructuring
and Gender Equality

CASHING IN ON PAY EQUITY?

SUPERMARKET RESTRUCTURING AND GENDER EQUALITY

by

Jan Kainer

SUMACH
PRESS

WOMEN'S ISSUES PUBLISHING PROGRAM

SERIES EDITOR BETH MCAULEY

NATIONAL LIBRARY OF CANADA CATALOGUING IN PUBLICATION DATA

Kainer, Jan, 1957-
Cashing in on pay equity? : supermarket restructuring and
gender equality

Includes bibliographical references and index.
ISBN 1-894549-14-7

1. Wages — Women — Canada. 2. Pay equity — Canada —
Case studies. 3. Wages — Grocery trade — Canada.
4. Supermarkets — Canada. I. Title.

HD6061.2.C3K35 2002   331.2'153'0971   C2002-900859-X

Copyright © 2002 Jan Kainer

Edited by Beth McAuley

*Sumach Press acknowledges the support of the Canada Council
for the Arts and the Ontario Arts Council
for our publishing program.*

ONTARIO ARTS COUNCIL
CONSEIL DES ARTS DE L'ONTARIO

Printed in Canada

Published by

SUMACH PRESS
1415 Bathurst Street, Suite 202
Toronto ON Canada M5R 3H8
sumachpress@on.aibn.com
www.sumachpress.com

For Diane Gale and Barbara Hall
who both gave ten years
to the pay equity struggle.

Contents

Acknowledgements

When I began this project over ten years ago, I was a doctoral student in the Department of Sociology at York University. I am now (thankfully) a faculty member in the Labour Studies Program in the Division of Social Science at York. Having made the transition from student to professor at the same university, I am in the position today of thanking my former thesis advisers, who are now my colleagues, for encouraging me to revise my dissertation into this book. I was fortunate to work with three women faculty whose area of expertise matched my interests perfectly. Pat Armstrong, my thesis supervisor, encouraged me to think about pay equity as a political and legal strategy. I am grateful to Ester Reiter for expressing enthusiasm about doing a project on the food retail industry, and assuring me that some people really do care about what goes on at the supermarket. Patricia McDermott encouraged me to pursue the topic of pay equity and suggested that I link the research question to feminist legal theory. She also took time to explain some of the technical details of Ontario's pay equity legislation to me that was crucial to my analysis of the pay equity application. Patricia and I worked on a research project on Sunday shopping while I was still a graduate student. The employment data on gender segregation in the Ontario retail sector collected for this project convinced me that the supermarket industry was well worth studying from the perspective of wage equity. Judy Fudge, who read the dissertation as an external examiner, was especially supportive of the idea of turning the research into a book.

Since completing my dissertation, other colleagues at York have expressed interest in my work. Deborah Barndt asked me to write an essay for her edited collection *Women Working the NAFTA Food Chain: Women, Food and Globalization*. Deborah introduced me to a number of scholars interested in food production and labour flexibility that furthered my understanding of the commodity food chain and renewed my enthusiasm for this study on the supermarket. Linda Briskin invited me to a workshop on women in unions where I presented a paper on pay equity in Saskatchewan. The Centre for Research on Work and Society at York University published two working papers directly related to my research. I thank Carla Lipsig-Mumme, Judy Fudge, Eric Tucker and Rosemary Warskett (who is co-author of the working paper on pay equity) for their support.

I am very appreciative to the workers who took time from their hectic lives to talk to me about their work experiences at the supermarket. A friendly cashier at my local Loblaws graciously offered me her telephone number and put me in touch with co-workers. While at a meeting of the Ontario Labour Board, I met a cashier who provided important details about the Miracle Food Mart strike and spoke to me at length about her experiences during and after the strike. Several interviews were conducted with a meat cutter whose critical commentary on labour and management relations proved invaluable. Some interviews were conducted with my labour studies students, whose willingness to provide me with names of co-workers, many of whom were long-term employees, helped enormously with the interview process.

Of course, without the interviews and information I received on pay equity from union officials at United Food and Commercial Workers Union and the Retail, Wholesale Department Store Union (now Retail Wholesale of the Canadian Auto Workers), this project would not have been possible. Several union officials at both retail unions granted me interviews, gave me copies of pay equity plans, and offered explanations about the pay equity process. Josefina Moruz at the UFCW National answered my questions about women in the union and sent me information on the Safeway strike, that continues in Thunder Bay.

A number of people helped me update the research for this book. Todd Marciano, a graduate of labour studies at York, provided invaluable research assistance on the supermarket industry. His enthusiasm for the project was evident from our first meeting when he launched into a lively and insightful discussion of the transformations in the supermarket. Harold Kim at Statistics Canada provided me with special runs on the Ontario retail labour force and Joseph Roman, a graduate student in political science, accessed tables from the Canadian census. Journalist Paul McKie alerted me to the Canada Safeway arbitration in Manitoba.

I was fortuante to have not one, but two, editors assist me in revising the manuscript. Beth McAuley at Sumach Press carefully edited the first draft and provided the basis for revising and updating the manuscript. Mary Anne Coffey offered friendly editorial suggestions throughout and assisted in reworking chapter seven. Her efficient and calm approach to the editing process was greatly appreciated.

Friends and family helped sustain me at different times and when I most needed it. I want to thank Tara Kainer, Anne McAllister, Marianne Parsons, Ann Porter and Stephanie Ross. A special thanks to Louise Leger for listening and for giving me articles from *Grocer Today* that simply are not available in Ontario. I am grateful to Janice Webster, Della McNeil and Aina Kagis for telling me about the Barbara Hall Nuttall human rights case, and to the Glebe choir who put up with my periodic absences.

Most of all, I am grateful to Bruce Smardon. He read through chapters, offered encouragement and helped me move forward whenever I ran into a conceptual roadblock. I never would have completed this project without his love and support.

This book is dedicated to former cashiers Diane Gale and Barbara Hall Nuttall who both filed human rights complaints of sex discrimination in employment against their supermarket employer. Both cases lasted ten years and neither was heard at a Board of Inquiry.

INTRODUCTION

PAY EQUITY has been on the political agenda of the women's movement in Canada for at least twenty-five years. In that time, political action by women and the labour movement has culminated in pay equity laws in six of ten Canadian provinces, an equal value provision at the federal level under the *Canadian Human Rights Act*, as well as many public policy and trade union initiatives aimed at eliminating gender-based wage discrimination in the workplace. Despite all of this activity, a gender-wage gap, ranging between 15 and 30 percent, continues to exist in Canada.[1] That gender-based wage discrimination persists in the labour market helps explain why labour and women's groups continue to demand equal pay for work of equal value in the workplace. Indeed, action around pay equity has not subsided. The Women's March Against Poverty in Quebec resulted in proactive pay equity legislation in that province in 1996. There were several strikes including an illegal strike by the Saskatchewan Union of Nurses in 1999. A five-week strike by Bell Canada telephone operators in the same year over an inadequate pay equity offer and a strike by teachers in Quebec in 2002 protesting the application of the *Pay Equity Act* in the province are further examples of the pay equity labour struggles in recent years.

Litigation over pay equity abounds. A recent court battle by retired women university professors at the University of Toronto claiming the university paid women professors much less than men of equal, or even lower, rank successfully concluded in 2002. After fourteen years, the Public Service Alliance of Canada, representing clerical workers in the federal service, finalized a major pay equity complaint in 1999; although a victory, issues around the settlement continue. After five years, Red Cross homemakers offering home-care services in Ontario concluded a $25 million out-of-court settlement. Bell Canada telephone workers await a decision from the Supreme Court of Canada over their federal human rights complaint, and several labour unions have launched a challenge under the Canadian Charter of Rights and Freedoms alleging that changes in government policy in Ontario on pay equity violates equality guarantees.[2]

Labour unions also continue the fight for pay equity. For example, in 2000, the Canadian Union of Public Employees (CUPE), the largest union in Canada, mounted a national campaign they called "Up with Women's Wages" to fashion bargaining strategies and revive ongoing gender pay struggles. The Canadian Labour Congress (CLC), the national union body representing labour in Canada, launched a Pay Equity Think Tank to revisit the problem of pay equity and re-examine its commitment to gender equity. In Saskatchewan, CUPE, the Saskatchewan Government Employees Union and the Service Employees International Union have combined forces to lead a pay equity struggle for women working in social service agencies.[3]

In spite of these struggles, the need for legislated pay equity has fallen out of favour under the politics of neo-liberalism. Attempts to introduce pay equity law in the provinces of British Columbia and Saskatchewan failed, and there are concerns that the Federal Task Force, appointed in 2001 to review the equal value clause (section 11) in the federal *Human Rights Act,* will not recommend proactive or mandated pay equity. Given the recent record on pay equity, analysts are now asking whether pay equity policy actually works. Does pay equity law result in better pay for women?

Cashing In On Pay Equity? helps to shed light on the problems of successfully achieving gender-wage equity in the workplace. Why does the gender-wage gap continue to exist? Is pay equity law an effective tool for eliminating workplace practices that contribute to gender-wage inequality? To date, a great deal of attention has been paid to the problem of implementing legislated pay equity. This book contributes to a perspective on this issue and provides a critical analysis of the utility of law in promoting social change.

Pay Equity at the Supermarket

This case study of pay equity implementation in Ontario supermarkets examines the law as it operates in practice. It investigates the social actors such as the retail unions, the economic and industry context in which pay equity was applied and the content of Ontario's pay equity law to understand the pay equity outcome. This combination of factors, including intense industry competition, economic restructuring and business unionism, worked together to prevent a more favourable pay equity result.

Not only does this book evaluate the success and failure of applying pay equity legislation, it also investigates the importance of the pay equity strategy at a conceptual and political level. What are the feminist principles that inform the struggle for equal pay for work of equal value? Pay equity has become strongly identified as depicting a narrowly defined procedural reform focused on technical issues like job evaluation. However, I analyze the reform from the standpoint of its feminist political agenda. Its political goals, I suggest, are grounded in a discourse that has the capacity to forcefully challenge the status quo. Taking issue with analysts who argue that pay equity endorses a liberal view of equality, I argue that the strength of pay equity is its potential to question and critique (1) the liberal view of the market, (2) the liberal conception of the abstract individual (encompassing a critique of the white male standard) and (3) the liberal premise of equality of opportunity (that ignores systemic sources of employment discrimination).

Pay equity's political agenda is based on an understanding that a gendered and, to a lesser extent, a racialized labour market upholds and privileges white male standards. This political program therefore recognizes that systemic discrimination at the workplace is responsible for women's low pay. Pay equity is most likely to meet with success when the reform effectively challenges liberal assumptions about the market, the male worker and systemic forms of employment discrimination. Conversely, it is unlikely to be an effective reform strategy when liberal ideologies are not adequately challenged. The difficulties of putting pay equity's vision of gender-wage equity into practice is the greatest stumbling block to achieving substantive equality for women in the workplace.

Using this analysis as my conceptual framework, I begin by analyzing Ontario's pay equity legislation to determine whether the law embodies key feminist demands for gender-wage equality. An examination of Ontario's legislation shows that while the *Pay Equity Act* is complex, contradictory and vague, its provisions are flexible enough to empower politically motivated groups to press for progressive change. This is not to say Ontario's Act is problem-free, but rather the legislation could be interpreted to produce desired outcomes for those with the political will and resources wishing to do so.

An investigation of the supermarket industry follows this analysis. The retail food sector is one of the largest employers in Canada with a significant percentage of female workers and a fairly high level of unionization, compared with other subsectors in the private service economy. In addition, supermarkets have long been characterized by a highly gender-segregated and white workforce with men concentrated in higher-paid managerial and production work and women in lower-paid service jobs. Today the majority of employees at the supermarket are women, many of whom work part-time as cashiers, meat wrappers and service clerks. Although part-time (flexible) work and gender segregation are not new to grocery retailing, the corporate drive for greater labour flexibility and cheaper wages intensified in the past decade in response to changing market conditions accompanied by post-Fordism, a term used to describe the changes taking place under economic globalization. As many analysts point out, a consequence of economic globalization is the rise of insecure or precarious work arrangements, such as part-time employment, that coincide with capital's need to improve productivity while reducing labour costs.

Beginning in the 1990s, Ontario supermarkets underwent significant reorganization as a consequence of post-Fordist pressures; retail management demanded significant wage concessions and greater labour flexibility from retail unions. This analysis is an account of pay equity implementation at the moment this restructuring takes place. It details the implications of this reorganization on retail food workers, especially the feminized workforce that is most in need of wage improvements. Did pay equity, then, achieve positive economic outcomes for women workers? I argue that despite union representation and a pay equity law that had the *potential* to deliver gender-wage fairness, obvious gender-wage inequities remained in the supermarket following pay equity. This failure occurred because arguments concerning the market, the male standard and systemic discrimination were not sufficiently advanced and fully articulated in the pay equity implementation.

The Market, the Male Standard and Systemic Discrimination

With respect to challenging wage discrimination in the labour market, I found that employers and the unions accepted the view that industry competition and global restructuring necessitated maintaining the status quo. For instance, the industry standard for wages paid to the part-time classification was not adjusted upward. The notion that pay equity should operate to revalue and upgrade wage levels for the part-time (female predominant) category was never seriously considered by the retail unions. As a consequence, this job classification was firmly entrenched as a low-wage category and part-timers continue to be used by employers as a flexible workforce.

Indeed, following pay equity implementation, industry restructuring destabilized wage structures in a way that had an especially detrimental effect on women. At most of the retail chains, workers experienced wage reductions as a result of concession bargaining, undercutting any benefits accruing from pay equity reform. The contradictory effect of pay equity is best illustrated in the example of the full-time cashiers, meat wrappers and deli attendants at Miracle Food Mart who received a fairly substantial pay-equity wage adjustment, but found that their jobs disappeared after a three-month-long labour dispute. The retail union did not adequately protect its female members who got singled out for layoff by an employer intent on reducing costs in a time of intense market competition. As a consequence, the gendered impact of economic restructuring was not curtailed by pay equity policy in this instance.

Nor were male standards or male norms operating in the supermarket effectively challenged under pay equity. Masculine definitions of work were inadequately challenged in the job evaluation process, which resulted in the female-predominant job classes of head cashier and deli manager being unfairly evaluated. Part-time workers, too, were not seen to be primary members of the workforce, since they deviated from the male norm of a "real" worker who is employed full time.

Lastly, many of the sources of systemic gender discrimination in the supermarket were not analyzed or questioned in the pay equity implementation. The fact that seniority systems advantage male workers was not acknowledged by the retail unions, despite evidence from an Ontario human rights complaint filed by cashier Diane Gale indicating that seniority systems are gender-biased in the Miracle Food Mart supermarket chain. It is very likely that merit systems also operate to disadvantage women, but the issue of merit pay was not investigated from a gender perspective in the equal pay evaluation. Both seniority and merit pay continue to maintain and reinforce systemic gender discrimination at some Ontario supermarket chains. A recent human rights complaint, discussed in chapter 9, filed by cashier Barbara Hall Nuttall in Saskatchewan alleges that cashiers at Safeway are paid less than stock clerks for work of equal value and that women are given less opportunity for full-time employment than men. Another compaint in Ontario, which, like Diane Gale's, identified a gender-based wage gap and barriers to promotion for women was never heard at a Board of Inquiry, despite ample evidence of systemic gender discrimination in employment.

While the objective of pay equity policy is to eliminate the wage-setting and workplace practices that contribute to gender-wage inequality, an analysis of the application of Ontario's pay equity legislation in the supermarket shows that the structural factors contributing to women's wage inequality were not dissolved. Both the retail unions and retail food corporations stood to benefit from maintaining the status quo. Ontario's pay equity law was not interpreted and applied in a progressive direction, rather its potential for promoting equity was squandered by the retail unions and corporations. In fact, the law was even misinterpreted and applied in ways that violated certain sections of the Act.

By examining law as it operates in practice, we can better determine why a legal reform either meets with success or fails. An effective equality strategy must take into account women's situated realities. As feminist legal theorists argue, an equality definition that rests on abstract, universal principles, like that proposed by the "sameness" or "difference" equality formulations, cannot achieve substantive equality for women. Rather, what is needed is an equality strategy that is flexible enough to ensure that feminist engagement with the law can present possibilities for social change. Women's equality cannot take place in the abstract — only through engaging in concrete political struggle can we further women's equality rights claims.

Chapter 1 of *Cashing In On Pay Equity?* reviews major theoretical debates advanced by legal feminists. Much of this literature focuses on whether legal efforts should be directed towards constructing a view of women as being "different" or the "same" as men. In the debate on "sameness" and "difference," feminists argued that it is important to move away from discussion of abstract definitions of equality, to an analysis of how equality claims are defined in particular social contexts. At issue is how specific social or institutional arrangements may enhance, or detract from, gender equality goals. In examining the limitations of "difference" and "sameness" equality arguments, it became evident, to some feminists, that approaches to equality that are informed by liberal doctrine are seriously flawed. These theoretical issues inform my discussion of pay equity as a feminist legal strategy in chapter 2. Of particular concern is whether pay equity offers a political agenda that can confront liberalism. I argue that the discourse of equal pay challenges dominant liberal conceptions of the market and the (masculine) individual by stressing the role of systemic discrimination in producing gender-wage inequities.

Chapter 3 explores the historical legal context of equal pay reform in Ontario. It examines the political struggle by pay equity activists to define Ontario's *Pay Equity Act* and finds that their efforts to advance a progressive and coherent law were compromised in the legislative phase of the reform. This political resolution resulted in legislation that is riddled with technical problems and inconsistencies, especially concerning legal definitions within the Act. While Ontario's legislation operates to "contain" pay equity in certain respects, the contradictory or ambiguous technical definitions in the legislation also provide an opening to press for gender-wage equality.

The following three chapters provide background on the economic and industry context of the food retail sector. Chapter 4 examines the historical development of the gender division of labour in grocery retail, chapter 5 investigates the history of unionization, and chapter 6 provides a discussion of women's labour participation in the supermarket. These chapters demonstrate how the competitive pressures and corporate strategies within retail food determined women's location within supermarket retailing, why the retail unions developed a conservative business unionist philosophy, and why women continue to be used as a flexible (part-time) labour force in the industry.

In recent years, the supermarket sector has become increasingly fragmented with the growth of franchises and independents, changes which have pressured corporate chains to compete against lower labour costs and to introduce flexiblization strategies. These policies have had a particularly detrimental effect on women who mostly work part-time because corporations want to maintain maximum flexibility over the labour supply. Within this context, pay equity negotiations in the supermarket chains took on added importance. How influential were company concerns in limiting the wage bill in the pay equity implementation?

The answer to this question is provided in chapter 7, where I discuss the process of pay equity negotiations at three Ontario supermarket chains — Miracle Food Mart, A&P Dominion Stores and Loblaws Supermarkets Limited. The outcome of pay equity negotiations operated negatively for a large percentage of the female workforce. The union culture, the labour leadership and corporate management played an important part in women workers receiving a low level of wage equity. Specifically, the pay equity evaluation committees were unwilling to challenge common cultural meanings of women's work. The male bias of the unions and management was particularly evident in their view of the part-time women workers who were not awarded pay increases in the equal pay implementation. In addition, the pay equity legislation was interpreted and applied in a way that undermined the potential of Ontario's *Pay Equity Act* to redress gender-based wage inequities.

Chapter 8 examines the changes in the supermarket industry after the pay equity implementation. Within a few years following pay equity, massive industry restructuring in the supermarket sector took hold in Ontario, and the retail unions found themselves negotiating collective agreements in a new economic context. A major strike at Miracle Food Mart resulted in concessions or "take backs" that undercut pay equity gains. This negotiated settlement set the tone for other settlements in Ontario.

Chapter 9 assesses the full implications of the equal pay exercise in food retail. Did the parties involved in the pay equity exercise recognize the roots of systemic gender discrimination and try to redress unequal wages paid to women? The whole approach to negotiating pay equity indicates that a gendered discourse of the "woman worker" informed the implementation. The potential of the reform effort to breakdown gender-wage hierarchies and to counter the effects of economic restructuring was not accomplished, and the capacity for pay equity to challenge established market wages paid to women was not realized in the supermarket case.

The failure to achieve pay equity in the supermarket industry points to the difficulties of challenging liberal notions of the individual in the market. As was shown by the logic shared by corporate management and the unions concerning pay equity, there was an inability to see that women's unequal position in the supermarket was not a matter of individual choice but the result of an entrenched structure of unequal gender relations. In the absence of a strong pay equity movement that promotes a vision of gender equity and places this at the forefront of its political program, the possibilities for positive social change are doubtful. As is shown in this case study, it is not enough to simply pass a law; fundamental social relations must be challenged.

NOTES

1. *Pay Equity: Some Basics* (Ottawa: Pay Equity Task Force, March 2002), 4.
2. See Judy Fudge, "Paradoxes of Pay Equity: Reflections on the Law and the Market in *Bell Canada* and the *Public Service Alliance of Canada*," *Canadian Journal of Women and the Law* 12 (2000), 313-44; Michelle Landsberg, "Pension Controversy Hurts U. of T.'s Credibility," *The Toronto Star*, 18 September 2001, A2; "Toronto Settles Pension Dispute", *CAUT (Canadian Association of University Teachers) Bulletin* 49, no. 5, (May 2002) A1, A12. The university women retirees won a successful mediated settlement resulting in compensation for sixty faculty, with the university acknowledging that systemic sex discrimination operated at the university; Joel Rubin, "Red Cross Homeworkers Facing Layoff Over Pay Equity Law Requires 45 Percent Wage Increase," *The Toronto Star*, 1 October 1997, A8; Jan Kainer and Rosemary Warskett, "Introduction to the Pay Equity and Resource Guide," *Just Labour* 1 (2002); Peter Gorrie, "Undervalued, Underpaid as Profits Roll In," *The Toronto Star*, 27 April 2002, A1, A28. The Charter challenge is led by the Service Employees International Union, the Canadian Union of Public Employees and effects women workers employed in seniors' homes, as well as other related industries.
3. Doreen Meyer, "Up With Women's Wages: The Fight for Fair Pay," *Our Times* 21, no. 1 (2002), 23-7. Meyer points out that a majority of workers in social service agencies earn between $7 and $9 per hour. The CLC Pay Equity Think Tank was formed in response to the Pay Equity Task Force review of section 11 of the federal *Human Rights Act* (Jan Kainer and Warskett, "Introduction to the Pay Equity and Resource Guide").

Chapter One

THE HAZARDS OF
FEMINIST LEGAL STRATEGY

THIS CHAPTER EXAMINES feminist legal theorists analyses of the law in connection to problems of feminist politics.[1] Pay equity proponents often advocate a legal route to achieving gender wage equity. Yet there is extensive debate among feminists as to whether the law provides an avenue to achieve meaningful social change. Since pay equity can be accomplished without relying on legislative reform (e.g., collective bargaining, gender-based salary audit), questions are raised about the role of the law in meeting pay equity goals. Legal theorists are divided on the question of using the law to effect substantive social change, and feminist legal theorists query whether a liberal legal framework can properly address the problem of sex discrimination under capitalism. Debates within feminist legal theory point to the limitations of liberal legalism in advancing equality for women.

This overview of feminist legal theory concentrates on the "equality versus difference" controversy that dominated early debates on sex discrimination and the law. The "equality versus difference" debate not only captured the central limitations of operating within a liberal framework, it also initiated discussion of alternative feminist legal perspectives to advancing women's equality. In this debate, emphasis is placed on contextual analyses to show

how complex power dynamics influence rights claims. The themes emerging from feminist discussions of equality law lay the groundwork for my discussion of the equal pay strategy in chapter 2. At issue is whether there is a convergence between pay equity strategy and liberal legal reform. Feminist scholars have argued that pay equity relies on a formal equality model and have criticized the reform for incorporating liberal definitions of equality.[2]

Before undertaking a detailed analysis of the pay equity legal strategy, we need to clarify the meaning of liberal legalism, spell out its basic tenets and review prevalent criticisms of liberal equality offered by legal feminists. This review of the "equality versus difference" controversy shows that the discussion has run a dead-end course. Feminists' preoccupation with trying to specify the importance of sameness or difference (to the male norm) led theorists away from establishing a meaningful definition of equality for women in liberal society. In response to the "equality versus difference" dilemma, feminist legal scholars emphasize the importance of contextual analyses to frame equality arguments. Greater attention is placed on the particularities of women's social circumstances including the diverse experiences of women based on class, race, ethnicity, sexual orientation and other social distinctions.[3] This attention to diversity led theorists to disavow analyses based on the commonality of women's experience, raising new questions about the implications of feminist theoretical engagement on political activism. In addition, the emphasis on social context shifted the debate to an analysis of the social meanings of gender difference and how these impact on equality. In spite of this emphasis on social context, however, feminist legal theorists tend to neglect the role of the political economy in shaping equality struggles.

Analyses of the law are often related to discussion of court decisions and are not situated within the economy or the wider political realm in which equality rights are exercised. In the context of neoliberal globalization, pay equity struggles are severely effected by broader economic and social forces. Today, pay equity is operating in an entirely different set of economic and political conditions than that of the 1970s or 1980s, when the reform was at its height.

Gender wage equity cannot be divorced from an analysis of the changing market and political circumstances in which women's struggles for equality in employment are being fought for. As chapters 4, 5 and 6 will show, pay equity is constrained by industry restructuring that is rapidly altering the work arrangements for women and men. Equality definitions and equality strategies cannot be detached from the new realities of the globalized workplace.

Equality versus Difference:
The Problem of Legal Strategy

Theorizing equality within the parameters of liberalism poses a major dilemma for feminist legal scholars.[4] Classical liberal ideology premises equality on the belief that all persons are equal and have equal rights under the law. Yet the principle of equal rights is complicated by the fact that women are different from men biologically and in social terms. Given the differences between men and women in society, it has sometimes been difficult to know how to apply the law so that women are given the same rights as men within the meaning of liberal rights discourse. A major controversy within feminist legal theory emerging from this "equality dilemma" is the "equal treatment" versus "special treatment" debate. That is, should women be viewed as having similar characteristics as men and on that basis be granted equality, or do women's differences require them to have special protections under the law?

The "equality versus difference" dispute was first voiced by nineteenth-century women's groups concerned about the long-term consequences of protective labour legislation on women's economic and legal status. In Canada and the U.S., statutes were passed regulating maximum hours of work, minimum wages and working conditions.[5] Legal distinctions were made between male, female and (earlier in the century) child labour. The rationale behind distinguishing women as a separate legal category was the notion that women, as mothers, needed special protections. While male trade unionists were concerned that preferential treatment for women may have negative effects on the economic competition between male and female labourers, women's groups debated the advantages and disadvantages of sex-specific legislation more broadly.[6]

In the U.S., feminists questioned the potential effects of protective legislation on women's equality rights. Opponents of protective labour legislation were afraid that presenting women as vulnerable and dependent would have an adverse effect on equality arguments in the courts. If women were regarded as "different" from men then it would be difficult to argue that women deserved the same rights and privileges as men's *equals*. Moreover, special protections could make employers reluctant to hire women. On the other hand, feminists supporting labour reforms believed women's heavy domestic burden, in addition to harsh working conditions and long hours at the workplace, necessitated special protections for women. Thus, proponents of gender-specific legislation were concerned to improve the actual life conditions for working-class women, whereas critics of the reform believed equality was better achieved through pursuing formal equality rights as a legal strategy.[7]

What is interesting about this particular strand of the "equality versus difference" debate is the extent to which the conflicting arguments around labour reform reflected the contradictory consequences of sex-specific labour legislation. While the obvious goal of women reformers was to protect women's health and well-being as workers and mothers, the overall effect of labour protections worked against women. Mimi Abromovitz summarizes the enduring consequences of labour protections on women's position in the home and labour market:

> Protective labor legislation based on motherhood, female frailty and special privileges for the home became a justification for barring women from certain occupations (particularly the higher paid ones occupied by men) and segregating women into lower paying "women's jobs." It contributed to the preservation of a sex-segregated labor market, the relative subordination of women to men, and the overall marginalization of women workers.[8]

Part of the legacy of protective labour legislation is that it reinforced the "ideology of separate spheres" or the belief that women belong in the home as wives and mothers whereas men's primary role is that of provider. On the basis of this ideological view, courts invoked the concept of "gender difference" to justify differential treatment of women. The effect was to relegate men to positions that encouraged their maximum participation in the labour force while women were encouraged to remain in the domestic sphere. For example, men were expected to engage in night work, shift work and "dangerous jobs" that were seen to be unsuitable for women. Some believe protective labour legislation operated as a method to protect men's earnings, rather than as a mechanism to protect women's health.[9] Subsequently, feminists became wary of introducing labour force protections for women because of the negative repercussions that may result. Later on in the twentieth century, for instance, the demand that men and women be paid equal wages for performing identical work had the paradoxical effect of reinforcing sex segregation at the workplace and defining women into the home because employers preferred to hire male employees.[10]

A central difficulty in arguing special female labour protections, then, was a growing realization of the uncertain material effects such reforms would have on women. Ironically, protections often had the opposite effect of undermining instead of strengthening women's labour market position. Ideologically, the dichotomy drawn between male and female social roles served to reinforce women's subordinate status. In certain important respects many of the issues associated with special labour protections for women were reproduced in the twentieth century. As late as the 1970s and 1980s, feminist legal scholars in the U.S. engaged in acrimonious debate over the special treatment-equal treatment approach as it relates to the issue of pregnancy-leave protections.[11]

Pregnant versus Non-Pregnant Persons

Under the equal protection doctrine in the United States, equality is granted to individuals who are "similarly situated with respect to the purpose of the law to other individuals."[12] This equality standard is based on the premise that "likes are treated alike." Women's capacity to procreate has engendered serious problems for equal rights claims because it must be demonstrated how pregnant women are similarly situated in comparison with men. The obvious fact that women give birth, and men do not, creates enormous difficulties within this "equal by male comparison" framework. Contemporary feminist legal theorists attempting to secure equal protection for women in the context of pregnancy claims were faced with the same dilemma as nineteenth-century feminists struggling for labour reform. Feminists became divided over the best strategy to achieve women's equality. Is it better to argue for equal rights principles as defined by the male norm, or is true equality for women obtained only through recognizing women's "special needs"? Again, the question is raised as to whether women should be seen as "different" from men and on that basis receive accommodation to ensure equal treatment, or, alternatively, should arguments be put forward that support how women are similar to men, thereby granting women equal rights and privileges?[13]

On the side of "equal treatment," Wendy Williams argues the sameness approach avoids sex stereotyping because it explicitly rejects assumptions about motherhood or fatherhood. She believes in treating pregnancy as a disability, thereby allowing women the same benefits of any worker faced with a disability claim.[14] For Williams, the strength of the equal treatment approach is that it prevents marginalization of women at the workplace. In particular, the equality model avoids the problems that arose in the nineteenth century over sex-specific protections because it does not premise disability claims on the basis of special privileges for women that entails extra costs for employers. Although Williams believes an equality approach to the law is the best way forward to eliminating sex discrimination, she is cautious about the possibilities of achieving progressive change within a legal framework:

> An anti-discrimination provision is a device for telling legislatures, governments and designated others what they may not do, thus setting parameters within which they must operate. It does not, and cannot, do the basic job of readjusting the social order. Fundamentally, the courts are not the place to seek such important changes.[15]

Williams thus does not subscribe to the view that the law has a transformative effect on social or gender relations.

Contrary to Williams, feminist legal scholars supporting the special treatment approach believe the law can operate to improve women's social and economic status. A central difference between the special treatment–equal treatment models of women's equality rests on differing assumptions about what the law can achieve to alter the concrete, material reality of women's social situation. Those supporting the special treatment approach argue that social arrangements must be altered to produce equality of treatment for women. Equality can only be achieved through modifying institutions to accommodate women and minorities special circumstances. As Linda Krieger and Patricia Cooney point out, "to view equality as the right to equal treatment as an equal, focuses on equality of effect rather than equality of treatment [as an individual]."[16] Here, emphasis is placed on developing social policy that promotes conditions that ensure disadvantaged groups receive the same treatment as the more advantaged in society.

Regarding pregnancy leave protections, preferential treatment adherents argue for "special rights" to secure women's equality. That is, pregnant women should be provided accommodations to ensure they are granted equivalent opportunities with men at the workplace. In addition, supporters of pregnancy-leave provisions believe pregnancy should not be viewed as a disability but recognized as women's special capacity to reproduce. Unlike the equal treatment perspective, the "difference" approach does not accept that women conform to a male norm in order to guarantee women's equality. Moreover, the difference approach strives to implement reforms that permit equality of outcome or equality of condition, as compared to granting formal equality rights that offer individuals equal treatment without ameliorating the material circumstances that underlie structured inequality.

Although the "difference" approach addresses the material realities of women's unequal position in society, the special treatment strategy is problematic in that it can open the door to discriminatory treatment. The potential drawbacks of preferential treatment for pregnancy harkens back to the same issues as were apparent in the case of protective labour legislation. Treating women differently from men may create a situation in which women are not accepted as equals, and thus special treatment may result in unequal treatment. For example, courts often use biological difference to justify differential treatment, yet this biological difference is used against women to support arguments that prevent women from receiving equal opportunities.[17] And as Denise Reaume explains,

> ... differences are usually regarded as justifications for disadvantageous treatment for women. Sometimes this treatment means their exclusion from benefits and opportunities open to men; sometimes it means the provision of "special treatment" that marginally compensates them for some substantial exclusion elsewhere. By contrast, whenever women do get some benefit that men do not it is usually decided that women do not differ from men substantially to justify such differential treatment.[18]

The struggles over gender-specific labour legislation and pregnancy protections uncovered another crucial problem for feminist legal strategists. In deciding whether feminists should demand either equal or preferential treatment, there arose the dilemma of determining what specifically is different or similar about women when compared to men. Along the dimension of preferential treatment, it needs to be determined what is unique about women that requires special accommodation. Alternatively, if a sameness strategy is followed it needs to be determined how or in what way women are similar to men. Several authors commenting on the "equality versus sameness" approaches have observed there is little consensus by legal authorities as to the definition of "sameness" or "difference."[19] Many of these authors have remarked that trying to argue equality in terms of "sameness" or "difference" categories fails to take account of the social context that gives rise to an equality claim. Courts have tended to regard sex differences as biological and immutable rather than socially constructed. Consequently, sex equality arguments that rely on abstract categories or typologies founder because the specific social conditions underlying women's disadvantaged status are not emphasized.

Feminists are thus left with the intractable problem of how to pursue women's equality from a perspective that recognizes their unequal social position yet insists on women's equal treatment as defined by liberal doctrine. While "sameness" arguments are inadequate because they overlook the relevance of gender in structuring inequality in society, forms of special treatment that attempt to improve the social position of women may actually reinforce women's subordinate status. The difficulties of attempting to satisfy the "equality dilemma" has led to further criticism of the liberal approach and encouraged new perspectives on theorizing women's equality. Many critiques of liberalism by feminists advance the notion that rights claims are abstracted from their social context. As mentioned above, various criticisms aimed at the "equality versus difference" debate address the problem of searching for sameness or difference categories irrespective of the broader social context in which sex equality claims are situated. Emerging from this discussion is a concern about pursuing equality based on the concept of rights. Feminist analyses of liberal legal approaches take the view that greater emphasis needs to be placed on knowing women's social situation in order to formulate a theory of women's equality. Catharine MacKinnon, Deborah Rhode and Carol Smart are legal theorists who attempt to transcend the problems of the "equality versus difference" dilemma by putting forward an alternative feminist strategy that centres on power relations in society.

MacKinnon: Male Power is Systemic

Catharine MacKinnon argues that focusing on gender difference ignores the important fact that men and women do not share equal power in social life. Neither the sameness nor difference perspectives, MacKinnon contends, can ensure women's equality because the assumptions underlying sex equality can never be fulfilled: "to require that one be the same as those who set the standard — those which one already is socially defined as different from — simply means that sex equality is conceptually designed never to be achieved."[20] Either women must be seen to be the same as men (which assumes women be similarly situated to men) or women's difference from men must be recognized (which deliberately sets them apart from the male norm and assumes women are socially unequal to men). Taken together, these models demonstrate the contradictions contained in sex equality issues:

> The legal mandate of equal treatment — both a systemic norm and a specific legal doctrine — becomes a matter of treating likes alike and unlikes unlike, while the sexes are socially defined by their mutual unlikeness ... a woman is legally recognized to be discriminated against on the basis of sex only when she can first be said to be the same as a man. A built-in tension thus exists between this concept of equality which presupposes sameness, and this concept of sex, which presupposes difference. Difference defines the states approach to sex equality epistemologically and doctrinally. Sex equality becomes a contradiction in terms, something of an oxymoron.[21]

The core of the contradiction in sex equality law is rooted in references to a male norm — if equality is "sameness to maleness" and sex is "difference from maleness," then neither the "sex" and "equality" twain shall meet as it is impossible to be simultaneously the same and different from men. Following either approach puts women in a double-bind because both accept men as the yardstick by which sex equality is measured. Viewed from this perspective, sex equality law is not in actual fact "gender neutral" but is grounded on male values:

> In its mainstream interpretation, this [sex equality] law is neutral: it gives little to women that it cannot also give to men, maintaining sex inequality while appearing to address it. Gender, thus elaborated and sustained by law, is maintained as a division of power.[22]

According to MacKinnon, sex equality law overlooks the fact that gender differentiation structurally orders gender hierarchy — that men are in a position to define what is valued in society. Men's power to shape reality extends to the very foundation of liberalism. Liberal epistemology is premised on a male viewpoint of what it is to be a person, an individual, a worker or a citizen. Basic philosophical assumptions concerning the nature of knowledge, reason and ontological views of the self rest on male constructions. The law assumes a "reasonable person" or legal subject who is "endowed with a specific set of characteristics that are presented as universal ... he is deemed to be able-bodied, autonomous, rational, educated, monied, competitive ..."[23] The market also assumes an abstract (male) individual who is free (of familial or community obligations) to pursue his self-interest. By accepting "objectivity as its norm," the state too embraces the male perspective of rationality. For MacKinnon, the male viewpoint is the source of male power which she argues is *systemic and hegemonic.*[24]

In order to eliminate male power and privilege, it is necessary to develop a feminist standpoint, according to MacKinnon. Since abstract liberal ideals do not reflect women's experience, feminists have to frame their own version of reality rather than correct sex bias to meet male standards. Consciousness-raising provides a method upon which women can resist taken-for-granted assumptions about male definitions of reality. Only a feminist standpoint can challenge male views embedded in law. For instance, the male viewpoint embodied in liberalism defines the legal subject or individual as rational, freely acting and autonomous of any group affiliation. The legal subject is "decontextualized" from the broader society and differences among individuals based on group or cultural membership are not acknowledged. Liberalism attempts to transcend difference by stressing universal principles of equality, and by maintaining that particular differences (based on race or gender) between individuals does not affect one's political or legal status.[25] This view runs counter to women's perspective that subscribes to a group identity and recognizes human behaviour as responding to social conditions that have been historically constituted. The feminist viewpoint does not perceive individuals abstracted from their social context but rather understands people as operating within a particular set of social relations.[26]

The feminist standpoint is able to effectively confront the male perspective because it is based on concrete analysis of women's lived experience. Abstract definitions of equality can therefore be countered with women's substantive view of equality. Critics of liberalism are at pains to show how discrimination is systematically embedded in social relations of domination. Liberalism's weakest link is its inability to acknowledge systemic or structural forms of discrimination. According to MacKinnon, feminist jurisprudence must be devised to counter male hegemony that maintains systemic inequality between men and women. As we will see in the following chapter, pay equity proponents challenge several male constructs embedded in the liberal paradigm by appealing to a "feminist standpoint" in debates on pay equity.

Ironically, the promise of equality presumed in liberalism presents the possibility of pressing the state to promote women's substantive equality:

> Equality is [also] what society holds that women have already, and therefore guarantees women by positive law. The law of equality, statutory and constitutional, therefore provides a peculiar jurisprudential opportunity, a crack in the wall between law and society.[27]

This opening — the "crack in the wall" — constitutes the basis upon which some feminists engage in political activity to promote women's equality. From this perspective, legal reform offers the potential to redefine dominant (male) values and alter social practices that institutionalize male dominance.

Catharine MacKinnon's work has provoked a great deal of response from feminist legal theorists. A common criticism of MacKinnon's approach is that it portrays women as "victims."[28] In her view of gender relations, women lose their ability to act as self-determined actors; women's subordination to men denies women "agency" or the collective will to resist male domination.[29] Yet, as we have seen, MacKinnon's overdetermined perspective of "women as oppressed" undergirds her view of feminist epistemology. It is women's position as "victim" that gives them a unique stance or a marginal viewpoint to construct an opposing point of view. For MacKinnon, standpoint epistemology offers the basis for developing an oppositional politic. Despite this proviso, MacKinnon has been criticized for presenting the category "woman" as a unified group with a common set of interests that assumes a single feminist standpoint is possible. In a word, MacKinnon's work has been critiqued for presenting an "essentialist" perspective of women.[30]

Feminists have emphasized that differences among women based on race, class, ethnicity, disability and sexual orientation are crucial to devising an equality strategy.[31] When women are treated separately from men in law, they are regarded as a unified group with common interests and needs. Assuming "gender difference" in the law imposes a unity on the category of women as a gender that may not reflect the variation in women's lived experiences. By focusing on the particular experiences of women, it becomes evident that there is a diversity of needs and a multiplicity of "subject positions" or identities that influence how equality for women can be achieved. From this perspective, MacKinnon's framework is seriously questioned since it becomes uncertain whose standpoint has the greatest merit based on an experiential methodology.[32]

Rhode: Theorizing Gender Disadvantage

Concerns about "difference" led feminists to embrace theoretical perspectives that take into account the divergent social experiences among women. Deborah Rhode's analysis of the law turns on the importance of gender distinctions that reinforce or sometimes mitigate against gender inequality. As Rhode explains, "[M]uch of the difficulty in conventional frameworks stems from two fundamental limitations: the law's traditional preoccupation with gender difference rather than with gender disadvantage; and its focus on abstract rights rather than social context that contains them."[33] Rhode argues that sameness and difference approaches to the law consistently fail to take account of women's unequal economic and social position. She suggests reframing feminist jurisprudence based on the concept of gender disadvantage:

> The alternative [to sameness and difference approaches to the law] proposed here is not to abandon rights discourse, but to reimagine its content and recognize its limitations. The central strategy is to shift from gender difference to gender disadvantage.[34]

Focusing on gender disadvantage means addressing how the law materially affects various groups of women. Rhode argues that only contextual analyses of the law can determine "which women benefit, by how much, and at what cost."[35]

By paying close attention to social context, she argues, it is possible to devise laws that can operate to benefit those most in need. While Rhode recognizes that the consequences of law reform may not benefit all women, and that the success of any legal initiative must be weighed in terms of the diversity of women's needs, she remains confident that contextualizing legal analyses is the best way forward to develop reforms that suit women's interests.

While I have sympathy for Rhode's objective to use the law to improve women's material condition, I question her assumption that it is possible to anticipate the impact of any given law reform. First, it is very difficult to predict how the law will be interpreted or applied. Second, the emphasis in liberal rights discourse on the individual makes it difficult to capture the diversity of group experiences that are affected by the law. As pointed out by Sherene Razack:

> Many feminists suggest that we determine whether or not a practice contributes to the disadvantage of the group and use this as a guide. In effect, we look at the *result* of a practice on the group and ignore individual rights. None of these prescriptions leave the judge or the human rights advocate much in the way of guidelines for concretely evaluating and comparing disadvantage; these activities have always been fraught with peril for women and minorities whose realities, defined by their various group situations, are actively suppressed and even *inadmissible* in rights discourse and in the liberalism on which rights discourse is based.[36]

Thus, although Rhode attempts to modify the liberal rights paradigm by concentrating on social context, she remains within its framework since the basic terms of liberal legalism go unchallenged.

The Unpredictability of Law Reform

Contrary to the views of MacKinnon and Rhode, Carol Smart is far more cautious about what feminists can achieve through legal reform. Drawing on the work of Michel Foucault, Smart investigates the power of law at a conceptual level. She argues that the "law constitutes a discursive field," which means it operates as a discourse to organize institutions and practices by extending certain social meanings, or "truth claims," to various areas of social life. The law is able to exert its viewpoint because it is legitimized by society as a self-contained knowledge system that operates outside, and sometimes above, other knowledges.

Smart is particularly concerned that the women's movement does not over-invest in pursuing new legal reforms. She remains leery of using law as a tool for social change because it is never certain how laws will be interpreted and put to use. The "refractory" or contradictory nature of law that she documents in reference to rape and child sexual abuse shows that law can have an injurious affect on people. Legal reform can just as easily be used against those it is supposed to protect, as it can be used to advance their interests. The unpredictability of law reform makes it a "dicey" strategy for feminist activists. Smart's analysis is a warning to feminists to become more aware of the ambiguity of law before seeking a legal solution to female inequality. For Smart, operating within the confines of liberal approaches to equality often has the effect of erasing women's point of view — of evading feminist challenge to law's androcentric standard: this constitutes a real danger of engaging the state.

A final concern is that advocating more laws only contributes to the legitimacy and power of law as a system of knowledge. In Smart's view, law needs to be "de-centred" or disqualified as the purveyor of truth. By agitating for new or different laws, the law is fetishized rather than questioned or invalidated.

Despite Smart's misgivings concerning law's resistance to feminist discourse, she insists that the legal forum, the judicial arm of the state, remains an important site of feminist struggle. According to Smart, "it is law's power to define and disqualify" that constitutes the bedrock upon which feminists can confront the power of law:

> It is in its [law's] ability to redefine the truth that feminism
> offers political gains. Hence feminism can (re)define harmless
> flirtation into sexual harassment, misplaced paternal affection
> into child sexual abuse, enthusiastic seduction into rape, foetal
> rights into forced reproduction, and so on. Moreover, the legal
> forum provides an excellent place to engage in this process of
> redefinition.[37]

As a feminist political strategy, then, Smart believes legal discourse must be met by the feminist challenge. However, she is well aware that redefining law in a feminist mould is not an easy task. In fact, she ultimately concludes that to achieve success following a feminist legal strategy requires such diligence that it may be better to move outside the legal realm, and into the sphere of political activism, to fight against women's oppression.

Although I accept Smart's conception of the state as a forum for feminist struggle around competing definitions of social relations, I question certain other aspects of her theoretical approach. My objection stems from her use of Foucault's framework, which omits the agents of power that enforce structured inequalities. As Annie Bunting points out, a Foucauldian model of power overlooks the importance of "people's abilities to exercise power that may be related to personal characteristics such as class, gender, race and sexuality."[38] In other words, Foucault's notion of power does not fully recognize that some people have more power than others to define knowledges or discourse. Foucault's theory stresses the diffuse nature of power relations — the omnipresence of power that permeates the political anatomy — to use post-structuralist language. He therefore dismisses a structural definition of power that gives greater weight to the importance of class, economic or gender relations.

Smart's analysis, as well as that of many other feminist legal theorists, pays scant attention to the wider political economy. In most feminist discussions of the law, we are not given an analysis that connects the production of discourse to the maintenance of capitalist economic arrangements that are beneficial to men. More generally, there is seldom any discussion of the economic implications of introducing a legal reform. This is especially apparent in the discussion on pregnancy protections in which there is often times only passing reference to employer costs associated with pregnancy leave. Yet it is pointed out by Joanne Conaghan that economic issues were not irrelevant.[39] Commenting on developments in the area of pregnancy leave, she argues economic considerations were critical in the political debates around pregnancy leave arrangements and that business in the U.S. and U.K. was strongly opposed to family-leave provisions:

> ... in the United States of America the main opposition to the federal parental leave proposals came from business and financial organizations, including the United States Chamber of Commerce, the National Association of Manufacturers, numerous small business groups, and a large coalition of assorted business groups. In Britain, the Conservative Government has systematically reduced the scope of maternity provisions in the interests of "efficiency," promoting small businesses, and "freeing" employers from the "burdens" of an "over-regulated" market.[40]

It seems the neo-liberal climate that has pervaded economies in recent years has affected the discourse on pregnancy leave, but this dimension has tended to be ignored by feminist legal theorists.

One of the reasons for the lack of regard to the economic is that many feminists, such as Smart and MacKinnon, have focused their analysis on male authority over women in the spheres of reproduction and sexuality. Since the core of female subordination is largely conceived in regard to issues of sexuality, there is less attention placed on economic structures that underpin male power.[41] This kind of analysis contrasts sharply with frameworks that highlight the material basis of women's oppression. Jane Ursel's perspective, for example, focuses on the spheres of production and reproduction that underlie capitalist-patriarchal relations.[42] According to Ursel, the state mediates between the spheres of production and reproduction to preserve patriarchy. In her view, legal reforms are enacted to ensure patriarchal structures, such as the family, are maintained. Rather than focusing on discourse, Ursel's formulation addresses how the state can be used as a force to dismantle patriarchal structures under capitalism. Her analysis brings a certain clarity to the problem of legal reform since the oppressive features maintaining women's subordination are easily identified. As Ann Phillips reminds us, analyses of capitalism and patriarchy provide us with guideposts as to what is fundamental to women's oppression, something, she believes, that is sorely lacking in debates on "equality and difference."[43]

The views of MacKinnon, Rhode and Smart provide important insights concerning the difficulties of formulating a feminist legal strategy. Critical to this strategy is identifying the systemic character of discrimination (or male hegemony), as MacKinnon points out in her analysis. Advancing women's interests is not simply a matter of distinguishing on the basis of gender and on those grounds putting forward arguments that promote women's special needs or concerns. As the review on equality and difference shows, arguments about difference can "backfire," leaving women worse off than they were before. If women are to make political gains it is necessary to confront the systematic forces, such as exists in gendered organizational hierarchies, that underlie female subordination. Rhode's analysis of gender disadvantage points us in that direction — she urges careful consideration be given to the social structures that engender sex inequality. However, even though her analysis emphasizes the importance of social context in framing equality arguments, Rhode's formulation falls short by staying within the confines of liberal rights discourse. To demonstrate or "prove" group disadvantage often requires methods and a point of view that are unacceptable within the liberal legal paradigm — and it requires that feminist legal arguments are acceptable to judges who sit on the court bench. Important here is Smart's observation that political progress resides in redefining social meanings through law.

Recently, Radha Jhappan has argued that the deficits of the "equality versus difference" debate are still unresolved, especially when viewed from the perspective of Canadian Charter litigation that shows the courts have yet to fully embrace a contextualized approach to equality. A key problem is demonstrating to the court the meaning of systemic inequality, particularly when systemic discrimination stems from intersecting oppressions based on race, gender, class, disability or other factors. Second, feminist litigation strategists have been unable to avoid the trap of the sameness/difference logic with the result that equality arguments remain firmly within a comparative and essentialist framework:

> "contextualized" has meant the context of the subordination of "women" to "men," not the specific contexts in which various aspects of ascriptive identity shape experience.[44]

A central difficulty of the "equality frame" is trying to achieve equality in a practical sense. Within this equality framework, "to be equal" is to be compared to privileged white men, creating a situation of widespread inequality since the privileges of white men depend upon the subordination of all other subjugated groups including women, gays/lesbians and so on. Jhappan argues that the way out of this problem is to argue for justice, meaning that the social processes of domination and oppression are fully taken into account and redress means bringing about a just outcome that is not at the expense of subjugated groups. From this perspective, "a political economy of justice approach that demonstrates the ways in which liberalism is fundamentally unjust is a better bet than an essentialist gender equality frame."[45]

MacKinnon, Rhode, Smart and Jhappan raise significant questions about feminist legal strategy. There is considerable disagreement among them about the potential of using jurisprudence as a strategy to empower women. Can the state be used as an instrument of positive social change for women? If MacKinnon and others such as Martha Minow and Carol Smart are accurate in arguing that the state actively contributes to the reproduction of male dominance through institutionalizing male norms, is the first task for feminists to transform social meanings in the law? Or is male bias so embedded in legal thinking and social practices that attempting change only reproduces male definitions of equality? Is it desirable to establish a unified political approach to promote women's equality or does attention to difference preclude a uniform strategy? How can legal feminists attend to the problem of essentialism and maintain a robust politcal strategy? Has there been a preoccupation by feminists with "discourse" and social meaning at the expense of issues related to the material basis of women's oppression?

These questions established the basis for a new focus in legal feminist theorizing. The concerns of post-structuralists, in particular, turned discussion towards analyses that problematized the unified subject "woman." Investigation of the multiple experiences of different women based on intersecting identities, drew a far more complex picture of "woman's experience." Yet in rejecting essentialist conceptions of "'women's identity," feminists avoided making any generalized claims about "woman" as a discursive category and concentrated analyses on particular groups of women in specific social and historical context.[46] In legal feminism, greater attention was paid to the importance of discourse and the formation of gender legal categories and their discursive effects on the law.

Recently, feminist legal scholars have begun to question some of the parameters of legal feminism, pointing out that attention to specificity has moved discussion away from any analysis of women's disadvantage. Joanne Conaghan argues that while post-structuralist concerns about generalized representations of "women" are well founded, it is important to acknowledge that invoking "women's experience" is appropriate in certain circumstances:

> Anti-essentialism is, in no sense, a prescription for abandoning a concern with women's disadvantage; it does, however, direct us to an understanding of disadvantage as multiple, intersecting, and complex and requires us to consider the implications of such an understanding of feminist theory and

strategy. It follows, too, that while there are clearly risks attached to talking about "women" and "women's experience" there are also risks involved in not so doing ... To recognize diversity among women and heed the risks of assuming homogeneity is not to deny the possibility of commonality at some level, or in particular circumstances.[47]

Conaghan takes seriously the criticisms of post-structuralist feminists on traditional feminist theory, yet she contends that anti-essentialism does not of necessity require jettisoning the notion of women's common experience in every instance. Indeed, for political reasons it may be necessary to frame legal strategies in reference to claims linked to women's subordination in society. Feminist legal theorists need to reconsider the importance of normative or political goals as the basis for feminist theoretical engagement and redeploy women-centred theory as the basis of feminist political strategy.[48] There is a growing awareness that far greater attention must be placed on the material as well as the discursive implications of the law if feminist legal engagement is going to make a difference for women.[49] This is not to say that the critique of legal liberalism or issues of difference and universality are entirely forgotten, but rather there is a need to bring together feminist theorizing with feminist political projects to promote political mobilizing and achieve social change on behalf of women.

The pay equity strategy encompasses many of the components feminist legal theorists identify as necessary for advancing transformative projects, and incorporates both discursive and materialist elements into its political program.[50] As explained in the following chapter, pay equity's legal strategy acknowledges both "sameness" and "difference" to the male norm, thereby avoiding the contradictions inherent in legal liberalism. Specifically, the policy overcomes certain obstacles of the sameness-difference approach by addressing gender power structures in the workplace. Through mandating employers and unions to follow procedures that measure the worth of women's jobs, pay equity has the potential to tip the balance of power in favour of women. By using feminist standpoint to confront male definitions and male standards of job worth, it indirectly challenges liberal masculine discourse through the process of job evaluation, and it contests liberal assumptions of the capitalist market by arguing that systemic gender discrimination disadvantages women in the labour market. Further, its political goal is premised on the notion that women collectively experience gender-based wage discrimination in the labour market and that pay equity policy should be enforced to pay women fair wages, thereby achieving substantive equality for women. Women's common experience of economic discrimination is fully acknowledged and constitutes the very basis for political activism.

NOTES

1. A revised version of this chapter appeared in the *Canadian Journal of Women and the Law* 8 (1995), 440–69.
2. Debra Lewis, "Pay Equity and the State's Agenda," in Judy Fudge and Patricia McDermott, eds., *Just Wages: A Feminist Assessment of Pay Equity* (Toronto: University of Toronto Press, 1991); Johanna Brenner, "Feminist Political Discourses: Radical Versus Liberal Approaches to the Feminization of Poverty and Comparable Worth," *Gender and Society* 1, no. 4 (1987), 447–65. Also reprinted in Karen Hansen and Ilene Philipson, eds., *Women, Class, and the Feminist Imagination* (Philadelphia: Temple University Press, 1990); Anver Saloojee, "Containing Resistance: The Neoliberal Boundaries of Employment Equity," in Mike Burke, Colin Mooers and John Shilelds, eds., *Restructuring and Resistance: Canadian Public Policy in an Age of Global Capitalism* (Halifax: Fernwood, 2000), 287–305.
3. See, for example, Elizabeth Comack, ed., *Locating Law: Race/Gender Connections* (Halifax: Fernwood, 1999).
4. My discussion of feminist legal theory is drawn from the following list of books. The edited volumes by T. Brettel Dawson (1993) Bartlett and Kennedy (1991) and D. Kelly Weisberg (1993) provide a selection of articles commonly referred to in the academic feminist legal literature. Although not a comprehensive review, the books and articles cited are representative of major themes in feminist legal theory. See Catherine Bartlett and Rosanne Kennedy, eds., *Feminist Legal Theory: Readings in Law and Gender* (San Francisco: Westview Press, 1991); Anne Bottomley and Joanne Conaghan, eds., *Feminist Theory and Legal Strategy* (Oxford: Blackwell Publishers, 1993); T. Brettel Dawson, ed., *Women, Law and Social Change: Core Readings and Current Issues* 2nd ed. (North York: Captus Press, 1993); Joan Brockman and Dorothy Chunn, eds., *Invesitgating Gender Bias: Law,*

Courts and the Legal Profession (Toronto: Thompson Press, 1993); Catharine MacKinnon, *Toward a Feminist Theory of the State* (Cambridge: Harvard, 1989); Sherene Razack, *Canadian Feminism and the Law* (Toronto: Second Story Press, 1991; now available from Sumach Press, Toronto); Carol Smart, *Feminism and the Power of Law* (London: Routledge, 1989); Deborah Rhode, *Justice and Gender: Sex Discrimination and the Law* (Cambridge: Harvard, 1989); D. Kelly Weisberg, ed., *Feminist Legal Theory: Foundations*, Vol. I (Philadelphia: Temple, 1993).

5. On the history of the minimum wage, see for example, Gillian Creese, "Sexual Equality and the Minimum Wage in British Columbia," *Journal of Canadian Studies* 26, no. 4 (1991-2), 120–40; Judy Fudge and Eric Tucker, "Law, Industrial Relations and the State," *Labour/Le Travail* 46 (Fall 2000), 264.

6. See, Mimi Abromovitz, *Regulating the Lives of Women: Social Welfare Policy from Colonial Times to the Present* (Boston: South End Press, 1989), 186; Rhode, *Justice and Gender*, 40; Jane Ursel, *Private Lives, Public Policy: 100 Years of State Intervention in the Family* (Toronto: Women's Press, 1992), 91.

7. Rhode, *Justice and Gender*, 36–7.

8 Abromovitz, *Regulating the Lives of Women*,188.

9. Rhode, *Justice and Gender*, 44; Ursel, *Private Lives, Public Policy*, 94; Julie White, 1993, *Sisters & Solidarity: Women and Unions in Canada* (Toronto: Thompson Educational Publishing, 1993), 31.

10. Alice Kessler-Harris, *A Woman's Wage: Historical Meanings and Social Consequences* (Lexington: University of Kentucky, 1990); Mary Lynn Stewart, *Women, Work and the French State: Labour Protection and Social Patriarchy*, 1879–1919 (Kingston: McGill-Queen's University Press, 1989); Ursel, *Private Lives, Public Policy*; White, *Sisters & Solidarity*.

11. See, for example, Wendy Williams, "Equality's Riddle: Pregnancy and the Equal Treatment/Special Treatment Debate" (1984/85), and Linda Kreiger and Patricia Cooney, "The Miller-Wohl Controversy: Equal Treatment, Positive Action and The Meaning of Women's Equality" (1983), both reprinted in Weisberg, ed., *Feminist Legal Theory: Foundations*, 121–56.

12. Weisberg, ed., *Feminist Legal Theory: Foundations*,123.

13. Much of the discussion concerning pregnancy leave arose in response to two U.S. Supreme Court decisions. The first, *Gedulig v. Aiello*, upheld the constitutionality of California's insurance program that excluded pregnancy from coverage. The court made a distinction between "pregnant and non-pregnant persons" thus arriving at the conclusion that pregnancy did not involve "gender discrimination, as such." The second court decision, *General Electric Co. v. Gilbert* also validated the view that pregnancy discrimination is not sex-based discrimination. These two decisions set off a lobbying effort by feminists to grant women pregnancy leave protections which culminated in Congress passing the *Pregnancy Discrimination Act* in 1978.

For a discussion of the Canadian judiciary's response to pregnancy-related equality issues, see Sheilah Martin, "Persisting Equality Implications of the 'Bliss' Case," and Beth Symes, "Equality Theories and Maternity Benefits," in Sheilah Martin and Kathleen Mahoney, eds,. *Equality and Judicial Neutrality* (Toronto: Carswell, 1987). Interestingly, judicial reasoning in Canada regarding pregnancy discrimination parallels the U.S. In *Bliss*, the Supreme Court of Canada made a "distinction between "pregnant people" and "non-pregnant people" and thus concluded that discrimination related to pregnancy is not sex discrimination (Martin, "Persisting Equality Implications," 198). The Supreme Court of Canada stated, in regard to the *Bliss* case that, "If section 46 [of the Unemployment Insurance Act] treats unemployed women differently from other unemployed persons, be they male or female, it is, it seems to me, because they are pregnant and not because they are women." Cited in Michael Mandel, *The Charter of Rights and the Legalization of Politics in Canada* (Toronto: Wall and Thompson, 1989), 256–7. But it is also important to note that the history of maternity benefits in Canada is quite different from that of the United States. Maternity benefits (paid leave) are tied to the Canadian federal program of employment insurance whereas parental leave (without pay) is provincially legislated under Employment Standards statutes.

14. In 1978 in the United States, an amendment to Title VII was passed, referred to as the *Pregnancy Disabilities Act* (PDA), which requires employers to extend to women the same sick benefits available to other workers. Williams is in agreement with the equal model approach inherent in the PDA, which provides that employment discrimination on the basis of pregnancy, childbirth and related medical conditions is sex discrimination for purpose of the Act.

15. Williams, "Equality's Riddle: Pregnancy and the Equal Treatment/Special Treatment Debate," 151.

16. Linda Krieger and Patricia N. Cooney, "The Miller-Wohl Controversy: Equal Treatment, Positive Action and the Meaning of Women's Equality," *Golden Gate University Law Review* 13 (1983), 513, reprinted in Weisberg, ed. *Feminist Legal Theory: Foundations,* 167.

17. See Rhode, *Justice and Gender,* 86–92. Rhode documents statutory and constitutional developments to illustrate the indeterminant legal standards inherent in gender equality cases. In many instances, biological difference is exaggerated to justify special treatment for women that serves to disadvantage them in the labour force, the military, the family and so on.

18. Denise Reaume, "The Social Construction of Women and the Possibility of Change: Unmodified Feminism Revisted," *Canadian Journal of Women and the Law* 5, no. 2 (1992), 480.

19. Mary Becker, "Prince Charming: Abstract Equality," *Supreme Court Review* (1987), reprinted in Weisberg, ed., *Feminist Legal Theory: Foundations;* Lucinda Finley, "Transcending an Equality Theory: A Way Out of the Maternity and Workplace Debate," in *Columbia Law Review* 86 (1986), reprinted in Weisberg, *Feminist Legal Theory: Foundations;* Rhode, *Justice and Gender;* Ann Scales, "The Emergence of Feminist Jurisprudence: An Essay," *The Yale Law Journal* (1986), reprinted in Weisberg, ed., *Feminist Legal Theory: Foundations.* Again, Deborah Rhode has carefully pointed out in her analysis of sex discrimination law in the United States, that after a century of court decisions "assumptions about [gender] difference have been indeterminate, inconsistent and often indefensible," 318. Rhode concludes that difference arguments are always somewhat of a gamble since it is unknown how courts will interpret differences between men and women. There appears to be no theory behind courts' decisions that can explain why women are "different" in some instances and not in others. Lucinda Finley remarks that a theory of equality based on equal or special treatment is weak or indecisive because "the theory cannot tell us how to define or identify what is a relevant difference and what is a relevant similarity." She further argues the

sameness approach forces assimilation or conformity to definitions of male behaviour whereas special treatment may have a stigmatizing effect on women. See Finley, "Transcending an Equality Theory."

20. Catharine MacKinnon, "Difference and Dominance: On Sex Discrimination," *Feminism Unmodified* (Cambridge: Harvard University Press, 1987), reprinted in Weisberg, ed., *Feminist Legal Theory: Foundations.*

21. MacKinnon, *Toward a Feminist Theory,* 216.

22. Ibid., 168.

23. Ngaire Naffine, *The Law and the Sexes: Explorations in Feminist Jurisprudence* (Sydney: Allen and Unwin, 1990), cited in Comack, ed., *Locating Law,* 23.

24. "Male power is systemic. Coercive, legitimated, and epistemic, it is the regime." MacKinnon, *Toward a Feminist Theory,* 170.

25. On the racialized character of legal liberalism, see David Goldberg, *Racist Culture: Philosophy and the Politics of Meaning* (Oxford: Blackwell, 1993); Patricia Williams, *The Alchemy of Race and Rights* (Cambridge: Harvard University Press, 1991).

26. MacKinnon shows how the male perspective enters masculine assumptions into specific laws. "Rape law assumes that consent to sex is as real for women as it is for men. Privacy law assumes that women in private have the same privacy men do. Obscenity law assumes that women have access to speech men have. Equality law assumes that women are already socially equal to men." MacKinnon, *Toward a Feminist Theory,* 169.

27. Ibid., 244.

28. Katherine Bartlett, "Feminist Legal Methods," *Harvard Law Review* 103 (1990), reprinted in Bartlett and Kennedy, eds., *Feminist Legal Theory;* Reaume, "The Social Construction of Women and the Possibility of Change," 480.

29. MacKinnon's view of female subordination is most clearly articulated in her discussion of sexuality. The basis of male power is men's dominance of women sexually. Women are incapable of possessing their own sexuality and are not given the social power to alter the conditions in which women engage in sexual or social relations with men. She goes so far as to say that "it does not seem exaggerated to say that women are sexual, meaning that women exist, in a context of terror," 159. MacKinnon's view contrasts sharply with socialist feminist Marianna Valverde who offers a very different perspective on sexual relations. In contrast to MacKinnon, Valverde sees male female relations as operating within a dialectic. Whereas men have generally been dominant and aggressive in the dialectic, and women passive; there is room in Valverde's conceptual analysis to allow women to act as agents of their own destiny. See Mariana Valverde, *Sex, Power and Pleasure* (Toronto: Women's Press, 1985).

30. See, for example, Angela Harris, "Race and Essentialism in Feminist Legal Theory," *Stanford Law Review* 42 (1990), reprinted in Bartlett and Kennedy, eds. *Feminist Legal Theory.* Marlee Kline, "Race, Racism, and Feminist Legal Theory," 12 *Harvard Women's Law Journal* 12 (1989), reprinted in Weisberg, ed., *Feminist Legal Theory: Foundations.*

31. See, for example, Harris,"Race and Essentialism"; Patricia Cain, "Feminist Jurisprudence: Grounding the Theories, " *Berkeley Women's Law Journal* 2 (1989), reprinted in Weisberg, ed., *Feminist Legal Theory: Foundations;* Martha Minow, "The Supreme Court 1986 Term, Forward: Justice Engendered, " *Harvard Law*

Review 101 (1987), reprinted in Weisberg, eds, *Feminist Legal Theory: Foundations;* Sherene Razack, "Exploring the Omissions and Silences in Law around Race," in Joan Brockman and Dorothy Chunn, eds., *Investigating Gender Bias* (Toronto: Thompson Educational Publishing, 1993); Joan Scott, "Deconstructing Equality-Versus-Difference: Or, the Uses of Poststructuralist Theory for Feminism," *Feminist Studies* 14, no.1 (1988).

32. Rhode, *Justice and Gender,* 335.

33. Ibid., 2.

34. Ibid., 3.

35. Ibid., 4.

36. Razack, *Canadian Feminism and the Law,* 18.

37. Carol Smart, *Feminism and the Power of Law* (London: Routledge, 1989), 164.

38. Annie Bunting, "Feminism, Foucault, and Law as Power/Knowledge," *Alberta Law Review* 30 (1992), reprinted in T. Brettel Dawson, ed., *Women, Law and Social Change: Core Readings & Current Issues* (Toronto: Captus Press, 1993).

39. For instance, Wendy Williams tells us that the Court ruled pregnancy could be excluded in the California disability insurance scheme if it could be shown that it represented a high cost to the employer. However, the state did not use this rationale, she says, "presumably because it could not argue that pregnancy disabilities would have constituted the most expensive category of disabilities" (Williams, "Equality's Riddle," 135). While this is a compelling argument as to why economic aspects of the matter are not more fully discussed, we are not given any empirical evidence to support this claim. And the matter of employer costs is seldom addressed by feminist legal theorists discussing pregnancy leave provisions. We, therefore, are not aware of the full relevance of economic issues in this matter. An exception to the discussion on the costs of maternity leave benefits is provided by economist Monica Townson. She estimates that the costs of maternity benefits in Canada under the federal unemployment insurance programme is minimal. For example, only 4 percent of total benefits paid out in 1985 was allocated to maternity leave provisions. See Monica Townson, "Economic Consequences of Maternity Leave," in Sheilah Martin and Kathleen Mahoney, eds., *Equality and Judicial Neutrality* (Toronto: Carswell, 1987).

40. Joanne Conaghan, "Pregnancy and the Workplace: A Question of Strategy?" in Anne Bottomley and Joanne Conaghan, eds., *Feminist Theory and Legal Strategy* (Oxford: Blackwell, 1993), 85–6.

41. MacKinnon argues that male dominance and female submission characterizing sexual relations extends to many social practices such as the division of labour in the home and the workplace.

42. Ursel, *Private Lives, Public Policy.*

43. Ann Phillips, *Democracy and Difference* (Philadelphia: Pennsylvania University Press, 1993).

44. Radha Jhappan, "The Equality Pit or the Rehabilitation of Justice," *Canadian Journal of Women and the Law* 10 (1998), 74.

45. Ibid., 107.

46. See Linda Nicholson, ed., *The Second Wave: A Reader in Feminist Theory* (New York: Routledge, 1997).

47. Joanne Conaghan, "Reassessing the Feminist Theoretical Project in Law," *Journal of Law and Society* 27, no. 3 (September 2000), 373.

48. Ibid., 384.

49. See, for example, Susan Boyd, "Family, Law and Sexuality: Feminist Engagements," *Social and Legal Studies* 8, no. 3 (September 1999), 369–90.

50. On the discursive and material dimensions of pay equity see, for example, Pat Armstrong, "The State and Pay Equity: Juggling Similarity and Difference, Meaning and Structures," in Patricia Evans and Gerda Wekerle, eds., *Women and the Canadian Welfare State: Challenge and Change* (Toronto: University of Toronto Press, 1997); Linda Blum, *Between Feminism and Labor: The Significance of the Comparable Worth Movement* (Berkeley: University of California Press, 1991), 201; Judy Fudge, "The Paradoxes of Pay Equity: Reflections on the Law and the Market in Bell Canada and the Public Service Alliance of Canada," *Canadian Journal of Women and the Law* 12 (2000), 315–16; Michael McCann, *Rights at Work: Pay Equity Reform and the Politics of Legal Mobilization* (Chicago: University of Chicago Press, 1994).

Chapter Two

THE POSSIBILITIES AND LIMITATIONS OF THE PAY EQUITY STRATEGY

THE COMPLEXITIES of the pay equity legal strategy are explored in this chapter.[1] Feminist scholars both in and outside the pay equity movement have criticized the reform effort for its failure to challenge social relations of inequality and for its inability to sufficiently resist liberal conceptions of equality.[2] Is there a sound basis for assuming a correspondence between the pay equity strategy and liberal reform? While equal pay is often discussed as a liberal equality strategy, I argue the radical capacity of pay equity reform resides in its social vision of gender-wage equality that directly challenges masculine liberal discourse. Specifically, there are three key strands in the discourse of equal pay: (1) it critiques liberal conceptions of the individual; (2) it confronts abstract universalism (or the male standard); and (3) it recognizes that unequal power relations between the sexes are systemic. All three strands rely on a contextual analysis of rights that appreciates the full context of the social conditions underlying gender-wage equity claims. Solving the problem of equal value in pay requires redefining the social meaning of the "woman worker" (and the market) from a feminist viewpoint. Pay equity reform makes it possible to question taken-for-granted assumptions about the gendered labour market and thereby revalue the work women do. Unlike liberal approaches to equality that assume individual effort is rewarded in the labour market, pay equity strategists argue that women as a collective have a right to equal value in pay because of unfair market forces that produce systemic discrimination.

Pay Equity: Sameness or Difference?

The pay equity strategy is sometimes criticized for accepting the principle of "equal treatment," that women similarly situated to men receive equality rights. In other words, pay equity accepts a definition of equality based on a male standard, and women's right to equality in pay is premised on the male worker. In this sense, pay equity policy is seen to embrace the liberal concept of the individual and to uncritically accept the language of rights discourse. Commenting on the liberal feminist approach to equality, Patricia Cain summarizes why the demand for equal pay falls squarely within a traditional liberal rights framework:

> If men are being paid x dollars for performing a job in the public sphere, then women should be entitled to the same pay for performing the same job. The equality argument is that women are just like men. It is this argument of similarity that makes it possible to expand women's rights.[3]

There are thus two aspects of the equal pay approach which seem to conform to liberal standards of equality. The first is that women have to be shown to be similarly situated to men, and the second is that the definition of female equality rests on a male norm.[4] As we have seen in the debate on "equality versus difference," both of these issues are seen to be severely problematic in framing equality rights for women.

Johanna Brenner's critique of comparable worth strategy offers an extensive analysis of why pay equity conforms to liberal discourse.[5] In Brenner's view, the hierarchy of rewards inherent in liberal democratic society are not sufficiently challenged by pay equity. Neither are meritocratic values embedded in liberal discourse repudiated in the comparable worth approach. According to Brenner, "comparable worth aims primarily to rationalize the sorting and selecting of individuals into unequal places and does *not* eliminate market criteria from evaluation."[6] Because comparable worth incorporates "a rationale within liberal hegemonic discourse," she argues, it reproduces and reinforces the hierarchies and social divisions based on class, sex and race. Since job evaluation cannot overcome cultural biases that maintain these divisions, the overall effect of the policy may do more to solidify gender, class and race segmentation in the labour market than eradicate it.

While it is not inaccurate to say that equal pay arguments rest on the principle of similarly situated, I would suggest that the politics surrounding pay equity are more complicated than that suggested by Cain. Similarly, although Brenner is correct to point out the meritocratic component of equal pay, she bypasses other crucial aspects of the pay equity strategy. Missing from Brenner's critique is a recognition of attempts by pay equity advocates to re-define the value of work on terms that contradict mainstream views of the market.

Challenging the Market

In addressing the problem of gender-wage inequality, proponents of pay equity have put forward a view of the market that contrasts sharply with liberal ideology.[7] According to liberal economic principles of the market, compensation is seen to be the function of supply and demand for labour. Neo-classical economists argue that the market operates according to objective standards to fairly distribute wages. Sara Evans and Barbara Nelson offer a succinct summary of the major tenets of the neo-classical view of the market:

> ... the neo-classical model makes three stringent assumptions: workers have perfect mobility; capitalists are competitive; information is costless. These assumptions contain radically individualist views about a populace unconnected to one another, to their past, to communities of place, or to institutions of any kind. The neo-classical market posits a world without history or memory.[8]

Contrary to mainstream interpretations of the economy that see individuals making free choices within an impersonal market that does not discriminate on the basis of group characteristics, equal pay advocates argue that the market operates unfairly for minorities and women.[9] Whereas opponents of comparable worth couch their arguments concerning women's low wages in terms of a woman's individual choice about education, training, occupation, marriage and motherhood, supporters of equal pay consistently counter their arguments with structural explanations as to why women are secondary wage earners.[10] From the perspective of pay equity activists, individuals are placed in economic and social structures that curtail personal choice. Moreover, historical developments within the labour market led to occupational and job sex segregation, placing women in a disadvantaged position in the workplace.

According to pay equity proponents, women's relationship to wage labour is distinct from men's because women are situated in specific segments of the labour market. The majority of women workers are located in sectors of the economy that offer low wages and provide little or no room for advancement to higher paying jobs. In this sense, pay equity adherents believe women are not participants in a free market. As Michael Gold explains:

> The value of labor may be its price in a free market, but women are not part of a free market. For women, the labor market is segmented and they are relegated to the secondary segment ...
>
> Women may participate in a competitive labor market, but their competitors are other women and the jobs for which they compete are artificially limited. The price of women's labor is not the result of supply and demand but of bloated supply and strangled demand.[11]

Consequently, the overall effect of the labour market on women is seen to produce *systemic* discrimination in respect of compensation. Systemic sex discrimination persists, in part, because of sex stereotypes and belief systems that reinforce structural barriers in workplace organizations.[12] Cultural assumptions about women's and men's appropriate social roles structures choice around jobs and family and define workplace practices. Moreover, bureaucratic and organizational processes benefit employers and male workers who have a stake in maintaining organizational and social arrangements that advantage their gender and class interests.[13]

In recognizing the broader social forces that engender women's low pay, scholars of comparable worth have analyzed the cultural meaning of the wage. Historian Alice Kessler-Harris demonstrates how struggles over the wage have been conceived in gendered terms. Reviewing the history of women's wages in the U.S. from the late nineteenth to the late twentieth century, she uncovers the varying social and economic contexts that altered the social meaning of men's and women's wages:

> Popular perceptions of the wage are far richer than economists' descriptions would imply ...
>
> These popular images alert us to look at the wage for meanings that transcend economists' models. They suggest the wage is neither neutral nor natural but rather contains within it clues to how the laws of economists manifest themselves in the real world of human relationships, political compromise and social struggle.[14]

According to Kessler-Harris, the wage is imbued with gender meanings. The traditional belief in the "family wage" encompassing dependent wife and male breadwinner, eventually gave way to a series of struggles around alternative meanings of gender in relation to the minimum wage, the right to married women's employment and the concept of equal pay. Contained in these struggles were deeply ambiguous notions about gender.[15] The struggle by women for equal pay for work of equal value has a rich and complex history that challenges long standing views about gender roles. From this perspective, the wage is an expression of society's value systems, and is a far cry from being upheld as a valid measure of an individual's "marginal productivity" or labour contribution to a firm.

We can see how pay equity arguments concerning the market violate masculine discourse. Explanations for women's low pay do not rest on a concept of the autonomous individual removed from community and history. Far from it. Women are understood to be members of a disadvantaged social group who have experienced a common history. Rather than having individual and unfettered choice to maximize their economic gains in the labour market, women are affected by economic and social structures that limit their work and earning opportunities. These social and economic arrangements operate systematically to restrict the structure of choices available to women. This perspective places individuals in social and historical context and flies in the face of a liberal economic conception of the isolated ahistorical (male) actor making rational decisions in a perfectly competitive labour market.

Confronting the Male Standard

There is a twofold meaning of the term "male standard" in pay equity discourse. On the one hand, the male standard refers to the fact that men as a group are the norm by which women are judged. Women's wages are compared to men's wages. Women's work is divided up into separate components and compared to men's work according to the same components. This direct comparison between female work and male work is the basis upon which people commonly understand pay equity to embrace the principle of "similarly situated." On the other hand, reference to the male standard is given expression in the language of abstract universalism.[16] Definitions of what it is to be a worker and claims to neutrality or objectivity (discussed in chapter 1) reside in job evaluation systems and implicitly invoke a male reference point. It is by using the second meaning of male standard that pay equity strategists attempt to challenge male norms. Despite claims that pay equity relies solely on a male standard, the equal value strategy has the potential to confront masculine discourse in two ways. First, the process of implementing job evaluation questions the meaning of the abstract individual (i.e., the male worker), and second, equal pay advocates confront the meaning of gender neutrality in job comparison systems by explicitly challenging masculine definitions of work.

Pay equity strategists advocate the use of job evaluation as a method to correct a flawed market that allows systematic underpayment of women's wages. As we have seen, the aim of comparable worth is to eliminate wage differentials that are the product of occupational sex segregation and which result in inequitable compensation for equal labour contribution to an organization. The use of job evaluation systems is regarded by equal pay strategists as a political solution to the difficult problem of how to "redeem the market" to make it fair to women and minorities. It is important to recognize that comparable worth proponents saw job evaluation as a kind of necessary evil to advance their political agenda. From the very beginning equal pay activists were aware of the problems of utilizing a management tool to press for radical change. As Ronnie Steinberg remarks, proponents of pay equity "defended the use of job evaluation, even though they were highly critical of the practical application of the technique."[17] While the technical difficulties of using job evaluation are well known, a primary concern of feminists that is less commented on, is the importance of identifying unstated male reference points that pervade job evaluation systems. It is here that pay equity proponents attempt to confront the male standard.

Joan Acker, drawing on the work of Carole Pateman, argues that job evaluation systems embody liberal suppositions about the abstract individual.[18] The rationale underlying job evaluation is that jobs are "abstract categories that have no occupants, no human bodies, no gender."[19] On a philosophical level, job evaluations assume an abstract job is occupied by an abstract worker whose only goal in life is to fulfill the duties required of a position situated in a rational hierarchy. Acker sees this as a masculine perspective of the workplace that, in reality, cannot exist:

> The closest the disembodied worker doing the abstract job comes to a real worker is the male worker whose life centers on his full-time, life-long job, while his wife or another woman takes care of his personal needs and children ... The woman worker, assumed to have legitimate obligations other than those required by the job, did not fit with the abstract job.[20]

Flowing out of Acker's analysis is a recognition that the basic tenets of liberal individualism exist in uneasy tension in job evaluation systems. Beneath liberal conceptions of the abstract individual, or abstract worker, is a "deeply gendered and bodied" male worker.[21] The "universal worker" present in liberal thought supposedly "represents anyone and everyone," but in actual fact, this universal being is a heterosexual able-bodied male. Critics have further pointed out that the abstract individual represents the dominant racial group constructed as "white" European. Job hierarchies are not only gendered, they are racialized and white males are situated at the apex of the occupational pyramid.[22] The power of job evaluation systems, then, is that they are presented as neutral and objective instruments of measuring job worth, when in fact they are infused with gender and racial bias.

It is the task of feminists and pay equity analysts to expose masculine assumptions embedded in the logic of job evaluation systems. The whole purpose of engaging in a job evaluation exercise is to uncover gender biases operating to devalue the worth of women's work.[23] Wage setting practices are inherently subjective and political processes and pay equity proponents enter the arena of wage setting with the explicit objective of challenging existing value systems that devalue women's work.[24] To confront racialized gender bias in job evaluation is to engage in a critical exercise concerning the meaning of the abstract worker or abstract individual that underlies liberal individualism. This is achieved by making visible the job content of women's work. Many women engage in emotion and caring work (aspects of work life omitted in conceptions of the abstract worker), the work women do can be complex and highly responsible even though it is placed on a low rung in an organizational hierarchy, and women working part-time often perform the same work as full-time (male) workers in the workplace, although their work is not equally valued.[25] Numerous other aspects of women's work that are devalued or invisible in job comparison and classification systems can be laid bare and reassessed in pay equity implementation.[26] The process of unmasking gender bias implicitly brings into question liberal assumptions, based on racialized masculine standards, which structure unfair wage setting practices.[27]

In challenging socially constructed masculine definitions of work, pay equity practioners adopt a woman's standpoint. There is an explicit attempt to develop factors and weightings in job evaluation that reflect the value or worth of work on *women's own terms*. This strategy parallels MacKinnon's formulation in that women's viewpoint is the foundation for arguing against male standards of what is valuable work, and by extension challenging the privileged position of the "abstract worker." In this way pay equity strategists politicize gender neutrality implicit in liberal conceptions of the individual.

Systemic Discrimination

Recognizing the force of systemic gender discrimination lies at the heart of pay equity discourse. To argue from the perspective of gender inequality constitutes a group rather than an individual rights-based strategy. That women share a common experience of economic discrimination in society is understood as resulting from cultural norms about men's and women's gender roles. These societal expectations reinforce structural inequalities by defining the sex division of labour at work, and in the family, that systematically contributes to women's disadvantaged position in the labour market. Men's power to define skilled and responsible work, that has historically been associated with trade union struggles and the politics of masculinity, plays a large role in sustaining and reinforcing gendered structures at the workplace.[28] Systemic gender discrimination operates indirectly to disadvantage women and "appears where there is inequality of treatment, based not on gender as such, but on the criteria that are used in relation to work typically performed by women and work typically performed by men."[29] Challenging systemic sex discrimination in employment recognizes the way in which market norms operate unfairly for women and is therefore central to the pay equity struggle.

Pay Equity Strategy: Gender Parity

Does pay equity, in holding to the principle of similarly situated, operate as a (male) liberal reform? To be sure, pay equity refers to a male standard (i.e., the male wage), and equality arguments revolve around achieving sameness with men. From this perspective, pay equity undeniably and visibly appeals to a male standard. Yet, there are two unique aspects of pay equity policy that need to be mentioned.

First, as was just discussed, "equal worth" is defined from a women's perspective and thus avoids conforming to the "male standard." Thus, it is not necessary to say that women must be "just like men" in order to receive equal pay, but it is said women should be *paid* like men for making an equally valuable contribution to the workplace. As Cynthia Cockburn points out, there is an important distinction to be made between arguing for sameness as compared to arguing for parity. "What we are seeking is not in fact *equality,* but *equivalence,* not *sameness* for individual women and men, but *parity* for women as a sex, or for groups of women in specificity."[30]

A second aspect of equal pay policy is that women's unequal position in the labour force is seen to result from systemic forces relating to gender structures in society. Pay equity advocates contend that women are in a different social position from men both in the family and in the labour market. For this reason, women are differently situated. Given the emphasis on women's experience as a subordinate group in society, it is not possible for men to identify with or take advantage of this "rights claim." Men (who are not in lower-paying female-predominant job categories) are thus prevented from benefiting from equal pay arguments.[31]

It is important to realize that, unlike "equality versus difference" approaches, equal pay allows "difference" as well as "sameness" by recognizing that women are a separate case in the labour force (difference), yet argues for equality (sameness) based on the equal worth of women's work. Rather than having to choose between "difference" or "sameness," pay equity encompasses both dimensions of these equality models and in this sense does not suffer from the same dilemma contained in the equality controversy. Pay equity is able to question the male standard by arguing from a women's perspective the meaning and value of women's work. Accordingly, the male norm works somewhat differently than in the case of "equality versus difference" models where sex equality law is a contradiction in terms. Whereas in most sex equality laws the male referent operates to uphold men's social status, pay equity dissolves male authority by equalizing women's economic status relative to men. The reference to the male wage is used to give women what men have and are loath to give up. Namely, more money, which undermines male power both at the workplace and in the home.

Another aspect of the equal pay strategy that deviates from the "equality versus difference" approaches is an appreciation of the diversity of women's employment circumstances. As Rhode emphasizes, it is imperative that legal strategies start from the premise of gender disadvantage, that *particular* women's unequal social situation be acknowledged. Pay equity attempts to do this by adjusting the process of equal pay implementation and the equal pay demand to specific workplaces. In implementing pay equity, the job-evaluation exercise is specific to a particular group or groups of women in one organization or industry. The operation of wage-setting practices can be analyzed and a remedy sought that is specific to the needs of women in a particular work setting.

We can see that there are moments in the pay equity reform strategy that touch on profoundly sensitive liberal issues. Arguments that address structural barriers to wage fairness in the market identify the limitations of individualist thinking by revealing the systemic nature of gender wage discrimination. And, rather than focusing on abstract standards of equality, pay equity reform has been formulated in regard to detailed knowledge of women's varying position in the workplace. Feminist critiques of job evaluation and job classification systems are rooted in an examination of women's on-the-job experiences that reveal deep philosophical liberal assumptions about the abstract individual. By dismantling or deconstructing prevalent notions about the male worker and male definitions of job worth, pay equity challenges liberal (white male) norms. To that extent equal value in pay has an inherent radical edge.

The Practical Hazards of Pay Equity Reform

The following discussion investigates two problematic aspects of the reform effort. The first identifies the limitations of the discourse of pay equity in respect of race. And the second points out the inconsistency and contradictory outcomes that result in trying to put equal pay policy into practice. The practical hazards of pay equity reform reveal themselves in the many barriers confronted by practioners attempting to live up to the feminist goal of achieving substantive equality for women.

PAY EQUITY AND RACE

While the strength of pay equity is uncovering male norms in liberalism, the reform is less forceful on the matter of race. As critics such as David Goldberg and Patricia Williams argue, liberalism is highly racialized.[32] Racialized expressions and racist exclusions dominate liberal modernity, encode our culture and normalize racism. It is important to address pay equity's approach to race as part of assessing the reform's potential to challenging liberalism.

While race is not central to the discourse of equal pay, the reform does acknowledge racial issues in employment. As mentioned, job evaluation can identify and ensure the elimination of race bias, and in this way pay equity has the potential to address racial stereotypes. Still, the literature on job evaluation places far greater emphasis on eliminating gender bias.[33] It is also well worth noting that all Canadian pay equity statutes require gender neutrality but not racial neutrality in job-evaluation or job-comparison systems. This is similar to the situation in the European Union where pay equity law is silent on race discrimination.[34] Because pay equity was never intended to dissolve barriers to employment or offer equality of opportunity at the workplace through representation of women and designated groups (Aboriginals, people with disabilities and visible minorities) as has been outlined under employment equity in Canada, the reform has paid less attention to racial and other forms of employment discrimination.[35] Instead, pay equity is specifically aimed at eliminating wage discrimination for all women workers, regardless of racial identity, who are employed in traditional female occupations.

From the early stages of the reform effort, pay equity proponents, particularly in the U.S., recognized the underpayment of wages to minorities. Studies of earnings differentials showed that marginalized groups earned substantially less than white men. These studies also indicated two important facts about the gender wage gap. First, they demonstrated that women, regardless of race and ethnicity, were likely to work in female predominant occupations (i.e., two-thirds filled by women). Second, both white and racial/ethnic women earned considerably lower wages compared to either white *or* racial/ethnic men.[36] Canadian labour force data support these findings. Women are clustered in a few traditional female occupational categories including teaching, nursing, clerical, sales (cashier) and service jobs. Moreover, the employment patterns of racialized women (immigrant, visible minority and Aboriginal) reflect the broader contours of employment for women as a whole. Further, women as a group earn considerably less than men in the paid labour force (as discussed in chapter 3), while visibile minority and Aboriginal women earned much less than their male counterparts.[37] For both these reasons, pay equity activists argued comparison of women's earnings with male earnings would secure the greatest wage adjustments. As a result, arguments for pay equity rested on upgrading wages for women that assumed that all women experience lower wages in the labour market, compared to the earnings of men. Representations of "women's" work experiences were often not clearly differentiated according to race or ethnicity but rather "minorities" got lumped together and subsumed under the category "women."[38]

By combining women into a unified category, pay equity is less sensitive to how the workforce is racially segregated. As many researchers have observed, different groups of women are situated in different sectors of the economy and are relegated to perform particular work roles, indicating the workforce is highly racialized. Women of colour and ethnic minority women have *historically* been excluded from certain occupations reserved for white women including clerical, secretarial, nursing and sales work.[39] By the same token, ethnic/racial minority women are disproportionately represented in the least desirable low-paying personal service jobs, particularly paid domestic labour or reproductive work. As these studies point out, white women's work is more highly valued as compared with work performed by racial/ethnic women because systems of social construction privilege white women.[40] This pattern of gender racialization along occupational lines is evident in contemporary labour force profiles that show visible minority women are concentrated in certain sectors of the labour market such as industrial homework, especially in the garment industry, in home-care work such as live-in caregiver, and in paid reproductive and domestic work.[41]

Pay equity has the potential to recognize the devaluation of various types of women's work but it does not make explicit the racialization of the labour force. Instead, the difference between women's and men's work is stressed at the expense of specifying differences among women. Arguments that value women's work are gender specific but not necessarily race specific. Racialized exclusions (i.e., the exclusion of racialized Others) are not given prominence in pay equity strategy and, as a result, the reform does not often confront racial stereotypes and other racialized social expressions that subjugate racial/ethnic minorities in the labour market. The lack of an explicit race-sensitive analysis in pay equity delimits the efficacy and potentiality of the reform to challenge taken-for-granted assumptions embedded in liberalism's racialized discourse. At the same time, assuming a unity of interest among women grounded the reform effort and established the basis for a broad-based political movement. By taking women as a category of workers who experience systemic gender discrimination in pay, the reform effort was, and still is, capable of appealing to the vast majority of working women.

Making Pay Equity Work

Whether or not pay equity actually works to improve women's wages would seem like a straightforward question. However, as Judy Fudge explains, it is actually a very complex issue and the answer depends on how one characterizes the goals of pay equity.[42] In this study, the political objectives of pay equity have been specified along three dimensions and can be characterized in terms of challenging the way in which patriarchal norms operate in the labour market to produce systemic gender-based wage discrimination. Taking this analysis into account, the strength of pay equity discourse lies in its ability to question sexist assumptions about the worth of women's work in a gender-segregated labour market. The reform fails, however, when pay equity strategists are unable to put their political program into practice. When pay equity advocates are unable to persuade opinion on the role of market factors in producing gender inequality in pay, when stereotypes about gender in employment are not fully challenged, when racialized masculine norms continue to systemically disadvantage women and racial minorities in the labour market, and when the balance of power at the workplace favours the dominant male workforce while marginalizing women and racialized Others, then pay equity is an abysmal failure.

Pay equity arguments about the market constitute the most powerful aspect of the reform effort; however, if these arguments are rejected, then the whole basis of the pay equity challenge breaks down. In the federal courts of the U.S., for instance, pay equity challenges alleging that the "market discriminates" initially met with success. In the 1970s and 1980s, advocates were at times able to convince the courts of the discriminatory effects of the free market on women's low wages.[43] However, by the 1990s, the courts largely accepted the neo-classical economic paradigm that "market forces and efficiency explain [gender-based] wage differences" — taking the wind out of the sail of pay equity legal challenges.[44]

In Canada, the "market defence" has not been an explicit focus of court challenges per se, rather arguments have been framed in reference to historic patterns of systemic gender discrimination. In fact, the courts have acknowledged that the undervaluation of women's work is an outgrowth of "long-standing social and cultural mores [that] carry within them value assumptions that contribute to discrimination ..."[45] In so far as the courts and tribunals in

Canada have recognized the unfairness of "employment systems" and other patterns of workplace discrimination on women in the labour market, then pay equity has countered assumptions concerning the role of market forces in producing gender wage inequities.[46] The problem in the Canadian context is not that the courts, or statutes, ignore market-based systemic gender discrimination in employment, but rather the problem lies in carrying through on a successful pay equity challenge that is backed by sufficient resources and fuelled by the political will of interested groups to mobilize and sustain the struggle. One of the biggest obstacles for pay equity proponents has been delays in pay equity proceedings resulting from complaints that challenge the independence and impartiality of human rights tribunals. The actual issue of pay equity may not be discussed for years as the parties wait to hear from the court whether the tribunal has the right to decide on matters related to the pay equity process.[47]

Another difficulty pay equity activists face in putting pay equity into practice is exerting control in the pay equity implementation process. If pay equity practioners cannot advance their perspective of women's job worth, or a feminist viewpoint is entirely absent in the equal-value exercise, then the reform is completely unsuccessful. Pay equity advocates often meet resistance from managers, management consultants, male employees and even male union leadership who attempt to block meaningful reform efforts. When this happens there is a great risk that pay equity will reinforce women's marginalized status in the workplace. Studies of pay equity implementation show that in some instances pay equity initiatives may actually operate to reproduce and intensify gender, class and racial divisions rather than undermine them.[48] As we will see in chapter 7, pay equity implementation in the supermarket did not remove pay inequities between the predominantly male core and the predominantly female peripheral workforce, reinforcing the marginalization of casualized workers.

Technical procedures used in pay equity implementation can drastically undercut the radical potential of the reform. As mentioned, pay equity advocates approach job comparison as a political instrument to improve women's wages but they often confront intense opposition from employers or management consultants who resist any modifications to job comparison systems, or resist applying job evaluations effectively to reorder the organizational gender hierarchy. The progressive aims of pay equity projects can be supplanted by male interests or by the economic interests of the employer. A central question that emerges from analyses of pay equity is whether the process of reform, involving a myriad of technical decisions over which feminists may exert minimal control, can achieve the goals of the pay equity movement.

The well-known Canadian federal pay equity complaint filed by the Public Service Alliance of Canada, the union representing over two hundred thousand predominantly women workers in the civil service, is a particularly excellent illustration of the incredible complexity surrounding technical decisions in the pay equity process. This complaint was filed in 1984 and concluded fourteen years later, after years of litigation between the union and employer over the appropriate methodology to use to determine wage adjustments.[49] In 1999 the dispute was settled, with the union (Public Service Alliance of Canada) winning wage adjustments ranging between $3.3 and $3.6 billion. The success of this case largely depended upon the union convincing the legal authorities of the appropriate methodology to use in comparing and evaluating jobs. The tenacity of the union leadership to pursue their interpretation of job comparison, combined with the political will of the majority woman membership to fight for their legal right to pay equity, lay at the heart of the PSAC victory.

Barriers to Pay Equity Implementation

Having some control over implementation of job evaluation, as well as taking a critical stance on the content of job comparison systems, is essential to the success of pay equity. Many pay equity scholars conclude that those with the power to define the value criteria contained in job evaluation systems ultimately maintain control over the outcome of the equal value process.[50] This argument would seem to be supported in the PSAC case.

Yet job evaluation systems themselves often operate as a significant barrier to achieving gender-wage fairness. Historically, the reliance on job-evaluation systems to establish wage grids entrenched their legitimacy as a proven device for determining wage structures, especially in the eyes of management. The problem, however, is that these systems are skewed in favour of masculine work.[51] Moreover, job evaluation is a very complex system for determining pay systems that requires a high level of knowledge and training to implement. For this reason, compensation specialists or management consultants are hired to execute pay equity procedures. When consultants are hired, pay equity proponents are faced with the difficulty of establishing themselves as credible participants in the pay equity process. While compensation consultants are given automatic legitimacy as "neutral and objective," pay equity advocates are viewed with suspicion since they are seen to bring a biased or radical political agenda that gets in the way of "objectivity."[52] This view is reinforced when pay equity proponents are associated with a trade union. As a result, employers prefer to hand over control of job evaluation to compensation "experts" who are often willing to fulfill the employer's objectives. Important technical decisions such as the definition of female-predominant job class or factor weights in job evaluation, which bear directly on the scope and efficacy of the reform, are often decided unilaterally by compensation consultants, without input from trade unions.

Alternatively, trade union representatives may be consulted but they may not have the training or expertise to make informed decisions about pay equity procedures. This is particularly problematic for smaller union locals without sufficient resources to hire lawyers or "labour friendly" management consultants. But even larger and better resourced locals may not understand the ramifications of job comparison under pay equity and make decisions that are not in the best interests of their members. As we will see in chapter 7, the United Food and Commerical Workers and their employer chose to hire a consultant to devise a job-evaluation system for the supermarket, however, the comparison method did not fairly reward all aspects of "women's work."

Even more problematic for labour are the internal union politics that swirl around gender-wage equity.[53] When pay equity is negotiated, union leaders sometimes face opposition from male members who perceive pay equity as a blow to their "manliness."[54] Gillian Creese's detailed study of pay equity struggles pursued by the Office and Technical Employees Union at B.C. Hydro shows how masculine privileges are largely invisible to union members until such time as these norms are challenged. Once the privileges of the dominant male group are threatened, the systemic norms at the workplace are suddenly acknowledged and aggressively defended by the masculine union culture.[55] This parallels the response of some men in the supermarket chains who resisted pay equity, seeing it as an attack on their status as male breadwinner.

The reaction of male workers to pay equity presents a major dilemma for unions as there can be concern by the labour leadership that they fairly represent *all* of their members in bargaining. Yet male members tend to be far more vocal about their interests, have more experience in organizing for their concerns and may even occupy positions of power within the union hierarchy. Women seldom have the political experience or resources to effectively voice their demands and may have to put considerable energy into mobilizing and educating the union membership on gender-wage equity. The head cashiers at Loblaws in Ontario found themselves in exactly this position having been excluded from the pay equity process; they had to learn about their legal rights and defend their right to fair pay. And in Saskatchewan, cashiers working at Safeway mobilized to convince both the male dominant leadership and the male membership to file a complaint of gender-based wage discrimination at the retail chain.

The concept of equal value in pay is extremely dificult to convey to the majority of working people who are unfamiliar with the notion of systemic discrimination. Dominantly held cultural values about the worth of men's and women's work override alternative, particularly feminist, interpretations of wage determination. The common perception that women work in pleasant surroundings performing labour that requires less effort, skill and responsibility than men's work still pervades cultural defintions of masculine and feminine work. Later we will see that certain female job classes in the supermarket were devalued because of the perception that they deviate from the male standard of job worth, being viewed as less responsible and less skilled than men's work, and involving extensive human relations work that is perceived as less demanding than physical labour.

As workers confront an increasingly competitive labour market, struggles among union members for scarce jobs and greater economic security intensifies. During periods of economic decline there is a real danger that equity isssues will be sidelined in favour of "traditional" union concerns that are perceived to benefit the broad base of the union membership.[56] Equity demands have been especially susceptible to challenge since the development of economic globalization in the 1980s.

Economic Restructuring and Pay Equity

A further barrier to pay equity operates at the level of the economy and concerns the problem of restructuring of labour markets. The impact of restructuring in Canada is discussed in greater detail in later chapters, but it needs to be pointed out here that wage polarization, the growth of non-standard employment such as part-time work, higher levels of underemployment and unemployment resulting from technological change, and public-sector and private-sector downsizing, represent major trends in the Canadian economy. Within this context of labour market reorganization, pay equity gains can easily be undermined or even obliterated by decisions of employers to restructure their operations. Not only are the long-term benefits of pay equity at risk under conditions of economic change, but new initiatives can barely get off the ground. A rather dramatic illustration of the vagaries of introducing pay equity in the current political economy is the case of Bell Canada.

The Communications, Energy and Paperworkers (CEP) union representing approximately twenty thousand workers, many employed as telephone operators at Bell, filed a pay equity complaint in 1993 under section 11 of the *Canadian Human Rights Act.* Since the complaint was filed, the case has undergone numerous court challenges, the workers engaged in a five-week strike over the issue of pay equity in 1999 and the company subsequently sold its telephone operator division to an American-based corporation. As Judy Fudge explains, "[a]fter the sale, the mostly female employees would see their wages drop from $19.50 per hour to $12 per hour, a pay decrease of approximately 40 percent."[57] This study of the supermarket tells a similar story of restructuring. At one of the major supermarket chains where pay equity was negotiated, the workers engaged in a lengthy strike only to find upon their return to work that many of the jobs which benefited from pay equity adjustments were eliminated by the company.

Whether or not pay equity actually works to improve women's economic situation depends to a great extent upon labour market stability. No matter how hard unions and other equal pay proponents try to promote and enforce equity gains achieved under collective bargaining or through legal challenges, all can be lost when a firm decides, as a cost-saving measure, to reorganize or restructure its operations. The overarching goal of pay equity to achieve substantive equality for women is heavily contingent upon the broader economic conditions in which the policy is introduced. In chapter 4 we take a close look at the history of women workers in the food retail industry to show how the gender division of labour was developed in response to competitive business pressures in the sector. We can understand why women, who were hired at low wages at critical times of industry restructuring, were a significant factor in the development of the supermarket industry. Maintaining low wages for the feminized workforce continues to be a prerogative of supermarket management.

In the following chapter, a discussion of equal pay policy shows that the struggle to achieve better wages for women was circumscribed by prevailing gender ideologies that either supported or challenged traditional views of women's proper role in society. As social and economic conditions altered women's social status, the demand for equal pay entered the political discourse.

NOTES

1. A revised version of this chapter appeared in the *Canadian Journal of Women and the Law* 8 (1995), 440–69.

2. See, for example, Linda Blum, "Possibilities and Limits of the Comparable Worth Movement," *Gender and Society* 1, no. 4 (1987), 394; Debra Lewis, "Pay Equity and the State's Agenda," in Judy Fudge and Patricia McDermott, eds., *Just Wages: A Feminist Assessment of Pay Equity* (Toronto: University of Toronto Press, 1991); Johanna Brenner, "Feminist Political Discourses: Radical Versus Liberal Approaches to the Feminization of Poverty and Comparable Worth," *Gender and Society* 1, no. 4 (1987), 447–65, which is reprinted in Karen Hansen and Ilene Philipson, eds. *Women, Class, and the Feminist Imagination* (Philadelphia: Temple University Press, 1990); Anver Saloojee, "Containing Resistance: The Neoliberal Boundaries of Employment Equity," in Mike Burke, Colin Mooers and John Shilelds, eds., *Restructuring and Resistance: Canadian Public Policy in an Age of Global Capitalism* (Halifax: Fernwood, 2000), 287–305; Susan Boyd and Susan Elizabeth Sheehy, "Feminism and the Law in Canada: Overview," in Tullio Caputo et al., eds., *Law and Society: A Critical Perspective* (Toronto: Harcourt Brace Janovich, 1989), 254–66; Rhada Jhappan, "The Equality Pit or the Rehabilitation of Justice," *Canadian Journal of Women and the Law* 10 (1998), 69.

3. Patricia Cain, "Feminism and the Limits of Equality," *Georgia Law Review* 24 (1990), reprinted in D. Kelly Weisberg ed., *Feminist Legal Theory: Foundations,* Vol. 1 (Philadelphia: Temple University Press, 1993), 238.

4. Michael McCann argues the sameness logic is evident in pay equity because a uniform standard of job worth is applied to men and women's work resulting in equitable rewards for both sexes. Michael McCann, *Rights at Work: Pay Equity Reform and the Politics of Legal Mobilization* (Chicago: University of Chicago Press, 1994), 250.

5. Brenner,"Feminist Political Discourses."

6. Ibid., 447.

7. See Pat Armstrong and Hugh Armstrong, "Lessons from Pay Equity," *Studies in Political Economy* 32 (1990), 29–55; Pat Armstrong and Hugh Armstrong, "Limited Possibilities and Possible Limits for Pay Equity: Within and Beyond the Ontario Legislation," in Judy Fudge and Patricia McDermott, eds., *Just Wages: A Feminist Assessment of Pay Equity* (Toronto: University of Toronto Press, 1991); William Bielby and James Baron, "Undoing Discrimination: Job Integration and Comparable Worth," in Christine Bose and Glenna Spitze, eds., *Ingredients for Women's Employment Policy* (Albany: State University of New York, 1987); Carl Cuneo, *Pay Equity: The Labour-Feminist Challenge* (Toronto: Oxford University Press, 1990); Paula England, *Comparable Worth: Theories and Evidence* (New York: Aldine De Gruyter, 1992); McCann, *Rights at Work,* chap. 2; Robert Nelson and Wlliam Bridges, *Legalizing Gender Inequality: Courts, Markets and Unequal Pay for Women in America* (Cambridge: Cambridge University Press, 1999), 3.

8. Sara Evans and Barbara Nelson, Wage Justice: Comparable Worth and the Paradox of Technocratic Reform (Chicago: University of Chicago Press, 1989), 46–7.

9. While not speaking from the position of pay equity, Sarah Salter presents an interesting feminist critique of the market. She argues that the concept of the undifferentiated individual in liberal theory coincides with assumptions about the

operation of the market and the need for males to assert their autonomy and power through access to property. Since men's self-identification is given expression by separation and independence, their search for individual self-autonomy is commensurate with property acquisition. Liberal views of the market are based on a male conception of the self in that impersonal transactions between individuals take place within a framework that assumes trade-offs can be made between personal needs for economic benefit. For women and minorities, however, access to property is often denied and their sense of self is shaped by group identity and participation. Consequently, the philosophical assumptions underlying market relations in liberal thought make "no sense" to powerless groups in society. Women seek identity through fostering group participation — a process of "extended identity" that contradicts political and economic goals put forward by men. I would suggest that pay equity discourse opposes some of the fundamental philosophical assumptions of liberal economic thought identified by Salter. See Sarah Salter, "Inherent Bias in Liberal Thought," in Sheilah Martin and Kathleen Mahoney, eds., Equality and Judicial Neutrality (Toronto: Carswell, 1987).

10. Evans and Nelson, *Wage Justice,* 58–67; England, *Comparable Worth,* 287–91; Cuneo, *Pay Equity: The Labour-Feminist Challenge,* 84–126.

11. Michael Gold, *A Dialogue on Comparable Worth* (New York: ILR Press, 1983), 45.

12. Bielby and Baron, "Undoing Discrimination," 221; McCann, *Rights At Work.*

13. For instance, Robert Nelson and William Bridges propose an "organizational inequality model" to argue that organizational processes operate in conjunction with market factors to produce gender inequality in pay. See Nelson and Bridges, *Legalizing Gender Inequality,* 4–11.

14. Alice Kessler-Harris, *A Woman's Wage: Historical Meanings and Social Consequences* (Lexington: University of Kentucky Press, 1990), 2.

15. Kessler-Harris's discussion of the minimum wage debates is particularly illuminating. She suggests that the competing views of women as either family members or secondary labourers was played out in the courts of the early twentieth century. The courts relied on "gender difference as a legal category" to determine whether, on the one hand, women should receive minimum wage based on their status as free wage labourers, or whether on the other hand, women as family members required state regulation to ensure a wage that could sustain their health and well-being as mothers. See Kessler-Harris, *A Woman's Wage,* chap. 2, especially, 51–6.

16. Martha Minow, "The Supreme Court 1986 Term, Forward: Justice Engendered," 101 *Harvard Law Review* 101 (1987), reprinted in Weisberg, *Feminist Legal Theory: Foundations.*

17. Ronnie Steinberg, "Job Evaluation and Managerial Control: The Politics of Technique and the Techniques of Politics," in McDermott and Fudge, eds., *Just Wages,* 196.

18. Carole Pateman, *The Disorder of Women: Democracy, Feminism and Political Theory* (Cambridge: Polity Press, 1989).

19. Joan Acker, "Hierarchies, Jobs, Bodies: A Theory of Gendered Organizations," *Gender and Society* 4, no. 2 (1990), 149.

20. Ibid., 149.

21. Ibid., 149–50.

22. Ronnie Steinberg, "Gendered Instructions: Cultural Lag and Gender Bias in the Hay System of Job Evaluation," *Work and Occupations* 19, no. 4 (1992), 387–423; Rosemary Morgan, "Pay Equity By Law: Is There A Better Way to Equality of Result for Female Faculty?" in Susan Heald, ed., *Ivory Towers, Feminist Issues: Selected Papers from the WIN Symposia, 2000-01* (Ottawa: Humanities and Social Sciences Federation of Canada, 2002), 59.

23. See Acker, *Doing Comparable Worth;* Heidi Hartmann, "Comparable Worth and Women's Economic Independence," in Christine Bose and Glenna Spitze, eds., *Ingredients for Women's Employment Policy* (Albany: State University of New York, 1987).

24. Although management consultants and compensation specialists often claim that job evaluation is a rational, scientific process to order the organizational hierarchy and set wage differentials, it is probably more accurate to say that the process functions to establish a value system for measuring job worth. See Maeve Quaid, *Job Evaluation: The Myth of Equitable Assessment* (Toronto: University of Toronto Press, 1993); Debra Lewis, *Just Give Us the Money: A Discussion of Wage Discrimination and Pay Equity* (Vancouver: Women's Research Centre, 1988).

25. Ronnie Steinberg provides a comprehensive feminist critique of the Hay job-evaluation system, a well-known and widely used job comparison method that became the model for subsequent systems used by management consultants in the United States and Canada. Steinberg explains that the Hay system sustains the status quo by "treating location in the formal bureaucratic organizational hierarchy as the underlying standard against which all other work is assessed." Since location in the organizational hierarchy is given primacy in judging job worth, women's work are devalued because their jobs are situated at the lower end of the hierarchy. Moreover, the type and range of work men do is likely to be measured by Hay whereas the various work tasks performed by women are not. For example, Hay consistently values managerial functions (i.e., work usually performed by men) over other types of job tasks. Supervising employees is assumed to require greater complex use of skills than those skills required to work with clients, patients, children and other human services work that is typically performed by women. Steinberg concludes that the job content of women's work is "treated as invisible, unskilled and less responsible." The 'standard' of job worth that Steinberg criticizes is, in fact, based on an ideology of the abstract worker, who, in the Hay system, is implicitly presented as the white male manager. See Steinberg, "Gendered Instructions," 405, 418.

26. Joan Acker, "Sex Bias in Job Evaluation: A Comparable Worth Issue," in Christine Bose and Glenna Spitze, eds., *Ingredients for Women's Employment Policy* (New York: State University of New York, 1987); Ronnie Steinberg and Lois Haignere, "Equitable Compensation: Methodological Criteria for Comparable Worth," in Bose and Spitze, eds., *Ingredients for Women's Employment Policy.*

27. Steinberg, "Gendered Instructions."

28. See Gillian Creese, *Contracting Masculinity: Gender, Class and Race in a White-Collar Union, 1944–1994* (Toronto: Oxford University Press, 1999); Cynthia Cockburn, *In the Way of Women: Men's Resistance to Sex Equality in Organizations.* (New York: ILR Press, 1991); Jane Jensen, "The Talents of Women, the Skills of Men: Flexible Specialization and Women," in Stephen Wood, ed., *The Transformation of Work? Skill, Flexibility and the Labour Process* (London: Unwin Hyman, 1989); Ruth Milkman, *Gender at Work: The Dynamics of Job Segregation*

by Sex during World War II (Chicago: University of Illinois Press, 1987).

29. Francois Eyraud et al., *Equal Pay Protection In Industrialised Market Economies: In Search Of Greater Effectiveness* (Geneva: International Labour Organisation, 1993), 3.

30. Cockburn, *In the Way of Women*, 11.

31. Thus MacKinnon's concern that "the sameness standard has mostly gotten men the benefit of those few things women have historically had" is averted. Catharine MacKinnon, *Toward a Feminist Theory of the State* (Cambridge: Harvard, 1989), 221. Michael McCann makes a similar argument, see *Rights at Work*, 252.

32. See David Goldberg, *Racist Culture: Philosophy and the Politics of Meaning* (Cambridge: Blackwell, 1993); Patricia Williams, *The Alchemy of Race and Rights* (Cambridge: Harvard University Press, 1991). For a specific discussion of how liberal values of equality and rationality operate in the university to privilege "Whiteness," see Carol Schick, "Keeping the Ivory Tower White: Discourses of Racial Domination," in Sherene Razack, ed., *Race, Space, and the Law: Unmapping a White Settler Society* (Toronto: Between the Lines, 2002).

33. Most books on pay equity focus on gender-based discrimination, see, for example, McCann, *Rights at Work;* Nelson and Bridges, *Legalizing Gender Inequality,* 11.

34. Jeanne Gregory, Rosemary Sales and Ariane Hegewisch, eds., *Women, Work and Inequality: The Challenge of Equal Pay in a Deregulated Market* (London: MacMillan Press, 1999), 9.

35. For an analysis of pay equity and employment equity from an equal opportunity perspective see Lesley Jacobs, "Equal Opportunity and Gender Disadvantage," *Canadian Journal of Law and Jurisprudence* 7, no. 1(1994) 61–72.

36. See Evans and Nelson, *Wage Justice*, 42–6; McCann, *Rights at Work*, 24–5. McCann explains that "white, Black and Hispanic women were paid 55.7 percent, 52.4 percent and 48.2 percent of what white men earned" in 1978. Deborah Figart explains that a majority, 62 percent, of minimum wage earners in the U.S. were women in 1997, and that "compared with their representation in the U.S. as a whole, minimum wage earners disproportionately are African American (15 percent) and Hispanic (20 percent)." See Deborah Figart, "Raising the Minimum Wage and Living Wage Campaigns," in Mary King, ed., *Squaring Up: Policy Strategies to Raise Women's Incomes in the United States* (Ann Arbor: Michigan University Press, 2001), 117.

37. See Christina Gabriel, "Restructuring at the Margins: Women of Colour and the Changing Economy," in Enakshi Dua and Angela Robertson, eds., *Scratching the Surface: Canadian Anti-Racist Feminist Thought* (Toronto: Women's Press, 1999), 147–50, for data on racialized women's labour force participation in Canada. It must be pointed out that racialized groups do not fare as well as white people in the labour market. Racialized groups experience lower employment earnings, are less likely to be unionized and suffer severe discrimination in employment. Racialized women are particularly vulnerable. See Grace-Edward Galabuzi, *Canada's Creeping Economic Apartheid: The Economic Segregation and Social Marginalisation of Racialised Groups* (Toronto: Canadian Centre for Social Justice, 2001).

38. There are a few exceptions, notably New York State, which mandated a comparable worth study which included evaluation of minority jobs. See Alice Hanson

Cook, *Comparable Worth: A Case Book* (University of Hawaii at Monoa: Industrial Relations Center, 1986), ix. But I think it is fair to say that gender-predominance has taken priority over minority-majority comparison in most jurisdictions.

39. Diamond Ashiagbor, "The Intersection Between Gender and 'Race' in the Labour Market: Lessons for Anti-Discrimination Law," in Anne Morris and Therese O'Donnell, eds., *Feminist Perspectives on Employment Law* (London: Cavendish Publishing, 1999); Irene Breugel, "Sex and Race in the Labour Market," *Feminist Review* 2 (Summer 1989) 49–68; Julie Matthaei, *An Economic History of Women in America: Women's Work, the Sexual Division of Labor, and the Development of Capitalism* (Brighton: Harvester, 1982); Evelyn Nakano Glenn, "Racial Ethnic Women's Labor: The Intersection of Race, Gender and Class Oppression," in Chris Bose, Roslyn Feldberg and Natalie Sokoloff, eds., *Hidden Aspects of Women's Work* (New York: Praeger, 1987); Tania Das Gupta, *Racism and Paid Work* (Toronto: Garamond, 1996).

40. See Dionne Brand, "Black Women and Work," *Fireweed* 25 (Fall 1987), 28–37, and "Black Women and Work: Part Two" in the following issue of *Fireweed* 26 (Winter/Spring 1988), 49–68; Wenona Giles and Sedef Arat-Koc, eds., *Maid in the Market: Women's Paid Domestic Labour* (Halifax: Fernwood Publishing, 1994).

41. For a full discussion of the labour market profile of women of colour in Canada, see Chris Gabriel, "Restructuring at the Margins"; on homecare workers, especially live-in nannies, see Sue McWatt and Sheila Neysmith, "Enter the Filipina Nanny: An Examination of Canada's Live-In Caregiver Policy," in Carol Bains, Patricia Evans and Sheilia Neysmith, eds., *Women's Caring: Feminist Perspectives on Social Welfare,* 2nd ed. (Toronto: Oxford University Press, 1998); and on reproductive work, see Giles and Sedef-Arat-Koc, *Maid in the Market.*

42. Judy Fudge, "The Paradoxes of Pay Equity: Reflections on the Law and the Market in Bell Canada and the Public Service Alliance of Canada," *Canadian Journal of Women and the Law* 12 (2000), 314.

43. See McCann, *Rights at Work,* 40–1. He explains that in *Gunther* the court was inconclusive on the market defence, but by 1985 in *AFSCME v. State of Washington* the court argued that neo-classical economic principles explained unequal pay between the sexes.

44. Nelson and Bridges, *Legalizing Gender Inequality,* 15.

45. *P.S.A.C. v. Canada (Treasury Board)* cited in Suzanne Handman and Karen Jensen, "Pay Equity in Canada: An Overview," *Canadian Labour and Employment Law Journal* 7(1999), 67. This article provides an overview of Canadian pay equity case law.

46. For a discussion of systemic discrimination as it has been defined by the courts in Canada, see *P.S.A.C.of Canada v. Canada (Treasury Board),* 1998, 70-2; P.S.A.C of Canada (Department of National Defence), [1996] 3 F.C. 789 at 800.

47. See Judy Fudge, "Paradoxes of Pay Equity," on the PSAC and Bell Canada cases. For instance in Bell Canada, the employer challenged the existence of the federal Human Rights Tribunal, the equal wages guidelines and appealed to the Supreme Court to dismiss the union complaint, causing years of delays. In chapter nine two human rights decisions are also discussed that describe years of delays over the issue of impartiality of tribunals.

48. Acker, *Doing Comparable Worth;* Creese, *Contracting Masculinity;* Cuneo, *Pay Equity: The Labour-Feminist Challenge.*

49. See Fudge, "The Paradoxes of Pay Equity," and Kim Hertwig, "Pay Equity Legislation in Canada: A Study of the Public Service Alliance of Canada Case," *Canadian Woman Studies* 19, nos 1–2 (1999), 186–93. As Hertwig explains, the union, the employer and the Pay Equity Tribunal all had chosen different wage adjustment methodologies resulting in legal disputes that went on for years. See also Anne Forrest, "Pay Equity: The State of the Debate," in Yonatan Reshef, Collette Bernier, Denis Harrison and Terry Wagar, eds., *Industrial Relations in the New Millennium: Selected Papers from the 37th Conference* (Lavalle, QC: CIRA/ACRI, 2000), 65–78.

50. Acker, "Sex Bias in Job Evaluation"; Ronnie Steinberg, "Job Evaluation and Managerial Control: The Politics of Technique and the Techniques of Politics" in McDermott and Fudge, eds., *Just Wages: A Feminist Assessment;* Quaid, *Job Evaluation: The Myth of Equitable Assesment;* Rosemary Warskett, "Political Power, Technical Disputes, and Unequal Pay: A Federal Case," in Fudge and McDermott, eds., *Just Wages.*

51. On the history of job evaluation, see Quaid, *Job Evaluation: The Myth of Equitable Assessment.*

52. Steinberg, "Job Evaluation and Managerial Control."

53. Acker, *Doing Comparable Worth;* Alice Cook et. al., *The Most Difficult Revolution;* Rosemary Warskett, "Can A Disappearing Pie Be Shared Equally?: Unions, Women and Wage Fairness," in Linda Briskin and Patricia McDermott, eds., *Women Challenging Unions: Feminism, Democracy and Militancy* (Toronto: University of Toronto Press, 1993).

54. Joan Acker describes the acrimonious debates between men and women on job evaluation committees over the worth of women's jobs. "Admitting that certain female jobs might be worthy of a similar respect [to men's jobs] seemed to be demeaning" to male employees. Acker, *Doing Comparable Worth,* 102; on the same point see Creese, *Contracting Masculinity,* 198–201.

55. Creese, *Constructing Masculinity.*

56. See, Linda Briskin, "The Equity Project in Canadian Unions: Confronting the Challenge of Restructuring and Globalisation," in Fiona Colgan and Sue Ledwith, eds., *Gender, Diversity and Trade Union: International Perspectives* (London: Routledge, 2002), 34.

57. Judy Fudge,"The Paradoxes of Pay Equity," 335. At the time of writing, the Supreme Court of Canada agreed to hear Bell Canada's complaint that the Human Rights Tribunal is not impartial and cannot offer a fair hearing. The Tribunal had ruled that Bell had to pay its female employees $150 million in equity claims. The Supreme Court hearings have yet to be concluded. "Bell Takes Battle Over Pay Equity to Top Court," *The Toronto Star,* 14 December 2001 A23; "Memory of Laura Sabia Invoked in Pay-equity Row," *The Toronto Star,* 30 May 2002, D13. In September 2002, Bell Canada agreed to pay $178 million to its 29,000 clerical and sales workers represented by the CTEA. At the time of writing the settlement had not been ratified. If CTEA members ratify the deal the union will withdraw its complaint at the Supreme Court of Canada. The company has not reached a settlement with its 4,000 female telephone operators represented by the CEP and as of September 2002 the union awaits hearings at the Supreme Court.

Chapter Three

PAY EQUITY: THE FEMINIST LEGAL CHALLENGE TO GENDER-WAGE DISCRIMINATION

IN THIS CHAPTER Ontario's legislation is analyzed from the perspective of the pay equity political strategy. How effective were feminist demands to define the purpose and technical details of Ontario's pay equity law? Did the law operate to undermine, or entrench, liberal views of the market and the individual? This analysis shows that while certain fundamental aspects of the pay equity movement's reform strategy were incorporated into the law, political compromise largely weakened the radical potential of the legislation.

In order to understand the content and meaning of Ontario's pay equity law, a brief survey of the history of the "equal pay" concept is reviewed. In this book, equal pay refers to policies and labour initiatives whose objective is to improve women's wages relative to men. Equal pay refers to both "equal pay for equal work" and "pay equity" policy. The "equal pay for equal work" principle requires employers to pay women and men at the same rate of pay for performing *identical* or *similar* work. Pay equity differs from "equal work" laws in that it requires employers to pay women equivalent male wage rates for performing work that is *different* from the work performed by men but of *equal value.*[1] Both of these concepts are explained as they evolved historically in Canada.

Equal Pay in Canada

The struggle for equal pay started over a hundred years ago when women's groups and labour organizations demanded that women performing the same jobs as men receive wages equivalent to men. The principle of equal pay for equal work was endorsed by the National Council of Women in 1893.[2] In 1882 the Toronto Trades and Labour Council included "equal pay for equal work for both sexes" in its political program. The Knights of Labor, an American based labour organization that flourished in Canada in the 1880s, also supported the concept in its platform of principles. Despite these endorsements, labour's position on equal pay was contradictory because of the uncertain effect equal pay had on the employment and pay of women. As Julie White explains:

> employers not only opposed the notion of equal pay for women, but refused to hire women if the same rates of pay applied. When unions insisted upon equal pay, women were not hired.[3]

Applying equal pay for equal work had the effect of segregating women to lower paying jobs in the labour force because employers would only hire women if they could be paid lower wage rates. For working-class men, equal pay caused problems because employers sometimes substituted women's, or children's, cheaper labour in place of hiring men. That women were favoured over men in the labour market created an enormous dilemma for labour. In the nineteenth century, this dilemma was resolved by the working-class demand for a "family wage," in which men were paid a wage that could support their wives and families, and women could stay out of the labour market.

In the early twentieth century, women's low pay continued to be a source of competition for men's labour. The problem of equal pay was reinforced in the First World War when women entered jobs in munitions factories as well as in railways, steel, cement and shoe manufacturing. Women in wartime performed jobs with identical skills and tasks required of men, but seldom received equal remuneration. The widespread presence of gender-wage inequities urged the Canadian government to issue a labour policy directive that established the principle of equal pay for equal work However, the declaration was not introduced until nearly the end of the war, and it specified that women should receive equal pay only where they were performing work ordinarily performed by men. It further qualified the directive by stating that women "should not be allotted tasks disproportionate to their strength," implying that women not be given heavy jobs — jobs "ordinarily performed by men."[4]

Eventually the issue of low pay for women was addressed by provincial minimum-wage laws. Although the law was intended to "protect" women from the abuses of the market, the laws did little to help women achieve economic independence:

> The problem of low wages for the mass of women employed in women's jobs began to be addressed in 1917 by provincial female minimum wage legislation. Minimum wage boards *were* empowered to set female wages on an occupational basis, but instead of adopting an egalitarian approach, they took a protective one which, at best, provided working women with the bare minimum needed to reproduce their labour.[5]

By the conclusion of the First World War, knowledge of the equal pay principle was fairly widespread at both the national and international level. For instance, the Treaty of Versailles, signed in 1919, included in its Labour Charter "the principle that men and women should receive equal remuneration for work of equal value," a concept that endorsed the equal pay for equal work standard. The International Labour Organization (ILO) adopted the identical equal pay principle in the same year.[6]

While there were important developments in the campaign for equal pay during the First World War, the merits of equal pay were quickly forgotten during the Great Depression of the 1930s. Widespread unemployment pushed the issue of gender-wage fairness far into the background, as a Labour Canada report points out, "there is virtually no record of action taken [by labour or government] during this period" that promoted or affirmed the implementation of equal pay.[7]

When the Second World War broke out in 1939, the demand for labour power ushered women into the labour force in vast numbers, and the issue of equal pay was once again reignited. The Canadian government was prepared fairly early on to regulate wages, and in 1941 it set up the National War Labour Board (with nine regional boards) to administer wage structures for the duration of the war. Similar to what occurred in the First World War, the policies of the Board were inconsistent and tentative on the issue of equal pay. The government vacillated, in part, because it was trying to respond to the contradictory concerns of organized labour. Some trade unions, echoing fears first articulated in the nineteenth century, opposed the principle of equal pay for equal work on the ground that women's presence in the labour force would undercut men's wages.[8] At the same time, the Trades and Labour Congress supported the principle of equal pay, arguing that wage inequality between men and women "constitutes an undermining of the wage rates and standards won by the trade unions over a long period of time."[9]

In attempting to mediate the contradictory concerns expressed by the labour movement, the Canadian state did not establish a coherent policy on equal pay.[10] Instead, the War Labour Board continually released policies and reports that clouded the equal pay issue. Ironically, it was not until after the Second World War when large numbers of women were ejected from the labour force that the federal and provincial governments began to enact laws based on the equal pay for equal work principle.

Equal Pay for Equal Work: "Sameness" Equality Standard

The growing consensus regarding equal pay that took hold in the post-war period was linked to two contradictory ideas.[11] On the one hand, men wanted equal pay to prevent unfair competition and undercutting of male wage rates. Without equal pay, employers would continue to hire women workers because they could be hired at cheaper wages relative to men. On the other hand, women's groups argued for equal pay for equal work because they supported women's rights, as workers, to fair pay. Women's wages, they argued, should be paid according to the *effort, skill and responsibility* that were required of an individual (irrespective of sex) in performing a job. The feminist demand was predicated on a gender-neutral principle of job worth, but the rate of pay was tied to a "sameness" equality standard in that women were to be paid the same wage as men for performing the same work.

Provincial governments enacted equal pay laws starting in the 1950s. Ontario was the first province to pass equal pay legislation in 1951, the same year the ILO passed Convention 100 on "equal remuneration for men and women workers for equal value."[12] By 1959, six other provinces had adopted equal pay for equal work legislation.[13] The provincial statutes were uneven in their coverage, with some acts covering provincial government employees and others excluding them. The acts also differed in their definition of equal work. Ontario required employers to pay men and women the same wage, if they performed the same work in the same establishment, whereas other statutes, like Manitoba's, required equal pay for work done by women that was substantially identical. In 1956 the federal government passed the *Female Employees Equal Pay Act,* that covered workers in enterprises that were interprovincial or national in scope, but excluded the civil service. There was one limitation common to *all* of the statutes: differences in pay "based on factors other than sex" including seniority, length of service, location or geographical area of employment" were permitted.[14] In addition, these laws were complaint-based, meaning that women had to file a complaint of unfair pay with a government agency. Given that employees were very reluctant to initiate a complaint procedure, very few penalties were invoked and the legislation was weakly enforced.[15]

The greatest shortcoming of these equal work laws, however, stemmed from the fact that occupational sex segregation prevented wage comparisons between men and women:

In spite of the relatively early passage of the equal-pay legislation [in Canada] it was a well-known fact that the statutes did
little to reduce the gap between male and female wages ... in a
labour force that was highly sex segregated, women were most
unlikely to obtain employment in the same occupations as
men. As the Women's Bureau of Ontario reported, "It was dis-
covered that classifying jobs as 'male' or 'female' was a greater
obstacle to equality than separate wage scales."[16]

In short, the effect of applying the equal pay for equal work principle served to reinforce segregation because the law did not address
how women are differently situated in the labour market.

The enactment of equal pay for equal work laws is an excellent
illustration of what happens when policy is formulated that
attempts to achieve greater equality for women, but ignores gender
difference. Women's groups, in appealing to universal arguments for
equality based on a notion of individual rights, did not fully address
the gender structure of the labour market. Although they understood that wage discrimination prevailed in the economy, their
arguments left untouched the entrenched sources of women's low
pay that were related to the social construction of skill and the ideological dimensions of the sexual division of labour at work.[17] Equal
pay laws were devised without a well-developed understanding of
how occupational sex segregation is embedded in systems of wage
setting. As a result, they had the effect of reinforcing women's
subordinate position in the labour market.

When the second wave of the women's movement emerged in
the 1960s, the equal pay for equal work principle underwent
revision. New feminist analyses of the labour market identified
occupational segregation as an underlying source of low wages for
women. The recognition that women work in dissimilar jobs, shifted the focus of equal pay laws from comparison between the same
or identical jobs towards comparison between similar jobs. In
Ontario, for example, the equal-work principle was inserted in the
Employment Standards Act in 1968 and revised several times. In
1983, the *Act* provided equal pay for "substantially the same kind of

work" in respect of skill, effort, responsibility and working conditions.[18] While this wording allowed comparisons to be made between jobs that were substantially similar, the provision did not provide for wage comparison between dissimilar jobs. A different kind of approach was required in order to redress wage discrimination resulting from occupational sex segregation.

The development of an equal pay approach that allows cross-gender job comparison was initially formulated by the International Labour Organization in 1951. ILO Convention 100 states that:

> Each member shall, by means appropriate to the methods in operation for determining rates of remuneration, promote and, insofar as is consistent with such methods, ensure the application to all workers of the principle of equal remuneration for men and women workers for work of equal value.[19]

Essentially, Convention 100 established what is referred to as the "equal value" approach to equal pay. Although the precise method of implementation was not spelled out in the Convention, the notion that different types of jobs can be compared by determining their value, was a breakthrough in the campaign for equal pay. Initially, Canada responded to Convention 100 by passing equal pay for equal work laws. However, it restated its commitment to enact equal value legislation at all levels of government in 1972.

In the mid 1970s, the National Action Committee on the Status of Women (NAC), a Canadian feminist organization, lobbied the federal government to enact equal value legislation. NAC argued for legislation that permitted comparison between dissimilar jobs performed by men and women using a job comparison system that measured the relative value of different jobs. In 1978, the *Canadian Human Rights Act*, which covers workers in the federal jurisdiction, was amended under section 11 to provide for equal value comparison. It was the first legislation in Canada to include the equal value concept that used "composite criteria of job value for gender comparison between occupational job groups."[20]

Pay Equity in Ontario

With the passage of equal value at the federal level, the provinces were given incentive to enact their own legislation.[21] Political lobbying, particularly by feminist groups such as NAC, raised awareness about women's low economic status in society, and increasing pressure was placed on governments to introduce policy to improve women's economic standing.[22] The recognition that women are economically disadvantaged was reflected in the 1985 *Green Paper on Pay Equity*, a report produced by the Ontario Liberal government to review options for implementing pay equity in the province. Its rationale for pay equity policy reflected the changing social context of Ontario's economy. The report explained that women's place in society has substantially changed with respect to women's participation in the paid labour force. It explained that a large percentage (40 percent) of women are divorced, single or widowed, are self-supporting or sole-support mothers and that the persistence of occupational sex segregation is largely responsible for the under-valuation of women's paid work.[23]

Attempts to pass pay equity legislation were unsuccessful up until 1985, when a major political shift in political power transpired in the province.[24] A provincial election held on May 2, 1985, left the Progressive Conservative Party, which had held office in the province for forty-two years, with minority status in the legislature. While the Conservatives still held a majority of seats, the Liberal and NDP parties were in a position to combine forces to form a coalition government.[25] An agreement reached between the Liberals and the NDP was that pay equity would be legislated.

When the Liberals took power in June 1985, procedures to introduce legislation on equal pay for work of equal value were quickly initiated. David Peterson, leader of the Liberal Party and premier of Ontario, announced in July that the minister responsible for women's issues was to develop the *Green Paper* on pay equity. At the same time that the Paper was being prepared, the premier had also appointed William Wrye, then minister of labour, to develop an options paper on implementation of pay equity in the public sector.

Both the *Green Paper* and the *Options Paper* were tabled in the legislature in November 1985. Following the release of these two papers, a Consultation Panel on Pay Equity was named in 1986, charged to hear the views of business, labour, women's groups and other sectors in the province. The Premier's Business Advisory Committee on Pay Equity and the Premier's Labour Advisory Committee were asked to discuss specific implementation proposals and possible contentious issues. Both Advisory Committees were established within the state bureaucracy and had close connections to the premier and to the attorney general, the minister responsible for women's issues and other senior bureaucrats.

Although the Advisory Committees operated in a closed forum, public consultations were organized around the province by the Consultation Panel on Pay Equity. This government-appointed panel was made up exclusively of members of the business community, leaving both labour and women's groups annoyed that they had been excluded. In response, the Ontario Federation of Labour appointed Janis Sarra, human rights director of the OFL, as a shadow panelist to "attend all of the hearings to ensure greater accountability and more balance in reporting."[26] During the Consultation Panel hearings, 149 oral and 236 written submissions were submitted to the panel. The Standing Committee received 239 written and oral submissions in its first set of hearings, and received over 350 briefs in total. There was, then, plenty of opportunity for discussion on how to best structure equal pay law in Ontario.

Soon after the tabling of the Report of the Consultation Panel on Pay Equity in September 1986, a cabinet submission was drafted outlining legislation to cover both the broader public and private sector. Bill 154 appeared in November 1986 and was referred to the Standing Committee on the Administration of Justice, with further public consultation to follow. Meanwhile, work on legislation that would cover the Ontario public service was also being devised. Bill 105 appeared in March 1987, but it had undergone so many changes in committee that a decision was made to combine Bills 105 and 154. A revised Bill 154 was reviewed by the Standing Committee, a series of amendments were adopted and ultimately approved upon third reading in the legislature on June 15, 1987. The *Pay Equity Act* received royal assent on June 29 and was proclaimed into law on January 1, 1988.[27] This legislation remains law in Ontario although the deadlines for compliance have long passed for the private sector and the narrow public sector, while adjustments in the broader public sector continue to be controversial due to budget constraints and, in some cases, legal challenges have ensued (see below).

Public consultation was an important factor in the process of enacting pay equity because of the "newness" of the legislation. Although Ontario had looked to other jurisdictions, including Manitoba, as possible models for framing legislation, none covered the private sector. The fact that all sectors of the Ontario economy were to be covered by the legislation was a crucial determinant in shaping the law. Another crux of the legislation was devising a method for determining equal value that could be applied in all sectors and that required mandatory compliance by employers. While these factors created a unique opportunity for implementing innovative legislation, it was also an enormous task that had to be accomplished in a relatively short time period. In fact, the government itself was unaware of the complexity of the task it had committed itself to, as Elaine Todres, then assistant deputy minister of the Ontario Women's Directorate, explained:

> Few realized the intricacies and extent of pay equity as a concept. Some thought it a women's issue and encouraged its assignment to the Women's Directorate — a directorate with very limited resources, a directorate without the infrastructure of a majority ministry to [m]arshal staff, and a directorate that had never initiated or written legislation. What we were asked to do was so new that I can only compare it to experiments in reproductive technology or bioethics. We weren't attempting to enhance legislation; we were inventing legislation and there weren't a lot of experts around to consult.[28]

Given the fact that the government was unsure of how to devise pay equity legislation, it was receptive to the views of experts, and accepted submissions on implementation issues from various groups. In this context, lobbying was an important factor in influencing state policy formation.

THE EQUAL PAY COALITION

A key lobby group in the policy formation process was the Equal Pay Coalition of Ontario. The Coalition was established in 1976 and included a number of women's and labour groups at the provincial and national level; groups such as the Business and Professional Women's Clubs of Ontario, Organized Working Women, the International Women's Day Committee, the Ontario Public Service Employees Union, Federation of Women Teachers' Associations of Ontario, the Ontario Federation of Labour and the National Action Committee on the Status of Women. Neither the United Food and Commercial Workers nor the Retail, Wholesale Department Store Union were member groups of the Coalition. In 1987, the Coalition claimed it represented over one million people in Ontario, and over three million nationally. While over 350 labour and women's groups operated under its umbrella, the actual number of people involved in lobbying the government was much smaller. The core group was composed of highly skilled union activists, academics, trade-union staff and feminist lawyers specializing in labour law, including the head of the Coalition, Mary Cornish. The high level of expertise within the Equal Pay Coalition was not ignored by the government or the media, and it played a pivotal role in the debate on pay equity.

The briefs submitted by the Equal Pay Coalition signalled to the government the specific expectations of labour and the women's movement on equal value legislation. From the beginning of the consultation process, the Equal Pay Coalition was unwavering in its demands. In its public response to the *Green Paper,* it asked the government to enact a single piece of legislation to cover both the public and private sectors, that the legislation include both a proactive and complaint-based approach to implementation and that the statute be flexible in its terms to accommodate a range of workplaces in various sectors in the economy. Moreover, the Coalition demanded that a Pay Equity Commission and Tribunal be established to administer, enforce and monitor the legislation.[29]

To ensure maximum coverage and high value adjustments, the Coalition demanded inclusive legislative standards that provided universal coverage of women in every size of workplace in all sectors as well as cross-unit comparisons, arguing that equal value comparisons needed to be broadly defined to encompass a wide range of possible male job comparators.[30]

Finally, it argued from the principle that systemic sources were responsible for gender-wage discrimination and that women's collective right to pay equity must entail structural solutions. The Coalition maintained that pay equity legislation on its own was not enough to ensure substantive equality for women. It asked the government to increase minimum-wage laws, enact mandatory affirmative action, improve access to child care, provide better training programs for women and amend labour relations law to facilitate unionization. It repeatedly explained to the government that the devaluation of women's work derived from many structural sources and that pay equity legislation was only a partial solution to the problem of women's low pay.

BUSINESS OPPOSITION

Business groups were also crucial players in the policy formation process. In general, business opposed legislated pay equity policy primarily on ideological grounds, arguing that it required government intervention in the private marketplace.[31] The cost of pay equity was also a major concern of business:

> many private sector companies [said they] would be unable to afford the cost of closing the wage gap, and that the higher wages would lead to higher consumer prices and would discourage foreign investment in Ontario.[32]

Yet business was still somewhat divided on the issue of pay equity.[33] Large firms had access to resources needed to implement pay equity and were in a better position to pass on any incurred costs to the consumer. Smaller firms, which operated with fewer resources and functioned in a highly competitive market, were not in a favourable position to implement pay equity. Big business felt it unfair that small firms be excluded from coverage under the proposed legislation since it would establish an uneven "playing field." The Retail Council of Canada reflected this sentiment in its submission to the Consultation Panel:

> while "Retail Council opposes pay equity legislation in principle ... if it were to be implemented then Retail Council on principle, would not support the exclusion of all small business, as a category, from the impact of the legislation. To do so would be discriminatory."[34]

Contrary to the position of the Retail Council, Ontario's legislation excluded firms with fewer than ten employees ("under tens"), and provision was included that smaller private sector firms with fewer than 100 employees be exempt from developing pay equity plans.

Given that business was basically opposed to the legislation, why did pay equity get the go-ahead? One reason was that Ontario was experiencing an economic boom during the 1980s when pay equity policy was being debated. Hence, arguments concerning the cost of pay equity for business did not receive a lot of sympathy.[35] The proposed Act also provided that 1 percent of the employer's total payroll per year be set aside for pay equity — not an exorbitant amount during a period of economic prosperity.[36] A second reason was that a number of compromises, like the exclusion of "under-tens," were incorporated into the legislation, which basically had the effect of undercutting the effectiveness of the Act. As Carl Cuneo points out, these compromises made pay equity more palatable to businesses:

> Despite its initial vociferous opposition to the legislation, business has been willing to go along with it because, compared to labour and women's movements, it did not appear to lose as much. By design or otherwise, devices were set up in the legislation whereby pay equity would not cost employers any more in terms of labour expenditures than they would otherwise have to bear in the absence of pay equity.[37]

POLITICAL COMPROMISE

Although the legislation contains provisions that operate to restrict the cost of pay equity for business, it is also important to recognize that Ontario's Act reflects a series of political compromises. The internal inconsistencies and ambiguous terms in the Act are the product of the political negotiations and "horse-trading" that occurred in the writing of the legislation.[38] The political wrangling between representatives of different political parties, who were largely responsible for writing the Act, resulted in ill-defined legal terms or the entire absence of definitions in the law.[39] Moreover, because the Equal Pay Coalition asked that the legislation be "flexible in its terms," language may have deliberately been included that was open to interpretation.[40] Paradoxically, because the Act contains vague definitions and imprecise legal terms, organized labour (and possibly other politically motivated groups) were granted the opportunity to define pay equity in a progressive direction. The open ended and flexible provisions allowed negotiating parties to construct pay equity in a manner that was most suitable to their particular work setting or industry and that could maximize pay adjustments.

On the other hand, political compromise also shifted Ontario's legislation away from a feminist interpretation of pay equity. As explained below, pay equity strategists were unable to successfully craft the legislation in a way that reflected their vision of gender equality in pay. While feminists stress the importance of exposing the "male standpoint" embedded in market relations and identify systemic gender discrimination to explain women's low pay, Ontario's legislation contains many complex technical definitions and statutory requirements that undermine, or contradict, the broader political goals of the feminist pay equity strategy. By examining the legislative requirements in the Act, it is possible to assess whether a feminist vision of pay equity was incorporated, or purged, in Ontario's legislation.

Ontario's Pay Equity Act

It is important to understand the content and operation of Ontario's legislation before beginning an in-depth analysis of how it reflects, or departs from, a feminist viewpoint of pay equity. (An outline of the legislation and a list of definitions are provided in the Glossary at the end of this book.) Ontario's *Pay Equity Act* is pro-active in that the law requires employers to comply with positive measures to reduce the gender-wage gap. As mentioned above, Ontario's legislation covers the broader public sector (e.g, government civil service, hospitals, elementary and high schools) and private-sector employers with ten or more employees. Pay adjustments in the private sector were phased in over several years, depending on the number of employees in the establishment. Where there is a union present, a pay equity plan or plans has to be negotiated with an employer. As explained below, Ontario's law requires job-to-job comparison, meaning that male and female job classes are evaluated and compared, and wage adjustments are made to female job classes that are of equivalent worth to male job classes.

To achieve pay equity under the Act, employers (and bargaining agents of the union) are required to follow six steps to implement a pay equity plan: (1) define establishment; (2) identify job classes; (3) choose job comparison method; (4) determine job rate; (5) compare job classes; and (6) determine pay adjustments.

Establishment

Defining establishment is the first step in the pay equity process. Establishment is defined in the Act along geographic lines and refers to a regional municipality, a territorial district or a county. Ontario's legislation does not have a definition for "employer." Hence, identifying the establishment settles the question of the employer relationship and is essential to the pay equity implementation since it determines the relevant employees to be covered under a pay equity plan. It identifies the corporate entities, such as franchises, that are included under pay equity, as well as determines the size of payroll.

Job Class

The second step identifies job classes, which are defined as positions within an establishment having similar duties and responsibilities, requiring similar qualifications, recruiting procedures and having the same compensation schedule or salary grade(s). A job class is a cluster of jobs, usually bearing the same title, and having a uniform salary range. Under the Act, a female job class consists of 60 percent or more female employees; male job classes comprise 70 percent or more male employees. Where there are 50 percent male and female employees in a job class, it is deemed gender-neutral. The percentage criterion is not the only factor that can be used to determine male and female job classes. Arguments can be made that a job class has been historically performed by men or women (historical incumbency), or that the job class traditionally has been occupied primarily by men or women (gender stereotype). Either of these arguments can be applied to determine gender predominance irrespective of the proportion of men or women in the job class. Finally, one person (single incumbent) can constitute a job class.

JOB COMPARISON METHOD

Once job classes have been identified, the third step in a pay equity exercise is to evaluate job classes to determine their job worth. The job comparison method is required by law to be a gender-neutral system (i.e., free of gender bias). However, the legislation does not define the term gender-neutrality, rather the onus is on employers to show that the job comparison system is not gender-biased. In addition to gender-neutrality, the Act specifies that the job comparison system place a value on the content of jobs using a composite of four factors: skill, effort, responsibility and work conditions. Where there is a union, the choice of job comparison method is negotiated by the employer and bargaining agent.

There are a variety of job comparison systems that have been devised to measure the worth of jobs. The most common type of job evaluation is the point-rating system, which assigns points to compensable elements in a job. As I discuss in chapter 7, the job evaluation system used in the retail food sector, called the Neutralizer, is a point system. It is important to recognize that "job evaluation is neither objective nor scientific"; rather, it is a highly political and subjective process which is shaped by the politics, biases and experience of people directing the job evaluation.[41]

JOB RATE

Before job comparisons can be made it is necessary to determine the job rate, or wage level, for each job class because comparators are determined by the job rate as well as by the job value. The job rate is defined in the Act as the highest rate of compensation for a job class, including "all payments and benefits" for the job class. However, there are provisions in the legislation, referred to as "permissible differences in compensation," that allow employers to exclude the highest job rate as the basis for comparison. The permissible exemptions allowing the exclusion of the highest job rate include (1) the presence of a formal seniority system; (2) the presence of a merit compensation system; and (3) the presence of a skills shortage where the employer can argue a higher wage is only temporary to attract workers. The legislation requires that all of these practices do not discriminate on the basis of gender.

If permissible exemptions are applied, the employer is required to arrive at a lower job rate, but one that reflects the "true rate for the job" if a seniority system, or merit system, were not in place. Where a bargaining agent is present, the "true job rate" must be negotiated with the employer.

COMPARING JOB CLASSES

Having determined the value of male and female job classes and the job rates, the fifth step establishes comparators of equal value. Equal value comparison is determined by the employer where there is no union, and where a union is present, comparison occurs within bargaining units. Cross-unit comparison is permitted only when a suitable comparator cannot be found within the bargaining unit. Another very important aspect of job comparison concerns the definition of comparable value. The Act provides that where female job classes are matched to more than one male job class of equal value, the female job class receives a wage adjustment corresponding to the male job class of comparable value but the *lowest job rate*.

PAY ADJUSTMENTS

The sixth and final step in pay equity implementation is establishing the payouts. As noted previously, an employer is required to spend 1 percent of its total payroll for pay equity until pay equity is achieved. In the private sector, the timing of when pay equity adjustments begin varies depending on the size of the establishment. The public sector was required to negotiate plans and make pay adjustments within two years of the date of proclamation of the Act.

The pay equity implementation process is not particularly straight-forward. The structure of the law itself is complex and the legislative requirements are subject to modification, depending upon the particular interpretation placed on them by the parties. At each step of the process, the application of the law requires a subjective deter-mination of the meaning of terms. For instance, the definition of establishment sets the parameters as to which employees are covered under a pay equity plan. The identification of female and male predominant job classes is negotiable as they can be defined in reference to historical incumbency or gender stereotype arguments, as well as other criteria. The choice of job comparison system and the specific weightings applied to compensable factors in job evaluation must be decided upon because these are crucial in deter-mining the value assigned to job classes. Since gender-neutrality is not defined in the Act, the issue of gender-bias may be taken up as a challenge by a complainant, such as a labour union. Under the law, the definition of job rate can be modified if permissible exemp-tions are applied by the employer. There is flexibility in the job comparison in any instance where there are several possible male comparators, and there may be disagreement as to whether a comparator must be sought outside a bargaining unit. Finally, the schedule of payouts may be expedited in order to conclude the pay equity exercise, or employers may drag their feet in meeting the legislative requirements for payouts, making a complaint to the Commission necessary, especially as there is no requirement for filing plans or a system to monitor settlements.

Given the flexible provisions in Ontario's *Pay Equity Act*, the specific labour relations context in which pay equity is applied will largely determine the success of the pay equity exercise, specifically the level of payouts achieved. For labour-feminist groups with adequate resources, there is the potential to eradicate gender-wage disparities by applying a progressive interpretation and aggressive application of the law. Nonetheless, for pay equity implementation to have fruitful results, highly skilled negotiators are required. Only those familiar with the nuances of the legislation are able to identify the "pressure points" in the law that will maximize the standard of wage equity. Groups having a weak connection with the pay equity movement and that are unable, or unwilling, to direct funds to the pay equity exercise are unlikely to explore the potentialities of the *Pay Equity Act*. As we will see in chapter 7, neither of the retail unions in the supermarket sector stretched the possibilities of applying Ontario's legislation.

Pay Equity Discourse: The Market, the Male Standard and Systemic Discrimination

How, then, is the legislation an expression of the feminist struggle for pay equity? In what ways do the implementation mechanisms reflect the feminist struggle to challenge how women's work is valued in the marketplace? Is there provision in the legislation to resist masculine definitions of job worth? And, does Ontario's Act adequately address the problem of systemic gender discrimination in compensation? In other words, has pay equity's "social vision" or political strategy been realized in Ontario's legislation?

THE MARKET

The legislative requirements in Ontario's Act that bear directly on the market concern the terms of coverage, particularly with respect to the establishment definition. As previously noted, one of the most important determinants in applying pay equity is the definition of the specific area for job comparison. At the very outset, the government of Ontario ruled out the possibility of cross-industry comparison, even though cross-sector comparisons could result in significant wage adjustments, given that women are concentrated in low-wage industries and men are concentrated in high-wage ones.[42] Yet, the Act was deliberately structured to avoid such comparison, since this was regarded as too threatening for business, and instead requires comparisons to take place within an employer's establishment.[43] Such a definition sets parameters on the market wage, since the market rate is restricted to a particular industry or subsector of an industry.

The most critical limitation of Ontario's *Pay Equity Act,* which was readily identified by women's groups and labour, is its failure to provide male comparators for employees who are employed in all female establishments. The establishment definition, combined with the absence of an employer definition, creates severe difficulties for pay equity implementation in large segments of the Ontario economy. Even the government recognized that the Act was unable to provide pay equity for women employed in such female predominant workplaces as childcare centres, nursing homes and libraries. In fact, the Act required the government to conduct a study on systemic discrimination in employment in female-predominant sectors where female job classes are unlikely to find a male comparator. According to some estimates, as many as 420,000 women were excluded under legislation passed in 1988.[44] The lack of comparators eventually led to amendments to the *Pay Equity Act* that could expand the potential male job classes for comparison in all female workplaces such as daycare centres and healthcare organizations.[45] Following the amendments to the legislation, the Ontario Progessive Conservative government introduced budget cuts that eliminated pay equity adjustments for women working in these work settings. This decision was challenged by a labour union under the Charter of Rights and Freedoms and the court ruled in 1997 that it is unfair to disallow pay equity to broader public sector workers while other women in other sectors were granted wage adjustments.[46]

A further restriction in the legislation is the exclusion of firms with fewer than ten employees. The Equal Pay Coalition protested the absence of "under-tens" from the very start of the pay equity debate, pointing out that over 12 percent of working women are excluded from coverage. Significantly, many of the women employed in small workplaces are immigrants or members of visible minorities and tend to be non-unionized. Moreover, the phase-in approach of the legislation, which establishes weaker legislative standards for employer compliance for smaller firms, inadequately protects unregulated sectors of the economy.

The definition of establishment and employer is of paramount importance in pay equity implementation. Given that the premise of Ontario's legislation is to change how the market values women's work, it is critical to adopt a definition of establishment and employer that can encompass a wide area of the economy. Only an expansive definition can incorporate a meaningful market wage for purposes of pay equity comparison. When large segments of the market economy are excluded from pay equity, there is little chance of reducing the gender-wage gap.

THE MALE STANDARD

There are three legislative criteria in Ontario's Act that refer to a male reference point: job comparison, job rate and gender-neutrality. As we have already seen, finding appropriate male comparators is a major pitfall of Ontario's legislation. The job-to-job comparison approach requires that female job classes be matched with male job classes of equal worth. In all-female establishments, there is no possibility of locating a male comparator. Hence, the male standard is simply not achievable. Even in workplaces where there are male job classes, it is still necessary to find corresponding male job classes of comparable worth, which may *or* may not exist. And, even where a female job class is able to locate male job classes of equal value, the legislation requires that the wage adjustment be leveled up to the *lowest* possible male comparator. In the process of job comparison, then, we find that the search for male comparators is entirely arbitrary, and that the male standard by which female job classes are compared is subject to a low level of wage equity.

A specific mechanism in the legislation, which functions to diminish the male standard, is the "groups of jobs" provision. This provision allows a series of *female* job classes to be combined to create, in effect, one job class. The problem of the groups of jobs mechanism is that by combining a whole series of female job classes, some individual female job classes in the series do not receive a wage adjustment that represents their true worth. This device operates to reduce the level of wage equity for women, since one male job class becomes the comparator for an entire series of female jobs. Similarly, the practice of "banding" in job evaluation operates to reduce wage equity for female job classes by locating job classes within a hierarchy of value bands so that a series of jobs are situated along a rating scale. Depending on the value ranges of the band, numerous female job classes may receive a low wage adjustment, or none at all.[47]

A further provision in Ontario's legislation that explicitly refers to the notion of a male standard is the concept of gender-neutrality. The requirement of gender-neutrality in job comparison, although not defined in the legislation, is crucial in challenging male bias in wage setting.[48] Job evaluation in pay equity implementation holds out the greatest promise of addressing masculine assumptions of job worth since Ontario's legislation requires that job comparison systems be free of gender-bias. Unlike other provisions in Ontario's *Pay Equity Act,* the requirement of gender-neutrality is founded on purely feminist principles of pay equity, and offers maximum leeway for resisting male standards of job worth. Gender-neutrality offers an opening for feminists to critique job evaluation systems, and to construct alternative value criteria for determining the relative worth of jobs. Of all the provisions in the legislation, the criterion of gender-neutrality stands out as offering the greatest potential for redefining social meanings which devalue women's work. As argued in chapter 1, the feminist critique of job evaluation uncovers assumptions about the abstract (male) individual, and thereby challenges liberal conceptions about valuable work and the valuable worker.

In answering the question of whether Ontario's legislation relies on a male standard, we can argue that insofar as women need to find a male comparator, the male standard is held up as the norm by which women's value is measured. Further, there are mechanisms in the legislation, such as the groups of jobs approach and the requirement that female job classes find the highest value match but with the lowest job rate, which clearly function to diminish the male standard for comparison. The process of job-to-job comparison operates in a direct sense to ensure that women are compared to men, while at the same time ensuring that women seldom reach the highest or optimal standard for wage comparison.

Systemic Discrimination

A crucial component of the pay equity strategy is founded on the principle that systemic gender discrimination in employment contributes to women's low pay. Ontario's *Pay Equity Act,* which identifies the need to "redress systemic gender discrimination in compensation for work performed by employees in female job classes," recognizes a fundamental principle of pay equity. The fact that the legislation includes reference to systemic discrimination was an important victory for the women's movement. However, as Judy Fudge points out, "[t]he paradox of the Ontario Pay Equity Act is that while it recognizes the problem to be systemic, its solution is not."[49] This contradiction, that the legislation is to remove systemic discrimination but does not provide structural remedies to correct wage inequities, is particularly apparent in the "permissible exemptions" provision in the Act.

As previously discussed, there are a number of ways for employers to argue the exclusion of the highest rate of compensation of the job rate for pay equity comparison. Seniority, merit pay, skills shortage and red-circling can all be invoked to exclude the highest rate of compensation for the job class, if it can be shown that they are not gender-biased. Undoubtedly, the provision of gender-neutrality was intended to mitigate against employers use of the exemptions. However, the requirement of gender-neutrality in this context is somewhat incongruous because all of the "exclusions" provided in the Act are built-in sources of discrimination for women at the workplace. Ironically, the Act identifies some of the traditional biases against women, while at the same time offering employers an opportunity to justify the continuation of those same discriminatory practices.

The factor of seniority is especially problematic. As this commentator observes, to find a seniority system that does not discriminate on the basis of gender is almost impossible:

> Seniority systems in the workplace ... create several kinds of potential barriers. They are structured to give preference and protection to long-service employees, and in many work-places, those employees will be males, and often from Caucasian backgrounds. To the extent that promotion is based on a collective agreement provision specifying that the senior qualified person gets the job, there is an obstacle to the promotion of the newer entrants to the workplace who... [may be] as well qualified or even better qualified than the longer-term employee.[50]

Under most seniority provisions women can find themselves disadvantaged, since they are typically in the workplace for shorter lengths of time as compared to men and are therefore placed at the lower levels of the seniority scale. Where seniority systems are structured by job classification or department, women are segregated from the better paying positions and cannot achieve the necessary work experience for advancement. During periods of restructuring, women may find that their entire division has been downsized or eliminated, while in times of layoffs, women may be the first to be let go by the employer[51] For a variety reasons, then, seniority systems have an inherent gender-bias.

The merit principle is another "exclusion" under the Act that must be shown to be gender-neutral. Like seniority, merit pay is supposedly based on neutral principles such as a person's abilities, qualifications and work-related experience. However, most decisions concerning merit pay are influenced by gendered assumptions. For instance, "a person's abilities" are often actually seen through a s exist lens, as this analyst explains, "when men and women perform identically on particular tasks, their performances are perceived differently."[52] Typically, men are seen as better able to perform in a variety of areas of work, while women's abilities are restricted to a narrow band. Women are judged to be care providers, as "naturally" performing well in emotional kinds of work, whereas men are seen to be better suited to difficult mental and physical labour. As such, merit pay is an elusive but highly political concept that is largely defined in reference to management's interests to sustain a masculine organizational culture. Even though merit systems are imbued with gender-bias, it is difficult to dispute subjective decisions made by employers about employee competency and job performance. Under Ontario's *Pay Equity Act,* it must be explicitly shown that merit compensation plans are biased in favour of male employees.

Similar arguments concerning gender-neutrality can be made regarding skills shortage and red-circling. Since women are over-represented in a few occupations, and because women's work is devalued in the workplace, they rarely are singled out as having skills that need to be protected by higher wage rates — only men's work is seen to suffer from market shortages. Hence, employers can argue that men's pay rates are higher due to the lack of skills in a male field, or that a training program is needed to fulfill a skills shortage. Red-circling is a provision that allows employers to exclude a position from pay equity comparison. Male predominant jobs are more likely to be red-circled since men's positions receive higher wage rates. Finally, the provision that differences in compensation are allowable after pay equity negotiations due to differences in bargaining strength overwhelmingly advantages men. Men are more likely than women to be organized in unions, and collective bargaining processes, which often include men in positions of leadership, invariably benefit male members. Collective-bargaining strength is a factor in the workplace that works to the advantage of men but to the disadvantage of women. Ontario's legislation, *which allows* employers to pay different wages based on bargaining skills and strength, perpetuates a historical inequality between the sexes.

*

The result of the legislative struggle for pay equity, as we have seen, is legislation that is weighted down with numerous technical requirements that detract from the stated goals of pay equity advocates. Whereas pay equity strategists emphasize the need to redefine how the market values women's work, the legislation places limits on the definition of the market wage. Ontario's law is structured to limit the scope of pay equity comparison by imposing a definition of establishment that requires comparisons between female predominant and male-predominant job classes *within* establishments, thereby limiting the potential of cross-organization comparisons.

A fundamental principle of pay equity is raising women's wages to meet the level of men's pay rates; the "male wage" is supposed to be the standard by which pay equity can be achieved. As we have seen, Ontario's *Pay Equity Act* was structured in a way that entirely eliminated the possibility of male comparisons for women in all-female establishments. Although changes were enacted to expand coverage of the legislation to female-predominant workplaces, the amendments also do not provide for direct comparison with male compensation rates, rather the "male standard" is arrived at by indirect and convoluted methods of comparison. Where direct job-to-job comparisons can be found, mechanisms such as "groups of jobs" or "banding" can diminish the amount by which women's wages can be raised.

The most favourable provision in the Act, from a feminist perspective, is the requirement of gender-neutrality in job comparison. Although gender-neutrality is not clearly defined, this provision invites proponents of pay equity to identify male assumptions of job worth in job evaluation systems and to reassess the value of women's work in an organization. Contrary to many other provisions in the legislation, the legal requirement of gender-neutrality is most closely articulated with the feminist strategy to achieve pay equity.

Many of the radical components in the feminist strategy to achieve gender equality in pay were redefined in the struggle to create an equal value law. As a result, the potential of Ontario's Act to critique the market, question male standards of job worth and redress systemic gender discrimination is quite limited. Still, the legislation leaves open possibilities to challenge gender-wage inequities, especially for groups possessing political will and resources to take up the legal challenge. Even though there are inherent contradictions within Ontario's Act, there is scope within the legislative framework to argue for a meaningful definition of gender-wage equity. What is important to recognize is that the outcome of the pay equity application depends more upon the labour relations context and the industry sector where women work, than on the indeterminate nature of Ontario's legislation.

In the following chapter the retail food industry is analyzed with particular emphasis on the market and institutional context in which pay equity was applied. An analysis of Ontario's food retail economy uncovers the particular economic pressures and institutional arrangements that operate to disadvantage women in the supermarket. As we will see, the orientation of the retail unions was not conducive to a radical or progressive interpretation of Ontario's pay equity legislation. The philosophy of business unionism which pervades these labour organizations, worked against a progressive interpretation of pay equity. Neither union had a strong feminist presence when pay equity was negotiated, and some women felt they were not fairly represented on the pay equity committees. As a result, there was little opportunity for advocates to promote women's interests in pay equity negotiations.

NOTES

1. Pay equity advocates have addressed the need for equal value in pay for racial minorities. However, the issue of race remains secondary in pay equity discourse. As I argue in chapter 2, pay equity has the potential to recognize the devaluation of work performed by racial/ethnic minorities, but the discourse does not make explicit the racialization of the labour force.
2. See *Equal Pay for Equal Work: The Growth of an Idea in Canada* (Ottawa: Department of Labour, 1959).
3. Julie White, *Sisters & Solidarity: Women and Unions in Canada* (Toronto: Thompson Educational Publishing, 1993), 37.
4. *Equal Pay for Equal Work: The Growth of an Idea in Canada*, 6.
5. Judy Fudge and Eric Tucker, "Law, Industrial Relations, and the State: Pluralism or Fragmentation: The Twentieth-Century Employment Law Regime in Canada,"

Labour/Le Travail 46 (Fall 2000), 264.

6. On the history of equal pay in the international arena, see Thomas Flanagan, "Equal Pay for Work of Equal Value: An Historical Note," *Journal of Canadian Studies* 22, no. 3 (1987), 5–19; Mary Cornish, *Equal Pay, Collective Bargaining and the Law, Prepared for the Department of Labour* (Ottawa: Minister of Supply and Services, 1986), 9.

7. *Equal Pay for Equal Work: The Growth of an Idea in Canada,* 6.

8. On the contradictory position of labour towards equal pay during this period, see Pamela Sugiman, *Labour's Dilemma: The Gender Politics of Auto Workers in Canada, 1937–1979* (Toronto: University of Toronto Press, 1994).

9. Ibid, 7.

10. The contradictory position of the government is reflected in the changing wage policies established during the war. The Board first passed an Order-in-Council enforcing wage scales currently in effect (as of November 15, 1941) to all employees, irrespective of sex of the worker. By the following year, however, a new order was issued that stipulated wage rates be established according to the experience and skill level of the worker. Since women had less experience and were placed in positions deemed to require fewer skills, they received lower wages. Later on, in 1944, the Board produced a report expressing ambivalence about the "practicability of applying the equal pay for equal work principle," because women came to the workplace with varying degrees of ability and skill, thus implying they did not warrant the same pay as men. It seems the Board was not quite convinced that women were deserving of equal pay and was reluctant to endorse the universality of this gender-wage equity principle. See *Equal Pay for Equal Work: The Growth of an Idea in Canada,* 5–8.

11. See Alice Kessler-Harris, *A Woman's Wage: Historical Meanings and Social Consequences* (Lexington: University of Kentucky Press, 1990), chap. 4.

12. See Flanagan, "Equal Pay for Work of Equal Value," 10.

13. These included Alberta (1957), British Columbia (1953), Manitoba (1956), Nova Scotia (1957), Prince Edward Island (1959), and Saskatchewan (1953). See ibid., 18.

14. *Equal Pay for Equal Work,* 11.

15. The reluctance of employees to file complaints is evident from archival records of the Employment Practices Branch for Ontario, which administered complaints under Ontario's Female Employees Fair Remuneration Act. As Jane Ursel summarizes, "In ten of the eighteen years [period of operation of the Act] less than three complaints were filed annually; in five of those years there were no complaints at all." *Private Lives, Public Policy: 100 Years of State Intervention in the Family* (Toronto: Women's Press, 1992), 248.

16. Ibid., 247.

17. See Joan Sangster, "Women Workers, Employment Policy and the State: The Establishment of the Ontario Women's Bureau, 1963–1970," *Labour/Le Travail* 36 (1995), 140.

18. Caroline Egri and W.T. Stanbury, "How Pay Equity Came to Ontario," *Canadian Public Administration* 32, no. 2 (Summer 1989), 285

19. Cornish, *Equal Pay, Collective Bargaining and the Law,* 9.

20. Egri and Stanbury, "How Pay Equity Came to Ontario," 284.

21. The province of Quebec enacted an equal-value provision in its Charter of

Human Rights and Freedoms in 1976, making it the first jurisdiction in Canada to legislate "equal value," however, its provisions are not as broad as that at the federal level. The equal value provision contained in human rights codes, such as Quebec, are complaint-driven. Six of ten Canadian provinces have passed proactive pay equity legislation mandating employers to comply with pay equity procedures. Manitoba was the first province to pass proactive pay equity legislation in 1985 that covers the broader public sector; Ontario enacted pay equity in 1988 that covered the broader public and private sector; Prince Edward Island passed legislation in the same year as Ontario that covers the broader public sector, while Nova Scotia also passed pay equity legislation in 1988 covering the civil service and broader public sector; one year later (1989) New Brunswick enacted legislation that covers public sector employees (civil service and other narrow public service); Quebec is the most recent province to pass legislation in 1996 that covers both the broader public and private sectors (covering employers in the private sector with more than ten employees).

22. NAC was formed in 1972 in response to the Royal Commission on the Status of Women, a government commission established in 1967 to review women's economic and social standing in Canada. The Royal Commission tabled its report in 1970. Equal pay policy was a major concern in its list of recommendations. See Jill Vickers, Pauline Rankin and Christine Appelle, *Politics as if Women Mattered: A Political Analysis of the National Action Committee on the Status of Women* (Toronto: University of Toronto Press, 1993); Barbara Crow and Lise Gottel, eds., *Open Boundaries: A Canadian Women's Studies Reader* (Toronto: Prentice Hall Allyn and Bacon, 2000), 63–72.

23. *Green Paper on Pay Equity* (Toronto: Ministry Responsible for Women's Issues, 1985), 7–15.

24. The legislative struggle to pass pay equity legislation began in 1980 when the Ontario New Democratic Party introduced a private member's bill. Two other bills were later introduced by the NDP, and a resolution accepting the principle for equal pay for work of equal value met with unanimous approval by the legislature in 1983. None of these efforts resulted in legislation though, as all three bills died on the Order Paper. The three private member's bills introduced by the NDP included Bill 157, *An Act Respecting Economic Equality for Women in Ontario,* introduced by Mr. Charlton, 6 October 1980, 4th Session of the 31st Legislature; Bill 108, *An Act to Provide for Affirmative Action and Equal Pay for Work of Equal Value,* introduced by Bob Rae, 1 November, 1983, 3rd Session, 32nd Legislature; and Bill 15, *An Act to Provide Affirmative Action and Equal Pay for Work of Equal Value,* introduced by Bob Rae, 27 March 1984, 4th Session, 32nd Legislature. MPP Sheila Copps introduced a resolution to accept pay equity in 1983. Following all of this activity, the Conservative government amended the *Employment Standards Act* to provide equal pay for substantially the same kind of work. See Muriel Deschenes, "Pay Equity in Ontario: Equity and Efficiency Revisited" (MA thesis, University of Western Ontario, 1990), and Egri and Stanbury, "How Pay Equity Came to Ontario," 285.

25. The Progressive Conservatives won fifty-two seats, the Liberal Party (Grits) held forty-eight seats, and the NDP had a total of twenty-five seats in the legislature. A coalition government is formed when the party in power meets with a vote of non-confidence. This allows the other parties to reach an alliance and form a government. In this case, the Liberals, who held the most seats after the

Conservatives, formed the government. In fact, four days following the election, the NDP caucus agreed to meet with the Liberals to form a coalition, referred to as the Liberal-NDP accord.

26. *Report on the Ontario Government's Public Hearings on Pay Equity* (1986), i.

27. For detailed reviews of the legislative history of pay equity in Ontario, see Deschenes, *Pay Equity in Ontario;* Egri and Stanbury, "How Pay Equity Came to Ontario"; Elaine Todres, "With Deliberate Care: The Framing of Bill 154," *Manitoba Law Journal* 16, no. 3 (Spring 1987), 221–26; and Carl Cuneo, "The State of Pay Equity: Mediating Gender and Class through Political Parties in Ontario," in Judy Fudge and Patricia McDermott, eds., *Just Wages: A Feminist Assessment of Pay Equity* (Toronto: University of Toronto Press, 1991).

28. Todres, "With Deliberate Care," 225–26. Also see Elaine Todres, *Managing Pay Equity: A Bureaucrat's View of Bill 154* (Toronto: Ontario Women's Directorate, 1987), 8; and Cuneo, "The State of Pay Equity," 35.

29. *Equal Pay Coalition Response to the Ontario Government's Green Paper on Pay Equity* (Toronto, January 24, 1986); *Ontario Equal Pay Coalition Response to Bill 154,* 1987.

30. The Equal Pay Coalition tried to convince the government that the Act required "a very broad definition of the employer's establishment." It specifically lobbied for a corporate definition of establishment that would clarify the employer relationship. For instance, a corporate definition makes clear that associated businesses and related employers, including franchises, are associated with a corporate entity. Unfortunately, the Coalition was unsuccessful in its demands, and Ontario's *Act* provides for a geographic definition of establishment that restricts the range of potential job classes for comparison. See *Equal Pay Coalition Response to Ontario's Green Paper* (1986), 13.

31. See Carl Cuneo, *Pay Equity: The Labour-Feminist Challenge.* (Toronto: Oxford University Press, 1990), 89–90 .

32. Todres, "With Deliberate Care," 223.

33. Pat and Hugh Armstrong, "Lessons from Pay Equity," *Studies in Political Economy* 32 (1990), 29–55; Cuneo, *Pay Equity;* Egri and Stanbury, "How Pay Equity Came to Ontario."

34. Retail Council, *Submission to the Ontario Consultative Panel on Pay Equity* (April 1986), 16.

35. Egri and Stanbury, "How Pay Equity Came to Ontario," 279.

36. The proposed legislation required the employer to allocate 1 percent of total payroll (including benefits) per year on the anniversary of the first adjustment until pay equity was achieved.

37. Cuneo, *Pay Equity,* 56.

38. See Egri and Stanbury, "How Pay Equity Came to Ontario," 290; Cuneo, "The State of Pay Equity."

39. See Pat McDermott, "Pay Equity in Ontario: A Critical Legal Analysis," *Osgoode Hall Law Journal* 28, no. 2 (1990), 381–407.

40. Both Elaine Todres and Barbara Falk comment on the deliberate approach of the Women's Directorate to devise legislation that was flexible in its approach to implementation. See Todres, "With Deliberate Care," 222; and Barbara Falk, "A Reasoned Response: Pay Equity in Ontario," in Richard P. Chaykowski, ed., *Pay Equity Legislation: Linking Economic Issues and Policy Concerns* (Kingston:

Industrial Relations Centre, Queen's University, 1989).

41. See *Job Evaluation and Equal Pay: A Discussion Paper by the Equal Pay Coaltion* (n.d.), 2. On gender bias in job evaluation schemes, see, for example, chap. 8 of Clare Burton, *The Promise and the Price: The Struggle for Equal Opportunity in Women's Employment* (North Sydney: Allen and Unwin, 1991); John Kervin and Marika Elek, "Where's the Bias? Sources and Types of Gender Bias in Job Evaluation," in Yonatan Reshef, Collette Bernier, Denis Harrisson and Terry H. Wagar, eds., *Industrial Relations in a New Millennium: Selected Papers from the Thirty-sixth Annual CIRA Conference* (Laval: ACRI/CIRA, 2001), 79–90.

42. See *The Green Paper,* 16.

43. On the government's position concerning cross-unit comparison, see Falk, "A Reasoned Response," 13.

44. Barbara Aarsteinsen, "Pay Equity Needed Now," *The Toronto Star,* 1 December 1992, A3.

45. The widespread recognition that Ontario's pay equity legislation excluded a large number of women in Ontario's economy gave rise to Bill 102, *The Pay Equity Amendment Act.* The amendments, which took effect July 1, 1993, were intended to cover women previously excluded under the legislation and included the provision that employers with 10 to 99 employees be required to post a pay equity plan outlining their obligation and program to achieve pay equity. More important, however, was the inclusion of two additional methods of job comparison: proportional value comparison and proxy comparison. Proportional value was to be applied in workplaces where female job classes could not find a male comparator. This approach examines the relationship between the value of a group of male job classes (or a single male job class), and the value of female job classes in the same establishment. Proxy comparison also applies to workplaces without a male comparator in the broader public sector, and requires comparisons with jobs in other broader sector organizations where pay equity has already been achieved. None of the amendments extended coverage to the "under-tens" in the private sector.

46. Kelly Toughill, "Pay Equity for 80,000 Likely to be Killed," *The Toronto Star,* 19 July 1995, A14; Kelly Toughill, "Pay Equity Limited to $500 million," *The Toronto Star,* 22 July 1995, A8. The government of Ontario capped the amount of money to be spent on pay equity at $500 million. The court challenge was led by the Service Employees International Union, Local 204. Although this court challenge was successful, the government did not fulfill its obligation and another Charter challenge has been launched by several labour unions. See note 2 in the introduction.

47. See McDermott, "Pay Equity in Ontario," 396.

48. It is somewhat puzzling that business did not vehemently oppose the requirement of gender-neutrality during the policy's legislative phase. The lack of opposition may be because business did not fully recognize the ramifications of this provision. On the other hand, a certain segment of the business class stood to benefit from the marketing of job evaluation systems. As one consultant remarked, "the [pay equity] law should have been called the Relief for Consultants and Lawyers Act." *The Toronto Star,* 3 September 1989, F2. Large consulting firms in Ontario benefit enormously from the enactment of pay equity.

49. Judy Fudge, "Limiting Equity: The Definition of 'Employer' under the Ontario Pay Equity Act," *Canadian Journal of Women and the Law* 4 (1991), 557–58.

50. Katherine Swinton, "Accommodating Women in the Workplace: Reproductive Hazards and Seniority Systems," *Canadian Labour Law Journal* 1, nos. 1/2 (1992), 136. Also see Francois Eyraud et. al., *Equal Pay Protection in Industrialised Market Economies: In Search of Greater Effectiveness* (Geneva: International Labour Organisation, 1993), 9.

51. See Gillan Creese, "Gender Equity or Masculine Privilege? Union Strategies and Economic Restructuring in a White Collar Union," *Canadian Journal of Sociology* 20, no. 2 (1995), 143–66; Pamela Sugiman, *Labour's Dilemma: The Gender Politics of Auto Workers in Canada, 1937–1979* (Toronto: University of Toronto Press, 1994).

52. Clare Burton, *The Promise and the Price: The Struggle for Equal Opportunity in Women's Employment* (North Sydney, AUS: Allen and Unwin, 1991), 26 and chap. 3.

Chapter Four

SETTING THE STAGE:
THE SUPERMARKET INDUSTRY

GOING SHOPPING at the supermarket is so familiar and uneventful to most of us that we would never think to inquire about who works at the store, what workers are paid, or why we so often see women operating the cash register and men stocking the grocery shelves. Many of us take for granted a gender divided-workforce and give little thought to its significance for working people. Today, the supermarket industry is one of the largest private-sector employers in Canada, and it is highly gender segregated.

Supermarket chains, such as Safeway, A&P, Sobeys and Loblaws, and smaller grocery stores employ over 300,000 workers, while another 66,000 jobs exist in the wholesale food sector. The food retail sector along with its distribution networks, then, represent about 4 percent of total employment in Canada.[1] Over half of all workers employed in supermarket retailing are women, many of whom are employed part-time and at lower wage rates than their full-time counterparts.[2] A myriad of factors influence the structure of wages in the industry. The age, race and gender composition of the workforce, the labour process, managerial personnel practices and union representation interrelate to determine wage structures at the supermarket. Understanding the economic conditions that shape the gender division of labour and the unequal gender-wage structure in the supermarket industry is absolutely crucial to a study of pay equity. Equally important is an understanding of the historical developments that initially created a gender-wage gap in the supermarket.

The brief historical account included in this chapter uncovers the process of sex-typing of grocery store jobs and it shows that women of European origin have tended to predominate in service work that is deskilled, part-time and lower paying than men's jobs. Situating women's particular employment position in the history of food retailing allows us to assess how pay equity policy affected women's labour market position in the retail food industry.

A second issue raised by a historical analysis of the supermarket industry concerns how workers have been affected by restructuring. From its earliest development, grocery retail has been driven by an overwhelmingly competitive market structure that has led employers to improve profitability by reorganizing work processes, resulting in the deskilling of workers and, consequently, the lowering of wages. Could labour market policies, such as pay equity, protect workers from experiencing a downward pressure on wages? A definitive answer to this question would provide essential information to advocates of workers rights in many sectors of the economy. However, before considering this question, we might ask who controls food retailing in Canada at present?

Who's Who in Food Retailing?

Unlike many manufacturing industries in Canada that are owned by foreign interests, food retailing is primarily operated and owned by Canadians.[3] Historically, the retail food industry has been competitive with the Americans because of consolidation in the sector; corporate concentration was almost twice that of the United States.[4] Recently, mergers in the U.S. have altered this historical pattern, initiating Canadian company buy-outs to bolster market position and to defend against possible foreign takeovers. This has further consolidated the food retail industry in Canada. The impact of corporate concentration has raised concerns about the business practices of the large chains, especially the high cost of "listing fees" that are charged to manufacturers and suppliers to stock products in their stores. The exorbitant fees are viewed as an anti-competitve practice that put independent supermarket chains at a competitive disadvantage. It also has implications for the super-market workforce, as independents may squeeze workers' wages to better compete in the marketplace.[5]

The structure of food retailing reveals vertical integration among grocery manufacturers, food wholesalers and retailers.[6] For example, George Weston Limited is involved in food processing, distribution and owns retail food chains.[7] The company is able to obtain a large share of the food dollar because of its vast holdings in food wholesale and retail food distribution. Included in George Weston's list of assets is Loblaw Companies Limited, Canada's largest food and wholesale distributor.[8] Loblaw owns several food wholesale distributors such as National Grocers, Agora Foods and Westfair Foods Limited. National Grocers is a major food distribu-tor in Ontario that services supermarket chains numbering 600 stores that operate under eighteen banner names, including the largest supermarket chain in Canada, Loblaws Supermarkets. It also owns Supercentres, Zehrs, Maxi, Provigo and Fortinos, among others.[9] Loblaw has over 100,000 employees, making it one of the largest private-sector employers in Canada. The company is also the most profitable food distributor in the country today.[10]

Another giant in grocery wholesale in Canada is the Oshawa Group. Sobey's purchased Oshawa Group in 1998 to service its 402 corporately owned and 949 franchised stores, such as IGA, Foodland, Price Chopper and Price Check.[11] Sobeys employs over 30,000 workers in its food distribution and food service operations. It is the only chain that operates without a significant proportion of unionized workers.

In addition to Loblaws and Sobey's there are two other major corporate supermarket chains in Canada: The Great Atlantic & Pacific Tea Company of Canada (A&P) and Canada Safeway Limited. A&P operates in eighteen U.S. states and within the province of Ontario, where it has 20 percent of the Ontario retail market. It operates over 200 corporate and franchise stores including A&P, Food Basics, Dominion and Super Fresh. In 1985, A&P acquired Dominion Stores, and in 1990 it acquired Miracle Food Mart from Steinberg's, although these stores no longer operate under the Miracle Food Mart banner. The company employs 20,000 employees in Ontario.[12] Canada Safeway is a wholly owned subsidiary of Safeway Incorporated, which is based in California. Like Loblaw Companies Ltd., it operates wholesale and retail. Its wholesale operations, which are run by McDonalds Consolidated, manage 215 retail stores from Thunderbay, Ontario, to Vancouver Island, British Columbia, and employ 192,000 employees across Canada.[13] Safeway is the most profitable food retail company in Canada and the U.S.

These supermarket chains dominate retail sales regionally. Loblaws and A&P are the major corporate chains operating in central Canada, while Canada Safeway serves Western Canada, and Sobey's stores dominate the Atlantic provinces. All four corporate retail food companies experienced significant gains in earnings and sales growth since the mid-1990s.

Out of a total 25,747 grocery stores in 2000 in Canada, only 1,656 or about 6 percent were supermarkets, yet the supermarket category captured over half (57 percent) of food store sales.[14] The chains lost market share to the independents throughout much of the 1980s but were able to regain their position in the 1990s. The independents (e.g., IGA) captured about 10 percent of market share from the chains in the 1980s.[15] However, from 1991 to 1999, the share of independents declined from 47.7 percent to 42.8 percent.[16]

The organization of food distribution and retailing in Canada is a fierce struggle among companies to obtain a greater share of the food dollar. Food retailing is a highly competitive industry with low profit margins. Retail analysts estimate profit margins in the industry are, on average, 1 percent per dollar of sales, before taxes. In the 1970s, net profit before taxes averaged 1.6 percent; it dropped to 1.4 percent in the 1980s, and in the midst of the recession of the early 1990s, fell to about one-half of 1 percent.[17] Today profit margins hover around 1 percent of sales.[18]

Competitive struggle has always existed between the corporate chains and the independents for market share. The struggle has not, however, meant that wages have been equalized between the two sectors. Rather, the supermarket sector has always found ways to maintain or improve its competitive position, despite higher wage levels and a higher rate of unionization. There are a variety of strategies, often centring on the use of labour, particularly women's labour, that have been used by the major food retailers to strengthen their competitive position.

The history of supermarket retailing is an investigation of retail managements' strategies to gain an edge over competitors. The vast array of food chains and modes of retailing evolved as a way for companies to expand markets and reduce operating costs. Various technological innovations in grocery retailing were introduced to maximize efficiency, improve productivity and profitability, and reduce labour costs. Restructuring in the industry was motivated by a corporate drive to capture market share. Supermarket workers, particularly women workers, were inserted into the restructuring process to lower the costs of corporate reorganization. Women were a particularly attractive labour supply because they could be hired at cheaper wage rates than men and because they were willing to work part-time to acccommodate the busy periods of the shopping day.

A Brief History of Food Retailing

THE DEVELOPMENT OF SELF-SERVICE, 1920–1940

Grocery chains entered the Canadian retail market in the 1920s when the movement to self-service food retailing took place.[19] The trend to self-service was the first of many significant developments to reduce or eliminate the need for wage labour in the grocery store. Before the First World War, groceries were sold in small family-owned shops that serviced all of a customer's needs. Shop employees would collect the merchandise, total the cost, credit the customer's account and deliver the order to the buyer's home. Food retailers reorganized the labour process to eliminate full clerk service during the First World War when labour shortages and rising wages increased service costs. When grocery chains began to appear in the 1920s and 1930s, self-service expanded and was widespread by the 1940s. Self-service in food markets was first adopted by food store chains as a method for competing against independents.

Self-service of grocery merchandise was made possible because of developments in national transportation systems, the shift to centralization of production and standardization of packaged goods. In addition, national advertising campaigns that made food products with private brands recognizable to customers homogenized tastes and promoted the transition to self-service. As self-service stores began to take hold, new technologies were introduced to further facilitate customer self-sufficiency.[20] An article from a 1942 issue of *Canadian Grocer* praises the marvels of the new machines in the food store and comments on the many benefits new technology will bring the store owner:

> The modern cash register today does the work of an accountant, cuts costs and provides greater accuracy; the meat slicer cuts waste and speeds up service. The refrigerated meat counter prevents meats from deteriorating; the computing scale provides rapid service because it computes as well as weighs; the coffee grinder not only improves store atmosphere, but provides grinds that satisfies four or five different brewing methods. Scientifically made floor fixtures promote self-service, thus increasing sales at no extra cost.[21]

Restructuring the labour process in food markets to achieve self-service clearly had a deep effect on the retail workforce. New store equipment saved labour time and reduced required skill levels of the store clerk. Nona Glazer summarizes the impact of self-service on waged labour in retailing:

> Because of the new labor process, workers lost their jobs, or their jobs were deskilled or became waged work rather than salaried or commission based, and often part-time. The gender composition of the industry workforce became predominantly women, who dominated as cashiers and clerks, but not as managers.[22]

The major benefit of implementing self-service was to save on labour costs, either by reducing the number of clerks required in the store or by hiring employees on a part-time basis. Self-service fulfilled a particular need because unlike production work, productivity depended on service to buyers. By allowing customers to serve themselves, retail managers solved the difficult problem of scheduling service clerks to meet intermittent customer demand. In other words, rather than employing clerks full days, full-time, to serve customers who came and went at various times during the day or night, it became possible to staff stores to adjust to the periodic needs of customers. Hiring staff part-time was a particularly effective method of providing customer service during peak times of the shopping day. As early as the 1930s, when self-service in grocery merchandise (excluding perishables like meat and dairy) was well underway in food stores, part-time employment was on the increase. Many of the part-time staff hired were women.[23]

Beginning in the 1930s and continuing throughout the Second World War, women were hired to replace the full-time male salesclerks. Food stores employed women to work as cashiers, a job requiring fewer skills and knowledge of store merchandise than that required for sales work. Twenty-two percent of all sales workers in 1931 in Canada were women; many likely were employed as cashiers. During wartime in the 1940s, employers found they could hire women more cheaply than men. Management preferred women to do what was seen to be easy work: operating the cash register, taking money and wrapping goods for the customer. Women (and youth) entered food retail when work was changing from full-time to part-time. Cultural attitudes that prevailed during this time assumed that women would fill part-time jobs, since men required higher wages to achieve their role as family breadwinner. Married women with previous retail experience were seen as an especially desirable workforce and were recruited as "contingent workers," as this commentator explains:

> Every large store needs a group of salespeople who may be sent to the busiest parts of the store during the busiest hours of the day ... This group of salespeople are usually called the

"contingent group" or "flying squadron" ... saleswomen, now married, come to the store during the rush season days, from the hours of 11:00 a.m. to 4:00 p.m. The shortness of the day permits the contingent saleswoman to complete her housework at home, perform the work in the store at the time it is needed most, and then get home in time to prepare dinner for her husband.[24]

Although data is not available on the percentage of part-time employees in retail trade, the Canadian census shows 19,000 women employed in food stores in 1941, this number jumped to 33,000 by 1951, an increase of 73.7 percent.[25]

While women were recruited for what were defined as the least-skilled jobs in retail food, men predominated in skilled job categories. Because self-service initially applied only to grocery items, the jobs of meat cutter and produce, dairy and meat manager were typically held by men. Indeed, men held sway over the majority of retail food jobs until the 1940s, when other industries lured men away by the offer of higher wages.[26]

Conversion to self-service in the meat and other departments occurred a bit later than in grocery. A major obstacle to introducing self-service in non-grocery was the need for refrigeration compartments. Display cases for meat were not designed until the late 1930s. However, once meat was made available in open cases, employers found that meat increased sales as much as 30 percent, without a rise in labour costs. Significantly, too, grocery management realized that there was a close connection between meat sales and other grocery items. Customers spent four dollars on grocery merchandise for every dollar spent on meat. The importance of meat sales in grocery stores spurred management to reorganize the labour process in the meat department.[27]

CENTRALIZATION OF PRODUCTION, DESKILLING AND THE FEMINIZATION OF WORK

Prior to the 1950s, meat cutting was craft work, and all workers in the meat department were either male journeymen cutters or apprentices. Starting in the post-war period and continuing over three decades, the labour process in the meat department was restructured and meat processing became centralized. Both the reorganization of work in the meat department and the centralization of meat production contributed to deskilling the meat cutter.[28]

Before meat wrapping machines were developed in the 1950s, meat cutters had responsibility for carving and trimming primal cuts, wrapping and pricing meat and cleaning the cutting room, as well as serving customers. Once meat wrapping machines were developed, however, the tasks of wrapping meat and handling customers were delegated to meat clerks or meat wrappers. The meat clerks who were hired were largely women. Grocery management preferred to recruit women for this work because they would not pose a threat to the meat cutters' privileged status. The clerks were paid significantly less than meat cutters, had responsibility for the least skilled tasks (such as cleaning) and were allocated a separate room away from the cutters. While meat cutters did not relinquish control over the meat department or encounter significant deskilling as a result of meat wrapping, they eventually experienced job loss because the meat clerks had taken over a significant component of meat department tasks, particularly service work.

Deskilling of meat cutting began in the 1970s with the introduction of boxed beef. Boxed-beef systems involve blocking sides of beef at central processing plants, wrapping the subprimal cuts in airtight, non-toxic plastic and shipping them in boxes to retail stores.[29] An important consequence of centralized meat production was the transformation of the labour process in the in-store meat departments. Much of the work that had traditionally been carried out by meat cutters now occurred centrally. Because meat cutters were the highest paid occupational group in the grocery store, shifting meat processing to a centralized facility represented significant savings for retailers. Moreover, boxed-beef programs reduced the amount of labour in meat departments by nearly half. [30] Although boxed beef eliminated much of the craft work done by meat cutters, the job of cutting meat was still required in the meat department. But the tasks demanded of meat cutting were simplified, as a Meat Manager explained:

> At one time there was what we called sides of beef, where we actually had to cut down sides of beef. Now you order primal cuts. Everything comes in prepackaged and precut ... You probably need about half the skills you needed in the past, now the skills you need, as opposed to knowing what to do, is more of an ordering type of position.[31]

By the 1980s boxed beef in Canada was well entrenched; the craft work of meat cutting was deskilled, and the status and bargaining power meat cutters historically experienced were gradually diminished.

FROM 1950S SUBURBIA TO DIVERSIFICATION IN THE 1970S

Suburban developments in the post-war era gave rise to the shopping mall and shopping centres. Developers of shopping malls offered retail space to well-known retailers for a cheaper rate to attract customers and smaller retailers to the mall. The advantages of locating in shopping centres led to smaller corporate stores in the downtown area being either closed or sold to independents. Large stores with parking lots were better able to service customers located in suburbia.[32] During the 1950s and 1960s, chain food stores across Canada grew at a rapid rate because of the expansion of shopping centres. According to a government report, "between 1951 and 1961 sales volume of the [food] chains rose by 179 percent."[33]

As corporate chains became widely dispersed in shopping entres, a niche opened in the food market for variety stores in neighbourhoods. In the 1970s and 1980s, chain convenience stores grew rapidly, filling a market need for convenience food shopping based on location, quick service and extended store hours. For example, an American-owned convenience store chain named its operation 7-Eleven because when it began the stores offered service from 7 a.m. to 11 p.m. Today, the chain operates 24-hours per day, seven days a week. In the 1970s, convenience stores of all types, including franchises, chains and independents, were the largest growing segment of the retail food trade in terms of dollar sales.[34] By the 1980s, convenience stores competed directly with the corner store and many small family-owned shops went out of business. Convenience store chains such as 7-Eleven and Mac's Milk grew in prominence as supermarket chains continued the trend to fewer and larger stores. As the post-war boom came to a close and population growth slowed, the competitive environment in supermarket retailing intensified. For the first time since the end of the Second World War, supermarket retailing experienced a decline in profitability. In response to the profit squeeze of the 1970s, corporate chains began to diversify store operations.[35]

Store size increased to accommodate larger volumes and floor space was added to include new specialty departments. In an effort to attract customers, especially women who were entering the labour force in larger numbers, supermarkets offered one-stop shopping in which all of a customer's needs were available in one location. This strategy served management's goal of improving profitability since new products had higher margins. Convenience foods with high markups were being offered that appealed to women employed in the workforce who had less time to cook homemade meals. Stores began selling health and beauty aides, specialty foods and health foods at high markups. As people's awareness of health issues expanded, consumption of meat, especially red meat, declined.[36] Management had to rely on other departments to make up the loss in sales.

In addition to the expansion of types of products sold within departments, specialty departments were introduced to broaden customer service. Deli, bakery, seafood/fish and floral departments provided greater variety and enhanced profitability because service departments had higher markup (gross margin) than general grocery merchandise. For example, bakery and deli departments contributed significantly to store sales and to overall gross profit. According to one estimate, 10 percent of total gross profit and 6 percent of individual store sales were attributed to these two departments.[37]

As in the case of the meat department, the newly hired employees recruited to work in the service departments were primarily women. Retail food management chose to hire women to staff the service departments for the same reasons they hired women as cashiers and meat wrappers: women's wages were considerably lower than men's. Another very important reason reflects ideological assumptions about gender and skill:

> Female workers are expected to enter the job with a bundle of competencies: the ability to cook, the ability to identify foods (different fruits for example), cleaning skills, and personal interaction skills (how to treat customers pleasantly, under any conditions). Managers assume that women have acquired these competencies during their socialization into the role of adult female.[38]

As many feminists have pointed out, skill definitions for women's jobs have been infused with gender bias.[39] Conceptions of femininity and masculinity were significant to definitions of skilled work as were "objective" measures of technical skill and knowledge. Sex-typing of occupations devalued the work women do but often upgraded skill definitions of masculine occupations. For example, jobs perceived to require heavy physical labour (i.e., male-defined jobs) were often rewarded with higher levels of compensation than jobs requiring less physical effort, that is, female-defined jobs. Work competencies associated with femininity, such as human relations or domestic work, were typically devalued. In this situation, baking, cleaning and interpersonal skills were assumed to be female competencies rather than learned ones. The particular work performed by women was closely associated with domestic labour performed in the home. Unfortunately, "paid housework" was not highly valued in the labour force. Retail food management underestimated the skill level of "feminine work" and paid female workers less than their job worth. John Walsh identified jobs in deli and bakery to be especially devalued based on gender. His statistical analysis of male and female wage rates showed that women earned about two dollars less per hour than men in supermarkets.[40]

Between 1941and 1961, food store managers' preference for female employees was evident in the large increase in employment of women. In this twenty-year interval, women's employment in food stores increased by an astonishing 176 percent. (See table 1.) "By 1967 more than one in three food store workers were women."[41]

Evidently women were actively sought out as the preferred worker for many jobs in the grocery store. The workforce was increasingly feminized as employers turned to women, especially part-time women workers, to fill important jobs in the supermarket.

TABLE 1

Employment in Food Stores, Canada (000's)

FOOD STORES	1941	1951	1961	% INCREASE
TOTAL	99	109	151	52.7
MALE	80	76	98	22.6
FEMALE	19	33	54	176.0

Source: Census of Canada, 1961. Labour Force, Occupations and Industry Trends (Cat. No. 94-551). Adapted from Table 3, *Part-Time Employment in Retail Trade,* Economics and Research Branch and Women's Bureau (Ottawa: Department of Labour, 1969), 11.

COMPUTER TECHNOLOGY: THE 1970S AND 1980S

When computerization entered the supermarket, the changes predicted were seen to be as significant as those that occurred in the development of self-serve retailing. Indeed, computer technology restructured store operations and profoundly altered work processes in the supermarket.

In the mid-1970s, a variety of computer applications were tried by grocery management in an attempt to improve efficiency and productivity of food retail functions. While some of the technology was rejected, the development of checkout scanners proved especially advantageous for reducing labour time and costs of in-store operations. At first, stores installed electronic cash registers that were capable of conversion to scanning. Later when scanning technology was perfected, fully automated frontends or checkouts became the norm.

Electronic scanners read bar codes, called Universal Product Codes (UPC), which were printed on products and identified the price on the checkout display.[42] Once the code was read, the information was passed "to the cash register and a computer ... Registers equipped with scanners [could] identify each item, check its price, ring up the sale, total a customer's order, and print-out an item-by-item tape of the purchases."[43] Considered revolutionary in the late 1970s, the operation of scanners are very familiar to shoppers today; 90 percent of stores now use the equipment.[44] The range of functions that electronic scanners potentially could perform made them appealing to supermarket management. An important application of scanner technology was the retailers' ability to electronically communicate with suppliers. As contemporary analysts have noted,

> widespread use of UPC codes enable most retailers to use point-of-sale (POS) scanning ... [that] transmit business documents in standard format among retailers, vendors, and manufacturers in a system called Electronic Data Interchange (EDI) ... The advantage of ordering by EDI, without paperwork and even, in some cases, without any human intervention, goes well beyond simply savings in time, from the moment when the need to order is determined until the goods are received.[45]

Although the possibilities of scanning technology were wide ranging, the initial cost of installing the equipment, especially in the 1970s, meant that only the larger supermarket chains were prepared to implement automated frontends.[46] However, the implementation of scanning was uneven among supermarket chains. For instance, Steinberg's was one of the first chains in North America to test automated electronic terminals; Loblaws and Sobey's were also aggressive in moving to the new technology in the seventies, but A&P was far more cautious.[47]

From management's perspective, a number of advantages accrued from electronic scanners. First, they sped up checkout and eliminated cashier errors. A cashier could scan one item per second and did not have to spend time looking for a price tag. A second cost saving was that items did not have to be priced individually. The work of the stock clerk, which used to involve manual pricing, was reduced to posting prices on gondola shelves and restocking. Third, computer technology had the capability of improving inventory control. Automated warehouses interfaced with store computers to "direct the flow of goods from the receiving of suppliers' shipments through to the filling of store orders" via an on-site computer.[48] As goods were sold, new shipments were automatically sent by suppliers to stores.

While scanning obviously reaped benefits for employers, the impact of microtechnology on supermarket workers was less positive. For cashiers, scanning made a low-skilled occupation even less skilled. A cashier explained some of the changes that occurred with scanning:

> From a cashier's point of view, this system is easier ... whereas before they had to key things in [and] key in the right department. Now, they take a roast and scan it, and it automatically goes on the meat department, so they don't have to worry about keying in $5 on meat ... In the old days we had to take the bill, [deduct] a fifty-cent coupon, the same was true of cheques; we had to manually figure out how much change to give back ... you used to have to count back the change. [49]

Electronic cash registers simplified the work of cashiers by reducing the amount of mental effort required to perform the job. However, the new technology modified the labour process negatively in several ways.

One modification made possible with computerized scanning equipment was monitoring or surveillance. Managers were now able to monitor the productivity of cashiers. Productivity sheets were posted (sometimes in the women's washroom) that indicated number of errors and whether the rate of speed at which a cashier worked was above or below average, by company standards. Eventually, the retail unions successfully argued that posting productivity sheets caused stress and embarrassment for workers and the practice was discontinued in unionized stores.[50] However, the practice of monitoring the work speed of cashiers re-emerged in the late 1990s.

The new technologies also created a number of serious health problems for cashiers. Laser scanning increased the pace and workload of putting through groceries; and poor checkout stand design required awkward hand and body movements to perform the work. Both of these factors contributed to repetitive strain injuries (RSI) or musculoskeletal disorders such as tendonitis, carpal tunnel syndrome and cervico-brachial disorders. According to a survey conducted in 1980, 80 percent of cashiers who worked on new checkout systems suffered physical health problems from their work.[51]

The cashier's workflow was modified (and consequently her health) because the new equipment significantly altered the arrangement of the checkout counter. Prior to the development of scanning, cashiers handled groceries twice: first they rang the items through the cash register and then they bagged them. The conventional approach did not require cashiers to do both tasks simultaneously. The new system, called ring and bag, was described in a 1983 study of its effects on the cashier's health:

> the cashier packages each item with her left hand while she rings in the price on her register with her right hand ... No longer does she ring in all items before bagging them. This means that her left side is doing virtually all the work — stretching, reaching, lifting and bending. A typical cashier will handle up to 10,000 items in one 8-hour shift.[52]

Consequently, within months of implementation, cashiers using the ring and bag checkout stands, reported suffering disabilities such as neck and back pain and wrist and elbow problems. Another difficulty for cashiers was that only about half of all items could be scanned; either the item did not have a UPC code or scanning was not reliable. Cashiers had to key-in as well as scan, creating pressure on the back by constant twisting.

While people recognized the problems with the ring and bag system, they anticipated that many of these health issues would be solved when all items had UPC codes, and when better scanning equipment allowed cashiers to scan with both hands.[53] Unfortunately, research on computerized checkout stands reports a continued high incidence of repetitive strain injuries among cashiers. In fact, studies show the incidence of musculoskeletal symptoms to be twice as high in checkout as compared with other departments in food stores.[54]

FEMINIZATION, FLEXIBILITY AND FOOD STORES

The history of supermarket retailing tells an important story about the origins of sex segregation in the retail food workforce. From the beginning, women were inserted into food retailing as low wage, deskilled and part-time workers. This information is critical in assessing pay equity. Systemic sex discrimination in compensation is visible in the historic process of creating gender skill definitions and gendered wage structures in food stores.

With the appearance of self-service, women were recruited to perform the work of cashier, a job requiring less skill than that required of male clerks. Although paid low wage rates, cashiers were recognized by management as important for customer relations. In addition, store managers preferred hiring women part-time to accommodate peak times in the shopping day. The "flexibility" of female labour urged retail management to hire women exclusively to work the frontend operating cash registers. The work of cashiers remained relatively unchanged until the 1970s when computerization entered the supermarket. Computerization further deskilled the work of cashiers, but made their job more stressful and arduous as compared with operating manual cash registers.

Similarly reorganization of the meat department increased the low-wage work available to women. Women were hired in the newly created position of meat wrapper or meat service clerk to fulfil tasks men found demeaning. Serving customers, cleaning, wrapping and weighing meat, although quite strenuous, were perceived as "women's work." When the job of meat cutter was deskilled with the introduction of centralized meat processing, meat cutters experienced job loss because so much of their work had been given over to meat wrappers. However, despite deskilling and a decline in customer taste for meat, meat cutters continued to be paid high wages, typically one of the highest wage rates in the store.[55] Meat wrappers earned considerably lower wages than meat cutters for performing routinized functions in the meat department.

Management recruited meat clerks to save on the wage bill but this also reduced the strength of retail unions.

When stores grew in size and added on service departments, women were again hired to manage and work such departments as deli and bakery. Not only was it acceptable to pay women less than men in production departments but it was also assumed by management as unnecessary to compensate women for performing "feminine" tasks, including customer relations (being courteous), cooking (making sandwiches or preparing barbecue chicken) and cleaning. Many of the job functions performed in the service classifications were customer related tasks that were simply not rewarded at the same wage rates as production work.

Women entered food retail, then, during times of store and retail industry restructuring. When new workers were needed because of a change in store format (self-service), a change in the labour process (meat department), delivery of new services (deli, bakery departments) or under conditions of retail expansion (the suburban shopping mall), women were sought out as the best workers to satisfactorily carry out specific job tasks, primarily service work, in the grocery store. Even though the jobs performed by women contributed to store profitability, women were paid lower wage rates than their male counterparts.

The history of food retail offers some insight into the development of the gender division of labour in the grocery sector. However, other aspects of the retail food sector require further investigation. While market competition has always been a feature of food retailing as seen in the competitive struggle between the independents and the corporates, the contemporary era of economic restructuring has intensified competition among food retail and non-food retail chains. Recent developments include the formation of new retail formats within food retail as well as external developments outside the sector that directly compete with supermarkets. In chapter 5, the competitive pressures that have developed from industry fragmentation are analyzed further in view of their implications for labour, particularly for the retail unions.

NOTES

1. These figures are for 1995. Employment in food retail increased almost 30 percent between 1983 and 1995. See *Creating the Future: Human Resources Study of the Canadian Food Retail and Wholesale Sector* (Canadian Labour Market and Productivity Centre, 1998), 21.

2. The percentage of women working in food stores in Canada was 54.33 percent (45.66 for men), according to the 1996 Census. See Statistics Canada, Labour Force 15 years and Over by Detailed Industry (Based on the 1980 Standard Industrial Classification) and Sex, 1996 Census (20% Sample), *Women in Canada*, 2000 Cat. No. 89-503-XPE.

3. In fact, most of the grocery business in Canada is owned by a few Canadian families. The Weston's started business in 1882 in Toronto and now control George Weston Ltd., which owns Loblaw Companies Ltd. The Sobey family dominates grocery retailing in Atlantic Canada and controls vast holdings through the Empire Co. Ltd., including wholesale operations and food retail stores such as Garden Market, Price Chopper and Sobey franchises. Oshawa Group, a large food distributor, was controlled by the Wolfe family until 1998 when Sobey's purchased it.

4. A government study of the retail grocery industry in Canada reports that only 18 percent of industry sales is attributed to foreign-owned companies. See *Industry Profile: Retail Grocery* (Ottawa: Industry, Science and Technology Canada, 1988), 2. As stated in the report, the major foreign-owned corporations operating in Canada were A&P, Safeway and Seven-Eleven stores. A second study conducted by Industry, Science and Technology Canada examines the entire retail sector and further reports that "in the 15 years following 1970, retail sales by the Canadian outlets of foreign-controlled firms fell from 21 percent to 12 percent. The decline in foreign ownership in this period was due to the 'Canadianization' of such major firms as Loblaw Companies and Hudson's Bay and to faster growth of the speciality-store segment, which is predominantly Canadian-controlled." See *Industry Profile: Retail Trade 1990–91* (Ottawa: Industry, Science and Technology, 1991), 2.

5. On Canadian corporate concentration, see Eleanor O'Donnel MacLean, *Leading the Way: An Unauthorized Guide to the Sobey Empire* (Halifax: GATT-Fly Atlantic, 1985), 51. In the late 1990s, acquisitions in the U.S. resulted in the top ten chains controlling 50 percent of the nation's grocery sales, as compared with 30 percent in 1993 (*Canadian Grocer* [November 1998], 10). In Canada, Loblaw Companies Limited purchased Provigo, and Sobeys purchased the Oshawa Group in 1998, thereby intensifying corporate ownership in the country. Concerns about corporate concentration in the food retail industry were expressed by MP Dan McTeague (Pickering-Ajax), who urged the Competition Bureau to undertake a full investigation of the buy-outs in view of concerns that "the concentration of ownership has enabled companies to obtain a level of market domination at both the wholesale and retail level" (Dan McTeague, MP, Press Release, December 13, 1999). He expressed deep concern about the business practices of the large chains such as the cost of "listing fees" that are charged to manufacturers and suppliers to stock their products in stores. According to McTeague's research, listing fees increased over 100 percent between 1997 and 1999 (*Aggregated Public Results of Confidential Inquiry Conducted by Dan McTeague, M.P. with respect to anti-competitive pricing practices under the federal competition Act in the Fall*, 1999).

6. Vertical integration allows a company to profit at various steps in the processing and distribution of food. Weston's expanded its operations to include food processing and fishery extraction so that the company has been able to reap profit at various stages of its food operations. "For example, fish is harvested on the east and west coasts and sold to the processing arm for a profit, packaged and sold to the wholesale arm for a profit, sold to the retail arms for a profit, and sold once again to the customer for an additional profit." See *The Supermarket Tour: A Handbook for Education and Action* (Toronto: Ontario Public Interest Research Group, 1990), 54–55. Also see Appendix 3 in *Industry, Science and Technology Canada Industry Profile, Retail Trade, 1990–91,* 33, for an overview of Weston's food processing operations. Links with agricultural producers was tried in the 1970s, albeit unsuccessfully. Interview with Industry Analyst at Canadian Council of Grocery Distributors, June 22, 1994.

7. For example, Galen Weston owns Weston Bakeries, Maplehurst Bakeries and Best Foods Company Inc., which was purchased in 2001, as well as Heritage Salmon., and other food processing companies.

8. *Loblaw Companies Limited Company Profile,* 2001. <www.loblaw.com/en/abt_corprof.html>.

9. Dana Flavelle, *The Toronto Star,* 21 February, 2002, C3. It is important to note that Loblaw Companies Limited is a retail and wholesale food distributor that owns the Loblaws Supermarket chain, among others.

10. Loblaw Companies Limited employs 119,000 people throughout its operations. *About Us: Company Profile* (2002), 1. <www.loblaw.com/en/abt_corpprof.html >. Loblaw Companies Limited return on sales as measured by EBITDA, short for "earnings before income taxes depreciation and amortization," increased from 3.8 percent in 1990 to 6.3 percent in 2000. See *Loblaw Companies Limited Annual Report 2000,* 49; Dana Flavelle, *The Toronto Star,* 21 February, 2002, C3. In 1996, Loblaws captured 20 percent of market share. This was before the company purchased Provigo, representing 12 percent of the market share in 1996.

11. *Sobey's Summary Annual Report, 2001.*

12. *Company Profile: The Great Atlantic & Pacific Company of Canada Limited, 1999,* 20.

13. *Company Profile: Canada Safeway Limited, 2000.*

14. *Canadian Grocer* (January/Febuary, 2000), 29.

15. Interview with industry analyst, August 8, 1994. Data on chain stores and independents market share is reported in *Canadian Grocer* (February 1994), 39, 41. The chains' share of sales in 1983 in Ontario was 71.1 percent; it dropped to 61.8 percent in 1993. Nationally, the market share for chains stores was 64.8 percent in 1986; in 1993 it dropped to 53.1 percent .

16. Julia Drake, "Growing, Growing ...," *Canadian Grocer* (2001), 29.

17. See note 13, *Retail Grocery: Industry Profile,* 3. The decline in profit margins in grocery retail in the early 1990s was one of the lowest ever seen in the industry. Reported in the *The Toronto Star,* 28 May 1992. It should be noted that estimates concerning margins vary. Duncan MacDonnell reports that "financial data from publicly traded Canadian grocery retailers shows recent corporate store margins ranging from 1.7 to 3.9%. Operating costs — excluding interest charges — are typically 95 per cent." He estimates the average margin at about 2 percent. See Duncan MacDonnell, "The Cost of Doing Business," *Grocer Today* (May 1995),

23–24.

18. *Creating the Future,* 9.

19. As far as I know, a history of grocery food retailing has yet to be written in Canada. The Directory of Retail Chains reports that A&P was first established in Canada in 1928, Dominion in 1919, Safeway in 1929 and Loblaws in 1920, to name a few. See *1994 Directory of Retail Chains in Canada* (Toronto: MacLean Hunter Ltd, 1994). The following discussion of the history of food retailing is taken from several sources. Unfortunately, I rely heavily on American literature but supplement my understanding of what transpired in Canada from *Canadian Grocer,* a trade journal first established in 1887. Julie White's paper, "Trouble in Store? The Impact of the Micoelectronics in the Retail Trade" (Ottawa: Women's Bureau, 1985), Anne Kingston, *The Edible Man: Dave Nichol, President's Choice and the Making of Popular Taste* (Toronto: McFarlane Walter and Ross, 1994), and Harry Bruce, *Frank Sobey: The Man and the Empire* (Toronto: Macmillan of Canada, 1985) were also very useful. In general, there appear to be close parallels between the U.S. and Canada regarding basic industry trends. On the history of food retailing in the U.S., see Nona Glazer, *Women's Paid and Unpaid Work: The Work Transfer in Health Care and Retailing* (Philadelphia: Temple University Press, 1993), especially chapters 4-6; John Walsh, *Supermarkets Transformed: Understanding Organizational and Technological Innovations* (New Brunswick: Rutgers University Press, 1993); James Mayo, *The American Grocery Store: The Business Evolution of an Architectural Space* (Westport: Greenwood Press, 1993); Andrew Seth and Geoffrey Randall, *The Grocers: The Rise and Rise of the Supermarket Chains* (London: Kogan Page, 1999).

20. See Glazer, *Women's Paid and Unpaid Work,* 50–59.

21. This article first appeared in the March 15, 1942 issue of *Canadian Grocer,* and was reprinted in a special issue, *Flashbacks* 106, no. 2 (January 1992), edited by Simone Collier.

22. Glazer, *Women's Paid and Unpaid Work,* 49.

23. See Glazer, *Women's Paid and Unpaid Work,* 60, 74. Unfortunately, data on part-time employment in Canada is unavailable until the 1950s. Data on part-time employment in retail trade was not collected until 1966. See White, "Trouble in Store?" 5.

24. Paul Nystrom, *Retail Store Management* (Chicago: LaSalle Extension University, 1920), 154–55.

25. Department of Labour, Economics and Research Branch and the Women's Bureau, *Part-Time Employment in Retail Trade* (Ottawa: Queen's Printer, 1969), 11.

26. See Mayo, *The American Grocery Store,* 159; Glazer, *Women's Paid and Unpaid Work,* 75.

27. According to the Canadian Bureau of Statistics, meat sales contributed between 15 percent and 50 percent of the total sales in food chain stores in 1966. See *Food Chain Stores: Operating Results 1966* (Ottawa: Dominion Bureau of Statistics, Cat. No. 63-403). Also see Mayo, *The American Grocery Store,* 159; Walsh, *Supermarkets Transformed,* 69.

28. For a detailed discussion of deskilling in the meat department, see Walsh, *Supermarkets Transformed,* chap. 3.

29. Interview, Industry Analyst, Canadian Council of Grocery Distributors, June 22, 1994.

30. *The Supermarket Tour: A Handbood for Education and Action* (Toronto: Ontario Public Research Interest Group, 1990), 27.

31. Interview, Meat Manager, August 24, 1993.

32. Beginning in the post-war period, a consistent management strategy to improve profitability in grocery sales was to expand volume-level of trade by increasing store size. The greater turnover per square foot on the store shelf, the higher the profit in the store. Rates of turnover per square foot were typically higher in bigger stores because they attracted a larger clientele. In addition, larger stores benefited from economies of scale and permitted cost items, such as advertising costs, to be spread over greater volume of store sales. Mayo, *The American Grocery Store*, 162–63; Avijit Ghosh and Sara McLafferty, "The Shopping Center: A Restructuring of Post-War Retailing," *Journal of Retailing* 67, no. 3 (1991), 253–67.

33. See *Part-Time Employment in Retail Trade*, 38. In 1960, Safeway, A&P, Loblaws and Dominion were all adding new stores, many of which were located in the new shopping centres. See "Twenty Years Ago," *Canadian Grocer* (July 1979).

34. For more about the 7-Eleven convencience food chain, see Mayo, *The American Grocery Store*, 205. For convenience store sales, see *Canadian Grocer* (September 1973), 33; (February 1977), 72.

35. *Canadian Grocer* (May 1972), 43; Mayo, *The American Grocery Store*, 199; Walsh, *Supermarkets Transformed*, 42–56.

36. *Canadian Grocer* (February 1972), 39; Anne Kingston, *The Edible Man*, 155.

37. Walsh, *Supermarkets Transformed*, 118.

38. Ibid., 141. That the cashier is female is assumed in much of the retail literature. See Ralph Towsey, *Self-Service Retailing: Its Profitable Application to all Trades* (London: Iliffe Books Ltd., 1964), 100.

39. See, for example, Ann Phillips and Barbara Taylor, "Sex and Skill," Feminist Review 6 (1980); Ruth Milkman, *Gender at Work: The Dynamics of Job Segregation by Sex during World War II* (Chicago: University of Illinois Press, 1987). On the devaluation of women's jobs in domestic paid work, see Wenona Giles and and Sedaf Arat-Kroc, *Maid in the Market: Women's Paid Domestic Labour* (Halifax: Fernwood Publishing, 1994); Bridget Anderson, *Doing the Dirty Work:The Global Politics of Domestic Labour* (London: Zed Books, 2000).

40. Walsh, *Supermarkets Transformed*, 141-44.

41. *Part-Time Employment in Retail Trade*, 10.

42. The Universal Product Code system is a 12-digit number that identifies the product and the manufacturer. Although called "universal," the code applies only in Canada and the U.S. Europeans use a different code that has 13 digits. *The Toronto Star*, 16 January 1994, F4.

43. *Canadian Grocer* (November 1980), 43.

44. *Creating the Future*, 10.

45. Dale Achabal and Shelby McIntyre, "Information Technology is Reshaping Retailing," Journal of Retailing 63, no. 4 (Winter 1987), 322. Annual growth of EDI in Canada grew from 172 registered users in 1987 to 1000 registered users in 1990. See Barbara Macrae, "Technology: New Tools that Bind," Canadian Grocer (December 1990), 16.

46. Julie White, "Trouble in Store?" 8-9.

47. Many independents, such as IGA stores, did not install fully automated scanning equipment until the Goods and Services Tax was introduced in 1990. See Macrae, "Technology: New Tools that Bind," *Canadian Grocer* (December 1990), 27. Steinberg's tested scanning equipment in its store at Dorval, Quebec, in 1974; Sobey's first installed automated frontends in 1979; and Loblaws had scanning in 100 of its 135 stores by 1985. See White, "Trouble in Store?" 8, and David Brisson, "Tools of the Trade: Sobey's Integrated Computer System Reconciles Sales with Labour Expenses," *Canadian Grocer* (December 1993), 33. As reported by Barbara Macrae, A&P "sat back and let the market carry on until [they] corporately decided to adopt a system that met [their] needs." "Technology: New Tools that Bind," 17.

48. *Canadian Grocer* (July 1976), 9.

49. Interview, Head Cashier, March 23, 1992.

50. Interview, Part-Time Cashier, March 18, 1991. Steve Smith found in his study of retail in the UK that "managers were reluctant to exploit this [monitoring] 'big brother aspect' as they called it, for fear of a backlash at the checkout." It is possible that supermarket managers were afraid of a revolt at the cash register too. See Steve Smith, "How Much Change at the Store? The Impact of New Technologies and Labour Processes on Managers and Staffs in Retail Distribution," in David Knights and Hugh Willmott, eds., *New Technology and the Labour Process* (London: MacMillan, 1988), 151.

51. It was estimated that RSI health injuries cost $100 billion per year in lost work time. See Frank Swoboda, "U.S. Plans Attack on Repetitive Stress Pain," *The Toronto Star,* 5 November 1994, C3. The health survey was conducted by UFCW Local 1000A and RWDSU Local 414 and surveyed cashiers working at A&P, Dominion, Loblaws and Miracle Mart. See "Ring and Bag Blues," *UFCW Canadian Action* (November/December 1983), 5.

52. "Ring and Bag Blues," 5.

53. White, "Trouble in Store?" 19.

54. Anthony Ryan, "The Prevalence of Musculo-skeletal Symptoms in Supermarket Workers," *Ergonomics* 32, no. 4 (1989), 359–71.

55. An examination of collective agreements covering various supermarket chains indicated that the wage level of meat cutters and meat managers exceeded wage rates of other departments and positions in the store. For example, in 1977, Steinberg's paid meat cutters a higher weekly wage than that of production clerks, and considerably more than service clerks. Assistant meat managers and meat managers were paid more than any other department managers in the store. This pattern was still in evidence in the 1990s, despite deskilling.

Chapter 5

UNIONIZING THE SUPERMARKET

THERE ARE TWO major unions representing food retail workers in Canada today: United Food and Commercial Workers International Union (UFCW) and Retail Wholesale Canada (RWC). Retail Wholesale Canada originated with the Retail, Wholesale Department Store Union, an American International, whose headquaters are in New York. It remained affiliated with the RWDSU (during the pay equity process) until 1993, at which time it merged with the United Steelworkers of America. In 1999 the union voted to merge with the Canadian Auto Workers (CAW), the largest private sector union in Canada, with a membership of 260,000. At this time the union changed its name from RWDSU to Retail Wholesale Canada (RWC). The RWC represents over 9,000 workers at A&P, Dominion, Super Fresh, Miracle Food Mart (Local 414) and other stores, as well as 450 workers in wholesale food.

The second union representing food retail employees is the United Food and Commercial Workers. The UFCW is the second largest private sector union in Canada with a membership of just over 200,000. The majority of the UFCW membership is employed in retail food stores and services and food processing and production. The UFCW is a fairly new labour union in Canada, having come into existence in 1979 through the merger of two retail unions (the Amalgamated Meat Cutters and Butchers Union and the Retail Clerks International Union). The UFCW head office directed the Canadian operations in 1988 to merge Regions 18 and 19 to form the unified region of UFCW Canada, now one of twelve regions within the UFCW International. Over 100 of the 830 UFCW locals are located in Canada. One of the larger locals representing food retail food workers is Local 1000A with a membership of 22,000. The majority of Local 1000A members are employed in the food retail industry, many at the Loblaws supermarket chain; over half of the members are women, two-thirds of whom work part-time.[1] The largest local in the UFCW Canada, and the largest in the country, is a combination of two locals that is known as Locals 175/633, which is located in the Greater Toronto area with a membership of 40,000. Locals 175/633 represent workers employed at A&P, Dominion, Food Basics, Ultra Mart, Miracle Food Mart and other stores. As discussed further in chapter 7, Local 175 represents food clerks, cashiers and other service job classifications, and Local 633 represents employees in the meat and deli departments.

Within the food retail industry, unions have been able to achieve a relatively high rate of union coverage, although the retail industry as a whole has a low rate of unionization. Union density in retail trade was only 12.7 percent in Canada in 2000. This compares with a rate of 32.5 percent for manufacturing and 29.8 percent for services.[2] In Ontario, union density was 11.7 percent in retail in 1999, which indicates a slight increase over the past thirty years. A report of the Law Reform Commission found that less than 10 percent of the retail workforce was unionized in 1969.[3] While the rate of unionization is low for the Ontario retail workforce, a large percentage of unionized workers in retail are in food stores. Union coverage in the Ontario retail industry was 14.4 percent in 2001; however, in food stores it was 43.5 percent.[4] The historical overview that follows explains why the retail unions have been particularly successful in organizing food stores.

A history of these unions also explains the origins of the UFCW and RWC in Canada and spells out why these two unions are involved in jurisdictional and other disputes. For instance, the animosity between the two unions was expressed in the early 1990s when the RWDSU (Canadian Division) refused to merge with the UFCW, a decision made by the American parents without the consent of the Canadian division. The refusal to merge with the UFCW resulted in litigation when a complaint by the RWDSU concerning successor rights was filed at the Ontario Labour Relations Board.[5] The Board decided that the RWDSU had followed proper procedures in disaffiliating with its American parent, and the union joined the United Steelworkers in 1993. As mentioned, the RW has since disaffiliated from the United Steelworkers of America to join the Canadian Auto Workers.

The unions actually share many similarities. Both unions originally organized in the meat packing and food retailing industries, developing along a similar trajectory and following a similar approach to organizing. In the period immediately following the Second World War, important changes occurred in the organization of labour relations that supported collective bargaining and that led to the growth of unions in a number of sectors of the Canadian economy, including the food retail sector. This period of economic expansion began in the mid-1940s and ended in the mid-1970s and is often referred to as the Fordist era. The implications of the Fordist economy on the development of unionism in the food retail industry is important to understand, as is the transition to post-Fordism and the contemporary period of global economic restructuring that has affected collective bargaining and employment patterns in the supermarket sector.

Fordism and Food Retail Unions

Under Fordism, policy norms were established in Canada that facilitated unionization. Collective bargaining legislation was enacted in the late 1940s that legitimized and regulated labour relations. This legislation required that employers recognize unions as collective bargaining agents as long as they were properly constituted and followed appropriate certification procedures.[6] In addition to collective bargaining legislation, certain non-legislative developments, such as the Rand formula that provides for compulsory check-off of union dues, created a new environment for the establishment and operation of unions. This new industrial relations framework was a crucial component of the post-war compromise between labour and capital that enabled workers, especially male industrial workers, to bargain a wage with which they could support a family and purchase goods and services being produced in the expanding economy.[7] In the post-war period, men's right to earn a family wage was an accepted cultural and industrial relations norm, although in practice, a family wage was not always achieved.

Along with its role in regulating labour relations, the state was also important in sustaining overall conditions of economic growth and development. Keynesian economic policy, which assigned the state responsibility for maintaining full employment levels (at least for men), was supported by governments to promote high levels of consumption and investment.[8] In Canada, universal social programs, also referred to as welfare state programs, were largely developed in the post–Second World War period and included unemployment insurance, pensions, family allowance and medicare (healthcare). These programs were established to supplement wages, encourage consumer spending and bolster economic growth. The rise of the Keynesian welfare state in Canada paralleled developments in other advanced industrial countries and formed part of a broad international framework to sustain rapid increases in trade and other economic developments that supported the expansion of domestic economies.[9] On the whole this epoch of economic development was characterized by low inflation, rising real wages (i.e., adjusted for inflation) and high levels of employment.

Beyond the overall positive policy and economic conditions associated with the Fordist economy that were favourable to unionism, there also emerged in the mid twentieth century particular circumstances conducive to unionization in the retail food sector. Although the history of retail unions in Canada is woefully understudied, a substantial literature on retail unionism has emerged in the U.S. Given the similarities in the retail food industry and the fact that American-based international unions organized in Canada, it is probably safe to assume that many of the factors that contributed to the retail unions' bargaining power and presence in the U.S. were also evident in Canada.

EARLY RETAIL UNIONS

The first retail unions were formed in the late nineteenth century in response to grievances over long hours of work when it was not uncommon for retail clerks to work over 100 hours per week.[10] The initial impetus giving rise to retail unionism was the demand to close stores at "early candle light" as well as Sundays, although there is little evidence that merchants heeded labour's demand. Retail clerks first joined the Holy Order of the Knights of Labor forming several assemblies, but they became disenchanted with this labour organization and eventually pursued affilation with the American Federation of Labor (AFL).[11] By the turn of the twentieth century, seven locals had been chartered by the AFL under the name Retail Clerks National Protective Association (RCNPA). In 1899, the first Canadian local, located in the city of Vancouver, British Columbia, was chartered and the name of the RCNPA was changed to the Retail Clerks International Protective Association.[12] This retail union went on to become a major retail union representing food retail clerks in the U.S. and Canada. Although the RCIPA experienced growth in membership immediately following its affiliation with the AFL, the union mostly stagnated thereafter:

> From 1908 to the end of the First World War, the Clerks Union just about managed to survive. There was a strong leadership, and sickness and death benefits served to hold some of the members together. After the war, it participated in the surge of unionism that took place, but from the early 20's on the history of the union was one of steady decline.[13]

In spite of the fact that grocery chains first developed in the 1920s with the rise of self-service retailing (see chapter 4) making labour organization easier, unionization did not flourish during this period. In fact, unionization in food retail declined precipitously and did not regain a foothold until the 1940s. The retail unions were not able to capitalize on the advantages of organizing chain stores during the 1920s due to the paternalistic practices of employers who offered pensions, profit-sharing and other "welfare" benefits to workers. In addition, store management strongly opposed work stoppages and withdrew union recognition wherever strikes arose.[14]

Other factors that prevented unionization during this period included the prevalence of part-time work, extremely high levels of employee turnover, the widespread incidence of small stores (many with fewer than ten employees) and the presence of young women workers, whom the unions perceived as difficult to organize, in part, because of their weak attachment to the workplace. Married women, on the other hand, who had a stronger connection to the labour market, were recognized by unions as supportive of unionization and capable of engaging in militant action.[15] In general, though, the retail unions (like the labour movement) expressed ambivalence, and sometimes outright hostility, towards female labour.

In the nineteenth century, serious debate arose within the RCNPA over whether women should attend union meetings or be admitted to union locals as members, despite the widespread presence of women in retailing. At the centre of the controversy was the question of female wage competition or whether women should be paid the same as men employed in the retail industry. In spite of the fact that the RCNPA adopted the principle of equal pay for equal work at its first Convention in 1891, "equal pay" remained an ongoing issue. The request by women to hire women organizers was raised at various union conventions up until the 1920s but without much response, a clear indication that the union did not undertake a serious effort to address the special needs of women retail workers.[16] The loss of membership in the retail unions stemmed from many sources, then, and meant that the retail unions stagnated until the Depression of the 1930s created a new environment for union militancy.

Labour militancy was renewed in the 1930s when the American labour movement was induced by the newly enacted National Labor Relations Act (referred to as the *Wagner Act)* to engage in union organizing. The legislation permitted workers the legal right to join a union and mandated employers to recognize and bargain with a union, assuming proper legal procedures were followed.[17] The passage of this law in 1935 greatly facilitated unionization, and labour aggressively organized in a variety of industries. In March of 1937 the RCIPA organized a series of sit-down strikes at department stores and other retail operations across the U.S. Its first sit-down campaign was organized at Woolworth's in Detroit where the auto union had successfully waged sit-downs at General Motors and Chrysler. The retail union's demands for a wage increase, overtime pay after 48 hours of work per week and other demands were swiftly met by Woolworth's, and more sit-downs at retail stores in Detroit, as well as other cities such as New York and Philadelphia, followed.[18] This wave of union militancy prepared the ground for further organizing in the retail field.

About the same time as the sit-down campaigns were organized, a split occurred within the house of labour. A group of union leaders who argued that union organizing should occur on industrial, and not craft lines, broke away from the American Federation of Labor (AFL) to form the Comittee of Industrial Organizations (CIO). The CIO formed a committee to establish jurisdiction within retailing, and in 1940 the United Retail, Wholesale and Department Store Employe[e]s of America (later named the Retail, Wholesale Department Store Union) was formed. Some locals of the retail clerks (RCIPA) supported the CIO strategy of organizing on an industrial basis because the numerous job classifications within department stores made organizing on craft lines too complicated and unwieldy. As a consequence of this split within the labour movement, two major unions came to dominate the retail sector in the U.S.: the Retail Clerks International Association (RCIA) and the Retail Wholesale Department Store Union. Both of these U.S.-based international retail unions organized in Canada.

The Retail, Wholesale Department Store Union began its development during the Second World War. It was created from a merger between the Canadian Retail Employees union and the CIO affiliate unions belonging to the CIO organizing committee, which was operating in Canadian retailing during the 1940s. It adopted the name Retail, Wholesale Department Store Union (RWDSU) in 1953.[19] As an affiliate of the CIO, the RWDSU was a rival of the craft-based unions, such as the Amalgamated Meat Cutters and Butchers, because of the behaviour of the craft federations (e.g., the American Federation of Labor and the Canadian Trades and Labour

Congress) towards the industrial unions. In 1939, all CIO-chartered locals in Canada were expelled from the Trades and Labour Congress, following a similar move by the American Federation of Labor in 1937.

As mentioned above, the other major retail union operating in Canada is the United Food and Commercial Workers (UFCW). This union was only formed in 1979 out of a merger of two AFL affiliated unions: the Amalgamated Meat Cutters and Butchers Union, known in Canada as the Canadian Food and Allied Workers, and the Retail Clerks International Union. There existed ongoing competition and rivalry between the UFCW and its predecessor unions, which had historic ties to the craft union tradition, and the RWDSU that affiliated with the industrial unions. Despite these differences, unionization flourished in the post–Second World War era as a result of the specific industry and Fordist conditions conducive to retail unionism.

ORGANIZING IN FOOD STORES

The retail unions were able to expand in both Canada and the U.S. because they were highly successful in organizing food retail chains, which began in the 1940s. Compared with general merchandise stores that were smaller and more expensive to service, food stores were relatively easy targets for unionization in the retail sector for several reasons. The size and structure of grocery chains meant that the cost of unionizing was lower than in other areas of the retail field, such as department stores. In the U.S., for instance, during the 1950s and 1960s, the Retail Clerks International Association (RCIA) was able to secure "accretion clauses" in their collective agreements that extended unionization to any new stores a supermarket chain opened. As well, secondary picketing was practised by unions whereby pickets were set up at non-unionized chain stores in an effort to pressure corporations to negotiate a contract.[20] Strikes were especially effective in the industry at this time because of the high cost associated with the loss of perishable goods. Grocery retailing was, and continues to be, highly dependent on the continuous shelving and reshelving of goods, and the low margins required high turnover of grocery products. A work stoppage would jeopardize profit margins associated with volume sales. The predominance of male workers was another reason retail food was better unionized than other areas in the retail industry.[21] The first employees to be organized in grocery were white male craft workers (i.e., meat cutters and butchers), only later were grocery clerks recruited.[22] The unions were able to gain a toehold in the industry on the basis of craft organizing, which then paved the way for extending unionization to other categories of workers. For all these reasons, unions were far more successful in organizing supermarket workers. For instance, in 1967, a government report found that of 79,000 union members in Canadian retail establishments, 64,000 or 75 percent worked in food stores.[23]

By the 1960s and 1970s, the retail food unions had established a bargaining structure that was based on either province-wide or regional negotiations. In Ontario, with the exception of Loeb, all of the corporate food retail chains entered into agreements with the retail unions that covered the entire corporate entity's operations within a province or geographic region.[24] Unlike most industries in the service sector whose bargaining units were very small and highly fragmented, grocery retail unions had the advantage of servicing very large locals under master collective agreements. This type of bargaining structure facilitated co-ordinated bargaining efforts that culminated in strong collective agreements. Indeed, retail unions collective bargaining strategy gained unionized food workers respectable wage rates and improved conditions of work from the post-war period up until the 1980s. Strong collective agreements became the norm by the end of the 1970s, reflecting the positive industrial relations environment established under the Fordist economy.

To be sure, there were areas of Canada where unionization was difficult. For example, Sobey's supermarket chain located in Atlantic Canada was fiercely anti-union in the 1960s. Frank Sobey, owner of the chain, tried to avoid unionization by "black listing" or firing employees who fought for a union. However, by the 1970s, when the retail unions had successfully organized and fought several strikes at Sobey's stores, Frank Sobey backed down and recommended to his management team that "it might be smart to 'sweeten things early' to get a long-term contract at the bargaining table."[25]

The bargaining strength of the retail unions in Canada was further evident in the establishment of *pattern bargaining,* a type of bargaining arrangement in which negotiations with one unit establishes the pattern of negotiations for other units in the industry. In Ontario, the UFCW and Retail, Wholesale Department Store Union established a bargaining pattern whereby the expiration dates of contracts were set to ensure co-ordinated bargaining and to secure similar content in the retail food agreements. Following this approach to bargaining, retail food unions in Ontario achieved high wages, generous benefits, good work conditions and other positive labour standards in the industry. The ability to make gains extended to the area of full-time and part-time work. Unions achieved a clause in some collective agreements that required a 60:40 ratio of full-time to part-time employment, meaning that 60 percent of the workforce would be employed full-time.[26] In 1967, a survey estimated the ratio of part-time to full-time employees ranged from one to one to approximately one to three, with the average being 1.5 for every full-time employee in Canada.[27]

The strength of the retail food unions was particularly evident in the 1970s. Despite the fact that corporate retail food chains were in the midst of a price war, and some chains were experiencing a decline in profitability, unionized retail food workers consistently received wage increases above the rate of inflation throughout the decade.[28] For instance, in the early 1970s retail unions successfully negotiated a 21 percent wage increase over a two-year contract.[29] At the end of the decade, the Centre for the Study of Inflation and Productivity reviewed wage settlements in unionized food retail stores and found increases of 10 percent and 11 percent on average per year for major settlements.[30]

Retail food unions were well positioned to demand higher wages at this time for two reasons. First, most of the operations in food stores during the 1970s had yet to be mechanized. As discussed in chapter 4, Canadian supermarkets had not fully implemented centralized meat processing or automated checkout systems until the start of the next decade. This meant that labour was in high demand since products had to be hand priced, and processing of meat and baked goods primarily occurred in the store. Second, retail workers were willing to strike for higher wages. Although not widespread, unions such as the Amalgamated Meat Cutters and Butcher Workmen of North America and the Retail Clerks International Association (Local 500, Steinberg's) did go out on strike for higher wages.[31] The threat of a strike at a time when supermarkets were in the throes of a competitive price war was enough to ensure retail unions the power to bargain higher wage rates.[32]

By the end of the 1970s, unionized food store workers were earning some of the highest wage rates in the retail industry. Moreover, both full- and part-time employees received benefits rarely received in other workplaces. Retail food workers were largely satisfied with their wages and work conditions, as this cashier explains:

> The union played a big role in improving work conditions, as I said, this company spent a lot of money in those days [mid 1970s], most of it was in concessions to the union. Whatever the union asked for in those days, it pretty much got. Besides the higher wages, we as part-timers got benefits that other industries don't give to full-timers, including a full dental plan.[33]

BUSINESS UNIONISM

The history of these retail unions in the post-war Fordist period lent itself to a particular approach to unionism, often referred to as business unionism. Business unionism is a labour philosophy that focuses primarily on making economic gains and improving conditions of work for employees through the collective bargaining process. A basic assumption is that employers and unions have certain mutual interests and that a compromise can be reached that will benefit both sides. When times get tough, modest gains, or even concessions, are often accepted at the bargaining table in the hope that companies will not lay off or eliminate the workforce. Such an approach is more likely to accept the logic of business rather than oppose it.[34] As the discussion of union organizing in the supermarket sector makes clear, retail food unions benefited enormously from this unionist stance during the decades following the Second World War. The particular economic and industry conditions, such as an expanding economy, the competitive price wars among the chains and the lag in labour-saving technology, significantly advantaged the unions vis-à-vis the employer during this period. Up until the late 1970s, the retail unions established a comfortable relationship with management in which the expansion of employment and improved wages and working conditions were continuously negotiated.

The favourable conditions that strengthened labour's bargaining position in the Fordist era began to change for the worse with the competitive economic struggles that began to occur in the 1980s and 1990s. The limitations of business unionism surfaced with a vengeance under economic restructuring.

Economic Restructuring: An Overview

By the mid 1970s, a breakdown in the labour process and the world economy disrupted the stability and profitability of the Fordist regime creating conditions for massive restructuring. James Rinehart notes that "the profit rate in the world's seven wealthiest countries fell from 25 percent in 1965 to 12 percent in 1980. Between 1965 and 1976 the corporate rate of return fell by 16 percent in Canada."[35] Firms, concerned about declining rates of profitability, searched for new methods of organizational and production design to improve productivity and to maximize efficiency. This drive on the part of capital to restructure production has been identified as post-Fordism. A central feature of the post-Fordist era is capital's systematic search for flexibility to control labour costs and labour unions. The extensive use of flexible labour by firms is referred to as "flexible specialization."[36]

A flexible firm operates with a segmented workforce that is divided between a core and a peripheral workforce. Typically, the core workforce is high-skilled and/or multi-skilled (i.e., functionally flexible), whereas the peripheral workforce is more disposable and encompasses workers who are employed part-time or on short-term and temporary contracts.[37] In addition to segmentation occurring at the firm level, divisions between workers occur within the labour market. The more secure, higher-paid and high-skilled workers tend to be employed in the core goods manufacturing sector, whereas the peripheral workforce is concentrated in the lower-paid, less-skilled service sector. The division between the sectors is sometimes referred to as "market dualism." In the Canadian economy, as well as in other economies, employment in the service sector expanded in the 1970s and 1980s, while the manufacturing sector, which implemented highly advanced labour saving technology, significantly reduced its workforce. Another aspect of segmentation is polarized wage differentials between sectors and between workers employed in the core and peripheral segments of an industry or firm. Two-tier wage structures have also emerged in which senior employees receive higher wages and better benefits compared with newer entrants in the labour force.[38] As discussed below and in chapter 8, two-tier and multi-tier wage grids have multiplied in supermarket collective agreements.

Accompanying the breakdown in Fordist relations of production was a shift away from Keynesianism. Starting in the 1970s, the Keynesian welfare state came under attack by conservative governments. Governments at the federal, provincial and municipal levels weakened welfare entitlements and other social security measures, and at the same time reduced taxes on corporations and the rich. Canada has pursued neo-liberal economic policies such as trade liberalization, market deregulation and privatization in order to promote business opportunities in the private sector. All levels of government stopped introducing social and economic policy that incurred costs for business because it was presumed such measures inhibited investment. Legislation that helped to protect wages and working conditions came under attack in this attempt to promote business investment. For instance, in the province of Ontario, the Employment Standards Act was amended in 2001 and significantly lowered labour standards. The legislation no longer provides a basic floor of rights as workers must now negotiate employment conditions such as hours of work and overtime with their employer. For example, under the Act employees can reach an agreement with their employer to work 60 hours in a week without being paid for their overtime.[39]

Another important legislative change that was particularly detrimental to retail workers was the deregulation of Sunday shopping. Until the early 1990s, Sunday openings were illegal in Ontario as well as in most provinces across Canada.[40] In Ontario, the issue of Sunday shopping sparked considerable debate. The constitutionality of Ontario's *Retail Business Holidays Act*, which regulates Sunday shopping, was subject to a Charter challenge in 1986, and again in 1989 and 1990.[41] The first challenge (referred to as the Edwards case) went to the Supreme Court of Canada, which held that it remained valid by virtue of section 1 of the Charter.[42] The Court emphasized that the purpose of the statute was for people to have a common-pause day, and second, that the Act protected the "special need for regulation of the retail trade."[43] In effect, the decision acknowledged that the *Retail Business Holidays Act* operated as a form of protective legislation for retail workers. In spite of this ruling, subsequent court challenges were pursued by retail businesses. In response, the NDP government led by Bob Rae, amended the *Retail Business Holidays Act* in 1992, allowing wide-open Sunday shopping. The government argued that the extension of Sunday retailing would boost business.

The retail unions voiced their disappointment with the NDP government, pointing out that the new legislation did not guarantee sufficient protections for retail workers such as double-time pay or 48 consecutive hours off.[44] In fact, shortly after Sunday shopping was legalized, double-time pay was abolished in food retailing.[45] The full implications of Sunday openings on retail workers were ignored by the NDP government, despite the fact there had been plenty of research and discussion on the negative effects of Sunday work shifts.[46] Moreover, Sunday shopping was not identified as a feminist issue, even though the majority of retail workers are women who do the majority of domestic work within their families. Women with children faced tremendous difficulty obtaining childcare on Sunday, and the possibility of assigned Sunday work exacerbated uncertainties over their weekly schedule.[47]

Supermarket Retailing Transformed

The changes accompanying post-Fordism were strongly felt in the supermarket sector and affected consumers, the operation of retail food chains and supermarket workers. The breakdown of Fordism in the 1970s provided the stimulus for retail food corporations to restructure their organizations, while inflation raised the price of food — in the cities of Toronto and Thunder Bay the cost of food increased 228 percent between 1971 and 1979. Competition for the food dollar had be be balanced against other rising costs such as housing, which rose 80 percent in the same period.[48] Declining real incomes in this period were offset by the employment of women who entered the labour market in unprecedented numbers.[49] The decline in real incomes combined with women's growing participation in the labour market affected supermarket retailing as the corporations sought out strategies to reduce costs and create efficiencies. There were at least two ways they did this: through developing new store formats, lowering the wage bill and introducing new technologies; and by introducing new food products and retail departments to accommodate the "working woman" who had little time to shop or cook and who had limited grocery income. Corporate reorganization and industry restructuring, particularly company buy-outs, that began in the 1970s accelerated and continued into the 1980s and 1990s as Canadian supermarket chains responded to the new market conditions.[50]

MARKET SEGMENTATION

A key feature of industry restructuring, which emerged in food retailing and which had a major impact on competitive conditions, was market segmentation. Compared with the post-war era in which grocery retail was dominated by a few store types (i.e., the corner variety store, independents and supermarket chains), the current retail context displays deep fragmentation. Today, superstores, warehouse clubs as well as deep discount drug stores and general merchandise stores, such as Wal-Mart, all sell grocery products. This wide range of retail stores selling grocery items has created an ever-increasing competitive market.

In an effort to gain market share, companies have created new modes of retailing that take advantage of large volume, limited overhead and lower labour costs. These expanded store formats first developed to satisfy shoppers' demands for lower prices during the recession of the 1970s.[51] However, they continued to expand, and by the early to mid-1980s, warehouse clubs and other megastores invaded the retail market.[52]

Warehouse clubs are a major competitor of the established corporate food chains because they have absorbed a greater share of the market.[53] Compared with supermarkets, warehouse clubs use a number of measures to minimize overhead. They generally locate on industrial parks or on inexpensive real estate, they occupy large buildings that range in size from 100,000 to 130,000 square feet, and carry a narrow range of food products with a broad product mix.[54] These stores also save on costs by not providing sales help, not advertising, not finishing stores (floors are concrete) and by moving inventory quickly.

Another very important factor that contributes to minimizing costs is cheaper labour. In Canada, warehouse clubs rely on a youthful, non-unionized labour force.[55] According to a union official of the Canadian division of UFCW,

> A high proportion of Price Costco [warehouse] employees work part-time. They're paid only about $10 an hour — far less than the union rate of about $14 plus benefits ... [t]he corporation is fiercely anti-union.[56]

Because there are fewer employees working at warehouse clubs and because companies pay lower wage rates, grocery supermarkets are at a competitive disadvantage.

Superstores also made their debut in Canada in the mid 1980s. Similar in retailing functions to the warehouse stores, superstores are much larger than traditional merchandise stores and supermarkets, occupying warehouse-style buildings that typically build on inexpensive land sites. With the development of superstores and warehouse clubs, a significant shift in the market structure of retailing took place. For the first time since the post-war period, large retailers chose to locate outside shopping malls and shopping centres.[57] The development of "power centres" — shopping centres composed of megastores designed to serve shoppers in a large geographic region, consisting of warehouses and superstores on big tracts of land — have altered the Canadian landscape.

WAL-MART

The introduction of Wal-Mart discount stores into the Canadian market was based on its takeover of 122 Canadian Woolco Stores in early 1994.[58] The company's entry into Canada raised concerns because of the spectre of intensified price competition. Wal-Mart is the largest retailer in the world, America's largest private sector employer and the most successful retailer in the United States with sales of U.S. $191 billion in 2000. Canadian grocery retailers are especially uneasy about the impact of Wal-Mart on supermarkets because the company has moved from selling only general merchandise to selling food. In 1998, food retail sales at Wal-Mart reached U.S. $32 billion, and in 2002 it was recognized as one of the leading supermarket retailers in the United States.[59]

A particular area of concern is the effect Wal-Mart has on labour relations in Canada. This issue is especially significant for the corporate chains such as Loblaws, Safeway and A&P which operate with unionized labour. When Wal-Mart entered Canada, it did not purchase seven unionized Woolco Stores because the company did not want to negotiate with a unionized workforce; as a result, 1,000 employees lost their jobs. In addition, 700 warehouse employees receiving competitive wages and benefits were laid off, and just months after stores opened another 2,700 employees who believed they had permanent jobs were let go. Former Woolco Supervisors were instructed to work 52 hours per week instead of the regular 40-hour schedule.[60]

In 1996, Wal-Mart opposed a unionization drive at its store in Windsor, Ontario. When the union, the RWDSU, then affiliated with the United Steelworkers of America, lost the organizing drive, it filed for remedial certification under the Ontario Labour Relations Act. The Ontario Labour Relations Board ruled that the company had participated in unfair labour practices and imposed remedial certification, which granted union certification irrespective of a negative vote by the workers.[61] This 1997 ruling established the only unionized Wal-Mart store in the world at that time. One year after remedial certification, the Ontario government passed legislation, referred to as Bill 31 or the "Wal-Mart bill," that repealed this provision to remedy an unfair labour practice. There has been no effort to unionize Wal-Mart stores in Canada since then. The existence of Wal-Mart in Canada represents a further splintering of the grocery retail business and introduces another major competitor that relies on low-wage, non-unionized labour.

FRANCHISES

Alongside the recent development of warehouse clubs and the growth of discount stores, has been the rapid expansion of franchises. Franchise organizations in retail food are certainly not a new phenomenon. In fact, they were first established at the turn of the century but their expansion did not occur until the post-war period, and it is only very recently that independent franchise stores affiliated with corporate chains emerged in large numbers. From the mid-1980s to the mid-1990s in Ontario, corporate franchise outlets, also known as associated retailers, grew significantly.[62]

Under this system, the franchisor (or the corporation) acts as a wholesaler to the franchisee (the retailer). The greatest advantage to the franchisee is the advantage of volume buying. Other advantages include access to private brands; the benefit of a particular company image or store identity; and the right to build or acquire a store in a specific market area (territorial rights). In addition, the costs of advertising and promotion are shared among retailers on the basis of sales volume.

Typically, the franchisee is obligated to pay a percent of gross sales for advertising. Finally, the franchisee may lease property from the franchisor, and receive loans in order to purchase equipment or renovate a store. In order to receive the services offered by the franchisor, the franchisee pays a service fee. The particular fee arrangement, the package of services available and other obligations of franchisor and franchisee are set out in a franchise contract.[63]

The franchise system may be of greater benefit to the wholesaler than to the franchisee for a variety of reasons. Wholesalers have tremendous market and contractual leverage over franchisees. Contract agreements require that all grocery products be purchased from specific wholesale suppliers or approved vendors, albeit certain products such as bakery items or produce may be purchased from individual suppliers. The wholesaler's merchandising program may determine which sale items will be featured and at what price as part of the wholesaler's advertising arrangement. Moreover, wholesalers may charge the same markup for wholesale goods to both its corporate stores and franchise outlets.[64] Franchising benefits corporate chains in other ways, too, such as improving the wholesalers' buying power with suppliers and strengthening negotiations with financial institutions.

Large corporate chains operating in Ontario turned to the franchise concept in the 1980s as a way to compete against independents in retail food. As discussed in chapter 4, for a little over a decade independents were taking away market share from the corporate chains. Establishing franchises was seen as a viable strategy to capture some of the lost business. Moreover, corporate chains were not realizing sufficient profits in their smaller stores. Many corporations had built properties in the 1970s that by today's standards are considered "small" to "medium-sized" stores. Rather than selling these properties, the corporations leased them to independent retailers, as this retail analyst explains:

> There was a period of time when everything went towards corporate chains, where, in fact, the corporation ran the stores and they had managers. That was a continuing situation right up until the 1980s, except in Quebec, where there was a strong independence presence. Since the latter 1980s, the trend has gone the other way. There has been a move towards

> corporate organizations arranging for independent ownership, and acting as a wholesale supplier, rather than owning corporately-owned stores ... They had these properties, and what they decided was to lease out these properties to former managers who know how to operate stores.[65]

Corporate retailers who no longer wanted to fund their smaller stores maintained their real estate through franchise retailing. In some instances, corporate stores sold properties to store managers or recruited investors to manage the stores.

Low labour costs is a key reason that independents or franchisees could compete against large corporate chains. In some cases, franchise owners joined an employer association, whereby a group of employers negotiated a province-wide collective agreement with a union representing workers at franchised stores. UFCW established an agreement with franchisees at No Frills Stores, and RWDSU negotiated a master agreement with Willett Foods Limited, a corporate relative of Dominion. While some franchise stores were unionized, their collective agreements were inferior to those at corporate stores. Unfortunately, data on unionization of franchised stores is difficult to obtain. But commentaries of retail grocery consistently remark that a competitive advantage for franchise owners has been lower labour costs. As one retail analyst pointed out, labour costs increased in the corporate chains because the unions were in place for well over twenty-five years and achieved mature agreements in the corporate sector. As a result, in the mid-1990s, labour costs as a percentage of total business were higher in the corporate stores as compared with the franchises:

> All grocery stores know you can only go so high in their labour [costs] as percentage of total business. On average, that is 10 percent of sales for all labour. You usually find independents at 10 or slightly lower, and you can find corporates at 9, or sometimes as high as 13 percent or 14 percent.[66]

More recently, in the latter part of the 1990s, franchise operations and independents experienced a decline in the proportion of sales as corporate retailers either bought up franchises or forced them to close by competing directly against them in an effort to consolidate their market share.[67] However, franchise operations and independents still retained a significant share of sales — 37.2 percent — in 1998.

Supermarket Technology, Deskilling and Job Displacement

As corporate food chains came under increasing competitive pressure, they turned to technology as a strategy to lower costs. As discussed in chapter 4, historically the supermarket chains have relied on innovation to counter competition from independents. In the current context, supermarket management continues to implement, and experiment with, new technologies as a method to improve efficiencies and decrease costs, especially the wage bill.[68]

Although there are risks associated with technology implementation in that the costs are high and payoffs are uncertain, retailers accept the risks because of the potential to save costs in the long term and because

> if you are the first in, you have an advantage in the sense that you are a learner ... In the beginning, there are trial and error costs, and if you can't support them they'll kill you because it's such a competitive industry. But the fact remains, if you're the last in, you'll get killed. It has to do with timing, and judging when you should get in, when progress has been made [69]

Typically, larger employers are more willing to take the risks involved in introducing new supermarket technologies. Corporate chains such as Loblaws or Sobey's are in a better position to advance the necessary capital to purchase equipment and computer software as compared with smaller chains or independents. The need to keep ahead of new technologies is one reason companies seek corporate mergers, as retail expansion allows more revenue to experiment with new technologies. Conversely, if a corporate chain is not performing optimally, then it will not invest in new equipment or technology.

Technology assists in reducing costs by providing closer monitoring of sales, inventories and profitability. These technolgies benefit the more proftiable corporate chains that have the funds to invest in them. For instance, Direct Product Profitability (DPP) is a software system that has been implemented to help retailers make decisions about buying and merchandising. Other software programs have been devised that use universal product codes to analyze sales. These programs have the capacity to decipher sales of products by specific product and product category, as well as analyze sales at the store and even chain level. Using this technology, it is possible to determine how many items are sold in a particular store on any given day. Furthermore, computer technology has the capacity to calculate profit margins of various products so that entire pricing structures can be revealed.[70]

In an attempt to gain greater control over merchandizing and sales, the retail industry adopted the Efficient Consumer Response (ECR) initiative. ECR is a system that facilitates careful management of specific product categories from manufacturer to store shelves. The introduction of computer technology, like the software program described above, in conjunction with electronic data interchange allow companies to conduct category management and just-in-time inventory. Category management (CM) helps retailers track product movement and monitor required shelf space. Although the ECR is expensive to implement, retailers are restructuring operations and purchasing the necessary technologies in the hope that it will improve efficiencies and generate cost savings. For instance, Oshawa Foods spent $17 million on ECR-related technologies in fiscal 1995.[71]

Another technology that benefits retailers is computer scanning, which allows employers to monitor the work of cashiers. Computer printouts measure the speed at which a cashier scans groceries, as Deborah Barndt explains:

> One cashier showed us a computer printout that tallied her week's work, to the hundredth of a second, according to the average number of scans per hour, and how much time she spent per hour scanning, tendering money, or in "idle time" (between customers); it also indicated her average time per item (4.64 seconds) and per transaction (1.45 minutes) as well as how much money she had tendered per hour ($1,808).[72]

This technology allows management to closely supervise the productivity of cashiers and encourages work intensification as cashiers attempt to push through customers as speedily as possible. Particularly troublesome is the high risk of injury associated with scanning. A study of cashiers found that on average, cashiers lift 11,000 pounds or 5,000 kilos of merchandise in a day. Ergonomic analysis of cashier work stations reveal a range of health problems such as neck, shoulder, back and lower leg injuries (related to standing in one place for long periods), and repetitive strain injuries.[73]

In addition to computerization, labour-saving equipment that uses computer technology is being implemented at a rapid rate. In the forefront is deli equipment such as automatic slicers with pre-set programs to slice in selected patterns for party trays, stacking slicers that can vacuum pack and interfacing scales with a computer memory. Meat-wrapping machines are available that can weigh, label and wrap meat in trays. Fingerprint resistant doors save labour-time cleaning, and thermal-controlled glass saves energy costs. The implementation of retail-ready meats has displaced meat cutters and butchers in stores.[74]

Testing of automated self-checkouts has been ongoing for many years but the machinery has produced mixed results. Supermarket chains introduced customer-scanning in an effort to save on labour costs (of cashiers) and to improve customer efficiency. While self-checkout is in use in the U.S. and Europe, the service remains a rarity in Canada.[75] Similarly, companies have implemented Internet grocery shopping; however, it has not been widely used by customers and even one of the larger on-line grocery firms that operates in metropolitan Toronto, Grocery Gateway, has not proved profitable.[76]

Both computer technology and high-tech equipment have been implemented to help cut costs, reduce in-store labour-time and improve productivity in the supermarket. While all employees are affected by computerization and new supermarket technology, retail workers employed *at the store level* are disproportionately affected by labour-saving technologies. Self-checkout systems have the potential to displace cashiers at the frontend; equipment such as automatic meat slicers and ready-retail meats reduce the amount of labour and skill level required in deli and meat departments. Even cleaning can be reduced by fingerprint resistant freezer doors and electronic labelling can reduce the number of stock clerks required to install labels in supermarkets. Department heads may find that decisions over labour allocation and scheduling is determined by computer reports produced by the store manager. Although the implementation of new technologies is uneven across supermarket chains, it is inevitable that as technologies are perfected, fewer employees will be needed, especially at the store level, in retail food stores. Just as significant is that fact that labour-displacing technology disproportionately effects workers in the service departments, the majority of whom are women, especially those employed in the frontend as cashiers and those in the meat department.

CONCESSION BARGAINING

Another crucial way in which supermarket management has tried to limit costs is through demanding concessions at the bargaining table. Retail unions began to face aggressive negotiations at the bargaining table in the early 1980s when the economy was undergoing a severe recession. The demand for concessions continued over the next two decades as employers tried to reduce business costs. By the 1990s, "slow economic recovery, poor sales growth, deflationary pricing, and increased competition from warehouse clubs ... all contributed to the drastic cost cutting demands supermarket chains [were] bringing to the bargaining table."[77] While there are numerous factors that contribute to cost effectiveness such as inventory control, implementation of new technologies and better equipment, controlling labour costs is viewed by management as the largest internal cost factor in the supermarket.[78] A brief overview of some of the contract negotiations in the retail food industry in Canada reveal wage reductions, two-tiered and multi-tiered wage structures, downsizing of the full-time workforce and the expansion of low paid part-time workers.

The first agreement to be negotiated, which departed from well-established wage structures in the industry, was achieved by the

Federated Co-operatives Limited and UFCW in the mid-1980s. The Saskatchewan-based employer argued that wage rollbacks were necessary to save the co-ops from bankruptcy. After opening their books to the union, the UFCW agreed to major concessions. In 1993, Co-op retail workers in Regina and Saskatoon were earning, on average, $3 less per hour in their wage rates as compared with Canada Safeway and Westfair Foods Real Canadian Superstore.[79] Both the union and employer argued concessions saved the co-ops from total financial ruin. However, the negotiations undermined industry standards of unionized wage rates.

A further decline in industry standards occurred in Alberta when Canada Safeway Limited threatened to withdraw from the province unless workers accepted $45 million a year in wage cuts and benefit reductions. The company said it would close eighty-three Safeway and Food For Less stores unless the UFCW agreed to open a contract in March of 1993 that was not due to expire for another eighteen months. The UFCW agreed to open the collective agreement, with devastating results for labour. The company's intention behind rene-gotiations was to reduce the full-time workforce and eliminate longer service part-timers by offering workers a lay-off payout or buy-out. According to the terms of the buy-out, long-service employees could opt to accept a lump-sum payment (up to a maximum of $25,000) and then return to work at a lower wage with no benefits. Thousands of workers accepted the buy-out because full-time employees feared store closures, while part-time workers thought they would experi-ence cut backs in their hours. As a result of the buy-out, hundreds of full-time jobs were lost, and in their place were hired two to three part-time workers at much lower wage rates. Following concessions at Safeway, other grocery chains (e.g. Real Canadian Superstore) in the province also demanded wage reductions.[80] The agreement reached with UFCW in Alberta was to be the benchmark for contracts negotiated in the 1990s in Ontario at Miracle Food Mart and Dominion stores owned by A&P. Further discussion of those contract negotiations will be provided in chapter 8.

A pattern of concession bargaining was thus established throughout the retail food industry in Canada, which had major implications for workers' wages and working conditions. At one time, unionized food retail employees were the aristocracy of labour within the retail sector, but they suffered a severe blow in their wage levels and work conditions. Retail unions were placed in a weaker bargaining position when internal changes, such as mechanization, took hold in food retailing. In the mid-1980s, when the retail food market was fragmented by diversified modes of retailing and the economy went into recession, retail unions were further weakened.

These problems were intensified by the commitment of the retail unions to business unionism. As was stated earlier, during the Fordist period, the retail unions could function in an environment characterized by a mutually supportive relationship with management in which employers responded to the demands of unions and agreed to improvements in collective agreements. This type of relationship was severely challenged in the post-Fordist era. However, the retail unions remained locked in the old pattern of negotiations even though a new, more aggressive environment emerged that could no longer sustain the type of business unionism practised in the earlier period.

The aggressive corporate demands for concessions in combination with retail unions that were unprepared for the onslaught led to an extended period of concession bargaining. As a result, the retail food workforce experienced a severe decline in their wages and conditions of employment. For example, in 1971 retail workers average weekly earnings was $90.62 as compared with the industrial aggregate of $127.11, or 71.3 percent of the Ontario average for all industries. By 1983, the percentage declined to 59.9, and by 2000 it had declined a further 15 percent to 45.5 percent of the industrial average.[81] Supermarkets reduced the number of full-time workers in stores by implementing an attrition policy and by aggressively negotiating with retail unions the elimination of full-time/part-time employee ratios in collective agreements. The shrinking full-time "core" workforce encouraged store managers to adopt various labour flexibility strategies. For instance, full-time workers were required to engage in multi-tasking and to intensify their work effort. Because unionized full-time workers were guaranteed 37 hours of work per week, managers tried to amplify the labour of full-timers through multi-tasking and other tactics, while minimizing the number of labour hours allocated to part-time employees. At the same time, part-time workers may be assigned full-time hours but work at part-time wage rates. Because part-time workers provide managers with optimal flexibility in assigning labour hours and are less costly to employ, there has been a steady increase in the growth of the peripheral part-time labour force in food stores since at least the 1960s.

The issue of labour costs has become so important to food retail management that supermarket chains have followed aggressive campaigns to eliminate their higher-paid full-time and part-time workers by offering them buy-outs. Many full-time employees accepted a buy-out settlement only to return to the supermarket as a low-paid, low-seniority, part-time hire. A major aspect of buy-out policies is that they allow companies to hire part-time employees at increasingly cheaper wage rates. Every major supermarket chain in Ontario has instituted multi-tiered wage structures in the part-time classification.

For the food retail corporations, the benefits of multi-tiered wage structures and buy-out programs are obvious. The buy-out permits companies to retain an already trained workforce at low wage rates. Eliminating full-time employees allows managers to displace higher-paid long-service employees with low-wage workers in the part-time classification. There is thus a splintering of the workforce into various tiers. Workers receive different wage rates, are entitled to different job guarantees and numbers of hours of work and are eligible or ineligible for benefits depending on seniority or length of service with the company. In the supermarket, not only is there a deepening of the dual labour market between a very small core labour force and a peripheral workforce, but even the precarious labour force is subdivided into segments. Retail food corporations have ensured there is flexibility within the flexible workforce. Multi-tiered wage structures for part-time workers places restrictions on the level of wages part-timers can earn, while provisions in collective agreements also stipulate limits on the number of hours part-time employees are allowed to work. Restricted entitlements on hours, wages and job placement has a further effect on benefits entitlement for workers in the part-time classification. All of these measures allow companies to save enormously on labour costs.

Women have been disproportionately affected by supermarket reorganization. Women retail workers, who are concentrated in the service departments both as part-time and full-time employees, have seen their hours of work reduced and their full-time jobs eliminated. Women's under-representation in union governance and the reluctance of the union to fully protect the wages and work conditions of part-time employees are two identifiable factors that contribute to women's inequality at the workplace. Of greatest importance in the post-Fordist economy has been employers' reliance on a female predominant flexible workforce. Women in the supermarket sector are concentrated in the part-time classification and in departments that are susceptible to labour hour reductions. In the following chapter, the implications of restructuring on women's flexible employment is examined in greater detail.

NOTES

1. UFCW Local 1000A. "Who We Are." < http://www.ufcw1000aorg>.
2. Ernest Akyeampong, *Unionization — An Update, Special 2000 Labour Day Release* (Ottawa: Statistics Canada, Cat. No. 75-001-XPE).
3. *Report on Sunday Observance Legislation: Ontario Law Reform Commission* (Department of Justice, 1970), 101.
4. Labour Force Survey Estimates in Ontario, 2001 Annual Averages. Special run from Statistics Canada. Union coverage refers to those workers who are covered by a collective agreement but who may not have signed a union card and are not union members. For a detailed discussion of union coverage see Akyeampong, *Unionization — An Update.*
5. For the complete story of the RWDSU merger, see Retail, Wholesale and Department Store Union, Canadian Service Sector Division of the United Steelworkers of America, Local 414, *Applicant v. The Great Atlantic & Pacific Company of Canada, Limited.* [1993] OLRB REP. SEPTEMBER at 894.
6. For more on the development of this industrial relations framework, see Judy Fudge and Eric Tucker, *Labour Before the Law: The Regulation of Workers Collective Action in Canada, 1900–1948* (Toronto: Oxford University Press, 2001),

especially chap. 10. *The Industrial Relations and Disputes Investigation Act* came into effect at the federal level in 1948 and became the model for collective bargaining in the ten Canadian provinces. Also see Rianne Mahon, "Post-Fordism: Some Issues for Labour," in Daniel Drache and Meric Gertler, eds., *The New Era of Global Competition: State Policy and Market Power* (Montreal: McGill-Queen's University Press, 1991), 318. Mahon provides a concise overview of the central elements of Fordism and post-Fordism as presented by the French regulationists.

7. On the post-war compromise, see Leo Panitch and Donald Swartz, *The Assault on Trade Union Freedoms* (Toronto: Garamond Press, 1988); Julie Guard, "Womanly Innocence and Manly Self-Respect: Gendered Challenges to Labour's Postwar Compromise," and Ann Forrest, "Securing the Male Breadwinner: A Feminist Interpretation of PC 1003", both in Cy Gonick, Paul Phillips and Jesse Vorst, eds., *Labour Gains, Labour Pains: 50 Years of PC 1003* (Halifax: Fernwood Publishing, 1995).

8. On the implications of Keynesian employment policy on women in Canada, see Pat and Hugh Armstrong, "Taking Women into Account: Redefining and Intensifying Employment in Canada," in Jane Jenson, Elisabeth Hagen and Ceallaigh Reddy, eds., *Feminization of the Labor Force: Paradoxes and Promises* (New York: Oxford University Press, 1988), 68.

9. See, for example, John Shields and Stephen McBride, *Dismantling a Nation: The Transition to Corporate Rule in Canada* (Halifax: Fernwood Publishing, 1997), chap. 2.

10. On the early history of retail unionism in the U.S., see George Kirstein, *Stores and Unions: A Study of the Growth of Unionism in Dry Goods and Department Stores* (Fairchild Publications Inc., 1950), chap. 1.

11. Kirstein, *Stores and Unions,* 10–11, discusses the disaffiliation of the retail clerks from the Knights of Labor.

12. Ibid., 13. This union local still exists today as UFCW Local 1518.

13. Michael Harrington, *The Retail Clerks* (New York: John Wiley and Sons, 1962), 7.

14. On the decline of unionization in grocery stores during the 1920s in the U.S., see Kirstein, *Stores and Unions,* 47–49. The Retail Clerks International Association membership hit an all time low of 5,000 members by 1933, a huge drop in its membership that had numbered 50,000 in 1903. Cited in Harrington, *The Retail Clerks,* 7.

15. Kirstein, *Stores and Unions,* 107–8.

16. Ibid., 29–36.

17. *The Wagner Act* provided the model for Canadian collective bargaining legislation enacted in 1944 under PC 1003. See John Godard, *Industrial Relations, the Economy and Society,* 2nd ed. (Toronto: Captus Press, 2000), 98–100.

18. Kirstein, *Stores and Unions,* 63–74.

19. Tom Collins, "The Retail, Wholesale Department Store Union: The Political Behaviour of a Union" (MA thesis, University of Western Ontario, 1975).

20. James Mayo, *The American Grocery Store: The Business Evolution of an Architectural Space* (Westport: Greenwood Press, 1993), 186.

21. Department of Labour, Economics and Research Branch, and the Women's Bureau, *Part-Time Employment in Retail Trade* (Ottawa: Queen's Printer, 1969), 17.

22. Historically, the butchers were segregated into separate bargaining units from the remainder of the store. The lack of storewide seniority prevented promotion of clerks to the higher-paid skilled jobs. Referring to the American situation in the 1960s, Bloom and Fletcher remark that "[s]ince Negroes, as a group, are more likely to lack skill and training, they generally are employed as clerks or unskilled grocery workers. They tend to remain in this department where wages are relatively good but below those of meat and driver groups. See, Gordon Bloom and F. Marion Fletcher, *The Negro in the Supermarket Industry* (Philadelphia: University of Pennsylvania, 1972), 139.

23. *Part-Time Employment in Retail Trade,* 16.

24. Loeb is a franchise-based supermarket, hence collective agreements are fragmented. One of the largest units represents 250 employees.

25. See Harry Bruce, *Frank Sobey: The Man and the Empire* (Toronto: Macmillan of Canada, 1985), 369.

26. Interview, Produce Manager, Food Basics, December 30, 2001.

27. The employment data was taken from eleven supermarkets at various locations. See *Part-Time Employment in Retail Trade, 39.*

28. Except for 1974 and 1975 when CPI was 10.9 percent and 10.8 percent respectively, the inflation rate during the 1970s was well below 10 percent in every year. For a table of the change in CPI in the 1970s, see David Wolfe, "The Rise and Demise of the Keynesian Era in Canada, 1930-1982," in Michael Cross and Gregory S. Kealey, eds., *Readings in Canadian Social History* Volume 5 Modern Canada 1930–1980s (Toronto: McClelland and Stewart, 1984), table 1, 51.

29. *Canadian Grocer* (January 1971); *Canadian Grocer* (September 1972). This included units at Dominion, Steinberg's, and Loblaws stores.

30. Cited in *Canadian Grocer* (March 1979).

31. *Canadian Grocer* (February 1971); *Canadian Grocer* (January 1976).

32. The reasons for labour's strong collective bargaining position were outlined by E.C. (Tim) Carter to a meeting of the American Marketing Association in Toronto. See *Canadian Grocer* (January 1973), 33–34.

33. Interview, Full-Time Cashier, February 1995.

34. Labour unions operating within a framework of business unionism do not question the broader economic power of capital but attempt to work within the parameters of management control. Business unions typically do not confront business on issues of major economic impact either at the company or societal level. For instance, challenges are not made concerning the political power of corporations to influence wider economic and social policy. A common criticism of business unionism is that the union position becomes blurred with the interests of the employer. A cashier provided a good illustration of this when she remarked to me that her union representatives, speaking at a union meeting, "sounded just like the company."

35. James Rinehart, *The Tyranny of Work: Alienation and the Labour Process,* 4th ed. (Toronto: Harcourt Canada, 2001), 149.

36. There are three types of flexibility that operate in the workplace: (1) *financial* or *pay flexibility* (cost-cutting measures to slim the labour force often through lay-offs; (2) *functional flexibility* (making better use of the existing labour force (i.e., by implementing quality circles, or multiskilling/multi-tasking); and (3) *numerical flexibility* (use of part-time labour, subcontracting and temporary workers).

37. An overview of the flexibility debates, including Atkinson's flexible firm and Sabel and Piore's flexible specialization model, is offered by Stephen Wood in the introduction to his edited collection, *The Transformation of Work? Skill, Flexibility and the Labour Process* (London: Unwin Hyman, 1989).

38. For an excellent overview of the outcome of "new Fordism" in Canada, including contracting out, downsizing, two-tier wage bargaining, flexible work arrangements, state deregulation of industry and labour markets, see Daniel Drache and Harry Glasbeek, "The New Fordism in Canada: Capital's Offensive, Labour's Opportunity," *Osgoode Hall Law Journal* 7, no. 3 (1989), 517–60.

39. The provisions of the *Employment Standards Act* allow an employee to reach an agreement in writing with their employer to work 60 hours a week without being paid overtime pay. However, the average number of hours over a four-week period cannot exceed 176 hours or 44 hours per week. *Review of Employment Starndards Act (Bill 147), 2001* (Toronto: Parkdale Legal Clinic, Employment Standards Group, June 2001).

40. See Paul Lanoie, Georges A. Tanguay and Luc Vallee, "Short-term Impact of Shopping-hour Deregulation: Welfare Implications and Policy Analysis," *Canadian Public Policy* 20, no. 2 (1994), 177–88. Table 1 provides an overview of Sunday shopping regulation. Both Quebec and Ontario permit wide-open Sunday shopping, while many provinces allow municipal governements to regulate Sunday shopping. Alberta, British Columbia, Saskatchewan and New Brunswick allow Sunday openings in some larger municipalities (eg. Vancouver, Regina, Saskatoon).

41. The Supreme Court ruled the Act infringed on freedom of religion, but that the infringement was reasonable as per section 1 of the Charter. For a complete explanation of this case and others on the Sunday shopping issue, see Ian Greene, *The Charter of Rights* (Toronto: James Lorimer, 1989), 70–81.

42. Section 1 of the Charter provides that legislation can be upheld "as a reasonable limit as can be demonstrably justified in a free and democratic society." The intention of section 1 is to provide judges with "some direction in determining limits to Charter rights." See Greene, *The Charter of Rights*, 54. In other words, Sunday observance legislation was considered a reasonable limit in that it provides people with a day of rest in which to spend time with their family.

43. *R v. Edwards Books Ltd.* [1986] 2 S.C.R. 713 (S.C.C.) at 747.

44. *Toronto Star*, 4 June 1992, A28.

45. Loblaws and Miracle Food Mart eliminated double-time pay and replaced it with a $1.60 hour premium pay; Dominion and A&P stores paid time and half.

46. The Select Committee on Retail Store Hours, 1997, the Standing Committee on the Adminstration of Justice Regarding Bill 113 and 114 held hearings and commissioned reports detailing the negative implications of Sunday work on retail employees.

47. In 1992, I attended a workshop at the Ontario Federation of Labour's Women's Conference on workplace childcare. The facilitator, a staff person from the Ontario Coalition for Better Child Care, commented that when grocery stores defied existing legislation and began opening stores on Sunday, she received numerous phone calls from female retail workers complaining about the need for childcare on Sunday.

48. These figures are cited in Joy Parr, ed., *A Diversity of Women: Ontario 1945–1980*

(Toronto: University of Toronto Press, 1995), 8.

49. See Pat and Hugh Armstrong, "Women, Family and Economy" in Nancy Mandell and Ann Duffy eds., *Reconstructing the Canadian Family: Feminist Perspectives* (Toronto: Butterworths, 1988), 161-62.

50. For several examples of company buy-outs in the United States with disastrous consequences for workers, see James Mayo, *The American Grocery Store* (Westport: Greenwood, 1993), 223–33. For a Canadian example involving the Dominion Stores pension fund, see John Deverell, "Shrunken Dominion Hits 75: New Owners Kept the Grand Old Banner," *The Toronto Star,* 22 October 1994, B1, and "Pension-fund Surplus will be Returned," *Calgary Herald,* 1 September 1990, D15. The retail union, RWDSU, took legal action against the company and in 1986 the Ontario Supreme Court ordered Black to return the money to the pension fund. Although Dominion employees' pensions were in jeopardy because of the sale, their right to union protection was assured under section 63 of Ontario's *Labour Relations Act,* which ensured "successor rights." This meant that when a business or parts of a business were sold, the company was obligated to recognize the trade union and the collective agreement that was in place under the previous employer. Since Dominion stores operated primarily in Ontario, the retail unions' right to represent workers at these stores remained intact.

51. Mayo, *The American Grocery Store,* 221.

52. Walter Levy, "The End of an Era: A Time for Retail Perestroika," *Journal of Retailing* 65, no. 3 (Fall 1989); "Food Store Sales Rocket Upward," *Canadian Grocer* (February 1975), 66; Interview, Industry Analyst, Canadian Council of Grocery Distributors, June 22, 1994.

53. Between 1990 and 1998, the grocery market share of mass merchandisers, warehouse clubs, drug stores and other non-traditional outlets increased 7 percent (from 11 percent in 1990 to 18 percent in 1998). US Department of Agriculture and Foreign Service. <http://www.corporateinformation.com/casector/Retail.html>.

54. Harlow Unger, "U.S. Supermarkets Seek Share of Warehouse Club Sales," *Canadian Grocer* (May 1991), 20D.

55. Richard Currie, president of Loblaw, commented that "retail warehouses in Ontario [pay] their employees about half of what Loblaw's workers earn." See Maureen Murray, *The Toronto Star,* 29 April 1992, F1.

56. John Deverell, "Costco Opening Two Megastores," *The Toronto Star,* 18 November 1994, B3. In 2000, only one Costco store, in British Columbia, was unionized. See Julia Drake, "Welcome to the Big Time," *Canadian Grocer* (May 2001), 23. Costco employed 11,000 workers in Canada in 2000.

57. Avijit Ghosh and Sara McLafferty, "The Shopping Center: A Restructuring of Post-War Retailing," *Journal of Retailing* 67, no. 3 (1991), 265.

58. See *The Toronto Star,* 11 November 1995, C7. On Wal-Mart in Canada and internationally, see George Condon, "Wal-Mart Watch," *Canadian Grocer* (April 2000), 53–7.

59. See Andrew Seth and Geoffrey Randall, *The Grocers: The rise and the Rise of the Supermarket Chains* (London: Kogan Page, 1999), 204. Also, CNN Money. <http://money.cnn.com/2002/06/06/news/supermarkets/index/.htm.>

60. For a discussion of Wal-Mart, see "Communities Challenge Waly World: Citizens' Fightbacks Control Wal-Mart Threats," Canadian Perspectives 13 (Winter 1995),

and "Anti-Union Strategy Fuels Attack: The Wal-Mart Invasion," *Technotes* (March 1995), 9.

61. See Judith McCormack, "Shopping for a Remedy: The Wal-Mart Case," *Canadian Labour and Employment Law Journal* 5 (1997), 341–58.

62. "Ten years ago, corporately-owned chain stores had about 60% of the nation's retail food business. Since then, the independent section of the market has encroached into the chain business due substantially to the rise of voluntary or franchised groups. From 1983 to 1993, the total market increased at a compound rate of 6.3% per year, with chains advancing only 5.4% on average. Franchised stores rose 9.3% annually during this period." See *Oshawa Group Annual Report,* 1994, 2.

63. See Taylor Gilbert and Douglas Jung. *Franchising in Canada: A Guide for Franchisors and Franchisees,* 2nd ed. (Toronto: CCH Canadian Limited, 1992).

64. Select Standing Committee on Agriculture, *Franchising in the British Columbia Food Industry* (Febraruary 1979), 39.

65. Interview, Industry Analyst, Canadian Council of Grocery Distributors, June 22, 1994. Also see Carl Cuneo, "Franchising Union Succession Rights," in Cy Gonick, Paul Phillips and Jesse Vorst eds., *Labour Gains, Labour Pains: 50 Years of PC 1003* (Halifax: Fernwood Publishing, 1995), 311–13.

66. Interview, August 8, 1994. The industry standard for labour costs is generally reported to be anywhere from 9 to 11 percent. See James Oakes, "The Cost of Labour," *Grocer Today* (October 1993), 7.

67. George Condon, "National Market Survey: 1998 in Review", *Grocer Today,* (January/February 1999), 18.

68. *Canadian Grocer* (December 1990), 18; (December 1992), 34.

69. Interview, Industry Analyst, Canadian Council of Grocery Distributors, June 22, 1994.

70. Ann Kingston, *The Edible Man: Dave Nichol, President's Choice and the Making of Popular Taste* (Toronto:MacFarlane Walter and Ross, 1994), 82–83.

71. *The Globe and Mail Report on Business Canada Company Handbook* (Toronto: Globe and Mail, 1995), 429.

72. Deborah Barndt, *Tangled Routes: Women, Work and Globalization on the Tomato Trail* (New York: Rowman and Littlefield Publishers, 2002), 132.

73. Kate Pocock, "Torture Chamber," *Canadian Grocer* (February 1994), 88–92; Anthony Ryan, "The Prevalence of Musculo-skeletal Symptoms in Supermarket Workers," Ergonomics 32, no. 4 (1989), 359–71.

74. Louisette Hinton, Josefina Moruz and Cheryl Mumford, "A Union Perspective on Emerging Trends in the Workplace," in Isik Urla Zeytinoglu, ed., *Changing Work Relationships in Industrialized Economies* (Philadelphia: John Benjamins Publishing Co., 1999), 175.

75. The automated self-checker operates by customer-scanning of all grocery products that carry UPC symbols. See "Loblaw Explores Self-Checkouts," *Canadian Grocer* (June 2000), 21.

76. Raju Mudhar, "Delivering the Goods," *Canadian Grocer* (April 2001), 19–21.

77. *Grocer Today* (October 1993), 7.

78. *Grocer Today* (June 1995), 17.

79. *Grocer Today* (October 1993), 9.

80. *Calgary Herald,* February, 1994, F9; *Calgary Herald,* 23 March 1993, B5; *Calgary Herald,* 8 May 1993, B11.

81. Statistics Canada, *Annual Estimates of Employment, Earnings and Hours, 1971, 1983–2000* (Cat. No. 72-002 and CANSIM — Series Number V283556, terminated in 2001). In 1983, food store employees earned $225.62 per week, on average, compared with $376.57 of the industrial aggregate. In 2000, food store workers earned $304.87, compared with $669.21 weekly industrial earnings.

Chapter Six

WOMEN IN ONTARIO'S
FOOD RETAIL SECTOR

THERE IS ONGOING DEBATE within political economy as to whether labour flexibility is new or a return to older forms of work organization.[1] An investigation of labour flexibility in food retail suggests that both analyses are correct in that corporations have long relied on flexible workers, yet the degree or extent of flexibility has intensified with the onslaught of globalization. Employment patterns confirm recent feminist analyses of gender relations in the global economy that show women as being negatively affected by economic restructuring and flexibilization.[2] Feminist political economists argue that the capitalist market operates in gender-specific ways to subjugate women in the labour market and in the home. Some of the gendered effects of restructuring identified by feminists include a rise in the percentage of women employed in low-wage service occupations and in part-time work; an intensification of the work effort and deterioration of working conditions in female-predominant sectors; and the polarization of wage rates between men employed in goods-production and women employed in services.

Employment trends in retail food support the findings of feminist political economists. Isik Zeytinoglu's detailed study of retailing indicates that an increasingly feminized work force in food stores corresponds with an expansion in part-time employment.[3] As discussed in chapter 5, specific factors have contributed to the growth of flexible work, including competive pressures from new store formats that have driven corporations to reduce wage costs, the development of new technologies that can deskill and displace trained, permanent employees and the shift to concession bargaining that has reduced the number of full-time workers through buy-outs and other measures. By examining the operation of the supermarket industry during a period of restructuring, we can better understand the changes giving way to flexible work, particularly the groundswell of part-time work, that has arisen in service industries. This chapter reviews some of the strategies used by supermarket management to reduce labour in stores. As explained below, the corporate goal is to maximize labour flexibility of all food store employees, irrespective of their full-time or part-time status, in order to lower wage costs.

Another purpose of this chapter is to provide a statistical portrait of the sex segregation and gender-wage differentials in the supermarket. An analysis of statistics Canada data on the retail industry in Ontario shows the high percentage of part-time work performed by women in the sector. The data showing gender divisions at the store level was gathered in the late 1980s, just prior to pay equity implementation. This detailed description of the gender divisions underscores the rigid gender occupational hierarchy and the level of gender-wage inequities that existed in the sector before pay equity was applied.

A New Labour Market

One of the defining features of the post-Fordist economy has been the expansion of the service economy. This development is especially important for women because of the increase in peripheral or non-standard forms of employment where women are concentrated and that dominate in service industries. There has been tremendous growth in the service sector over the past three decades in Canada, with approximately seven out of ten jobs found in service sector industries. Significantly, the vast majority (86 percent in 1999) of women employed are in these industries, while 70 percent of women work in traditional female-predominant occupations (clerical, nursing, sales, service). Earnings in traditional services, where women predominate, are particularly low. For example, in the service occupation category women earned $21,516 on average in 1997, compared with the male average of $33,225.[4] But overall, earnings for those employed in services can be much lower than the above figures suggest because of the prevalence of part-time work.

Part-time employment has increased significantly in recent years as a response to capital's drive for flexibility. In 1953, part-time workers made up just 3.8 per cent of the Canadian labour force.[5] By 1998 almost 19 percent of all employed workers in Canada worked part-time. A large proportion of part-time workers, about 7 out of 10, were women in 1999.[6] Women working in non-standard employment has also increased. As Karen Hadley explains, "In 1999, 41 percent of employed women aged 15–64 had a non-standard employment arrangement compared with 35 percent in 1989."[7] The level of earnings for non-standard workers is incredibly low: women in non-standard, non-unionized work earned just $10,067 in 1999.[8]

The nature of service sector work, especially in the area of personal services, is particularly conducive to the demand for part-time labour. Employers achieve numerical flexibility in industries such as retail trade, health services, food and beverage, entertainment and accommodation services through the use of part-time work. Often the work performed by part-timers is labour intensive, physically or emotionally demanding, or extremely routine. The nature of part-time work encourages employers to place high demands on these employees. "Employed for only short periods of time, [part-time] women can work at speeds or under conditions which would otherwise be intolerable."[9] Although part-timers are more productive than full-time employees, part-time workers are the first to receive cut backs in hours during slack periods in the business cycle.

The large percentage of women in the part-time category has urged feminists to examine the social construction of gender and part-time work in the labour market.[10] Women are drawn into service-related jobs as marginal, low-paid workers, and their work is defined as unskilled. The tasks assigned to women are associated with feminine attributes, particularly tasks involving interpersonal or emotion work.[11] As was discussed in chapter 4, retail food managers recruited women as part-time workers to work in service departments to meet intermittent customer demand and to service customers. Historically, women have been viewed as the most desirable workers to perform part-time work in food stores. In the present context of restructuring, in which managers are driven by the prerogatives of flexible specialization, women are especially vulnerable to exploitation.

The expansion of part-time employment in retail food represents a key flexible-labour market strategy on the part of corporations. Before reviewing the strategies used in the super-market to maximize labour flexiblity, I present a statistical overview showing the gender distribution of employment in the retail industry to illustrate that the workforce is highly feminized and dominated by part-time employment.

The Retail Workforce in Ontario

The retail workforce is rigidly divided by sex and divisions exist between full-time and part-time employees.[12] While a significant proportion (37 percent) of Ontario retail employees work part-time, women represent about two-thirds (66 percent) of the total part-time workforce in retail (see Appendix B, Tables B.2, B.4).

The incidence of part-time employment among women, especially between the ages of 25 and 44, is particularly high in retail trade and represents 30.7 percent overall compared with 19.3 percent for all industries (see Appendix B, Table B.5). Middle-aged women have the highest percentage of part-time employment in the industry. For example, almost 90 percent of women between 35 and 44 years of age worked part-time in 2001 (see Appendix B, Table B.6). As Isik Urla Zeytinoglu explains, the workforce in food retail is composed of two main groups, "the majority being middle-aged women (34 to 55 years) with children or single mothers (24+ years of age), and the minority being female and male students (16 to 24 years of age)."[13] Indeed, women represent about 70 percent of all food retail employees over the age of 45.[14] The data show that men work part-time in their youth and drop out of the part-time workforce once they have completed their schooling. For example, about 25 percent of all part-time jobs in retail are held by young men between 15 and 24 years of age. Only 3.5 percent of all part-time jobs are held by men in the 25 to 44 age group (see Appendix B, Table B.2). Even more telling is the data that show the share of male part-time employment as a percentage of men's total employment in retail trade. For men between the ages of 15 and 24 years, 64.1 percent work part-time. This percentage drops to 7.5 percent for men in the age category 25 to 44 years (see Appendix B, Table B.4). In contrast, women's part-time labour force participation rate remains higher in all age categories, ranging from 33.6 percent in the youngest age category (15 to 24 years) to 19. 2 percent in the 25 to 44 age category (see Appendix B, Table B.2). Women's share of part-time as a percentage of total employment also does not decrease as much as for men. The share of part-time employment as a share of total employment for women between the ages of 15 and 24 years is 73.5 percent; this figure drops to 30.7 percent for women between the ages of 25 and 44 years (see Appendix B, Table B.4).

Men and women retail employees are segregated by industry and by occupation. About 54 percent of the total retail workforce are women (see Appendix B, Table B.1), and in food stores women represent a slightly higher majority — about 56 percent of the total workforce.[15] While it is very difficult to obtain data on the gender occupational distribution of the workforce at the level of food stores, recent studies confirm that the pattern of occupational segregaton that began in the 1920s (see chapter 4) remains starkly apparent today. Men continue to occupy managerial or supervisory positions, and dominate the stock clerk and meat cutter jobs; they are also are more likely to work full-time. Women work as cashiers and service clerks, especially in the meat and bakery departments.[16] The gender job divisions that exist today are very similar to those found in 1987 at Miracle Food Mart, and are discussed more extensively later in this chapter.

As one might expect, the divisions between men and women

translate into a significant gender-based wage gap. The data on gender divisions at the store level discussed below showing the rate of pay for male and female jobs indicate that women earn less than men in every full-time job category. However, recent data on gender wage differentials in food retail are not readily available. A study conducted in 1994 found that 57 percent of women employees in food stores earned less than $15,000 per year, whereas only 36 percent men earned this amount.[17] Data from the Canadian 1996 census provide another measure of the wage differentials between men and women in the retail sales and cashier category; although not as precise as the retail data provided above, it is a good indicator of gender wage differentials in the sector.[18] In 1983, men in the retail sales category earned an average of $30,796, compared with the women's average of $19,647 or 63 percent of men's earnings. In the cashier classification, men earned an average $20,557 and women $16,977, or 82 percent of men's earnings.[19]

RACIAL COMPOSITION

There is almost no data on the racial characteristics of workers employed in the retail industry. Again, the most recent available data from the 1996 Census offers information on racialized minorities but uses job categories that include workers in the "retail and non-retail sectors." The percentage of visible minorities employed as cashiers in this category was 13.1 percent. About 10 percent of all women in the cashier classification belonged to visible minority groups.[20] Historically, racialized groups have been excluded from customer service occupations. American studies of retailing indicate that historically workers were hired from the white population, and only later when retail work (especially in department stores) was largely part-time were racial minorities recruited.[21] A detailed study of Black workers in the U.S. supermarket found that "[b]oth Negro men and women barely had a foothold in supermarket employment in mid-1960," and by 1970 represented only 7 percent of total employment in the industry.[22] The authors explain that managers at the store level determined hiring practices and that workers were drawn from surrounding communities.

From my interviews with retail food workers, it seems that store managers have tended to recruit workers who reflect the ethnic or racial characteristics of the population from the surrounding neighbourhood. Within an Italian neighbourhood, Italian youth may be hired who can speak the language and who may also be familiar with "ethnic" foods. Further, recruitment practices often rely on word-of-mouth communication so that friends and relatives of existing employees are often hired. As this retail food manager explained:

> We had families working for us ... It's not just one family but a network of families in the community. We had couples, families, spouses, people marrying, cousins, and everything ... We have a thousand employees and that was how hiring was done, originally was done. A cousin, a brother-in-law, and they'd evaluate the individual that made the request and they would say yeah or nay. [23]

The very limited data on the racial composition of retail workers suggests that the majority of supermarket workers are drawn from white European groups and that retail food companies follow informal hiring practices that ensure the ethnic and racial character of local neighbourhoods is reproduced in their staff.

GENDER SEGREGATION

The most reliable measure of gender segregation in the food retail sector is an analysis of the gender divisions that occur at the store level. The data provided in Table 1 show the gender distribution of jobs at Miracle Food Mart, one of the supermarkets analyzed in the pay equity process in chapter 7. This 1987 data offer a picture of the gender-wage differentials and the gender divisions that were in place prior to pay equity in Ontario. The data are typical of the gender divisions that existed not only at the Miracle supermarket chain but also at other corporate chains. Moreover, the gender divisions have not changed significantly in the years since these data were collected.

TABLE 1

*Gender Distribution of Bargaining Unit Employees
in Ontario Miracle Food Mart Stores
(UFCW Locals 175/633), May 1987*

JOB TITLE	TOTAL	MALE	FEMALE	% FEMALE
Production Clerks	656	621	35	5%
*Service Clerks, Wrappers, Attendants	414	123	291	70%
Bookkeeper	77	0	77	100%
Grocery & Produce Managers	183	179	4	2%
Night Production Foreman	66	66	0	0%
Assistant Production Manager	25	25	0	0%
Meat Cutter	197	195	2	3%
Deli Head	81	1	80	99%
Assistant Meat Manager	76	75	1	1%
Meat Manager	78	76	2	3%
Baker's Helper	20	17	3	15%
Journeyman Baker	48	45	3	6%
Decorator	4	0	4	100%
Bakery Manager	33	20	13	39%
Fish Responsible	24	11	13	54%
PART-TIME	6,164	2,854	3,310	54%
FULL-TIME	2,095	1,454	641	30%
TOTAL	8,259	4,308	3,951	48%

* Service clerks include cashiers and meat wrappers.

Table 1 shows that most positions within the food store — in this case Miracle Food Mart — were sex-typed. Women were concentrated in service positions, while men predominated in production jobs. For example, about 70 percent of the service clerks and attendants were female. Although the position of cashier and meat wrapper were not specifically listed, data from other sources indicate that the position of full-time cashier in unionized settings was 96 percent female, while 92 percent of all meat wrappers represented by collective agreements were female.[24] Furthermore, the bookkeeper position, sometimes referred to as head cashier, was 100 percent female, as was the position of (cake) decorator, while the deli manager position was 99 percent female. All of these positions resided in service departments; that is, the job tasks involved service to the customer. Men, on the other hand, worked in production jobs in meat, grocery, and bakery departments as well as being employed as production or stock clerks. Males were hired in the production departments because of assumptions that they had the necessary competencies, such as lifting heavy objects, that are required in production work. Ninety-five percent of production clerks, 97 percent of meat cutters, and 94 percent of journeymen bakers were male.

With the exception of deli head, men also dominated in managerial positions. Men overwhelmingly occupied managerial positions in the meat, produce, and grocery departments in the 173/633 bargaining units as shown in table 2. Bakery, a service department, had more female managers than other departments, but even there women represent less than half of bakery managers.

TABLE 2

Gender Distribution of Department Managers, 1987

Classification	Male	Female	Total	% Male
Meat Manager	80	2	82	98%
Produce Manager	82	1	83	98%
Grocery Manager	82	1	83	98%
Bakery Manager	12	11	23	52%
TOTAL	256	15	271	94%

Accompanying job segregation were pronounced pay differentials between male and female classifications. Not surprising, perhaps, we find significant differences in pay between full-time male production and female service jobs even in unionized workplaces. According to the collective agreement, the wage differential between production and service clerks (meat wrapper and bakery wrapper attendant) at the weekly start rate was $11.23, while the end rate differential was $28.30 weekly (see Appendix B, Table B.7). Women who occupied the female-predominant positions of bookkeeper and deli head/manager earned considerably less than the male-predominant departmental manager positions such as grocery/produce, assistant meat manager, meat manager or bakery manager. For example, the bookkeeper's start rate was $30 less than the produce/grocery manager start rate and $52 less than the end rate of the produce/grocery manager classification. Even compared with the bakery manager, the bookkeeper earned $48 less at the start rate and $72 less at the end rate. The deli manager was the lowest paid department manager. Her start rate was over $300 less than the meat manager start rate and a little over $100 less than the meat manager's end rate. The deli manager, in fact, earned less than all of the other male managerial positions, and her weekly wages were less than the female-predominant bookkeeper position.

Comparing women's and men's wages in the food store showed that the loss of income on a yearly basis (excluding premium pay) was considerable. The deli manager earned about $5,350 less per year than the meat manager, the service clerks earned about $1,472 less than production clerks, and the bookkeeper earned about $2,700 less than the grocery/produce manager.

While these amounts may not seem significant, wage differentials represent a substantial loss of income for retail food workers, which in turn has a direct effect on their standard of living. The level of income of full-time workers also has a signficant impact on pension benefits since pensions are principally based on salary level as well as length of service. Women retail workers are differentially affected in respect to pensions because of the gender-wage gap in food stores.

Part-time Work

Food retail analysts and union representatives estimated in the early 1990s that about 70 percent of workers in grocery retail worked part-time. Notably, only 30 percent of women at Miracle Food Mart worked in full-time jobs. The data in table 1 show that almost 75 percent of the total bargaining unit membership was in the part-time classification. Women were concentrated in part-time jobs, with 54 percent of the total bargaining units' part-time workforce comprised of female members in 1987. By 1989, data on Locals 175/633 indicated that 60 percent of the 28,000 members in retail food were women.[25] These figures are similar to those found for the A&P/Dominion local represented by the Retail, Wholesale and Department Store Union in which 70 percent of the total 6,651 workforce was part-time, and 62 percent of part-time workers were women.

All part-time employees received wage rates based on a part-time wage grid. Unlike the full-time classification, which paid workers different rates of pay depending upon the specific job title, part-time workers progressed through a wage grid that paid automatic increases according to length of service with a company. The part-time classification did not have gender wage differentials because all part-time workers earned wages based on a part-time wage classification scale. Part-time employees earned lower wage rates and received fewer benefits compared with full-time employees. Although eligible for certain benefits such as vision and dental plans, they were excluded from disability and pension entitlements. The full-time benefits package at the Miracle Food Mart chain, which included such benefits as pension, disability and dental coverage, cost approximately $8,000 annually.[26] The more limited benefits package for part-time employees was obviously less expensive for the employer. Most collective agreements at the corporate food chains (e.g., Loblaws) specifed that part-timers must have a minimum length of service with the company to be eligible for benefits (e.g., six months or a specific number of hours of work per month).

Collective agreements also restrict the number of hours worked per week for part-time employees. While most full-time employees work 37 hours per week, part-time employees typically work a maximum of 24 hours per week in most supermarket chains. As will be discussed in greater detail in chapter 8, trade union negotiations in Ontario have resulted in a further reduction of the weekly hour maximum for a large number of part-time workers.

One of the most important issues for part-time workers is scheduling. Seniority, which is determined by a worker's date of hire, is crucial in determining how many hours are available to a part-timer. The higher a part-timer is on the seniority list, the greater choice he or she has over scheduled hours of work. Competition among part-time employees centres on maximizing hours of work, and workers pay close attention as to where they are positioned on the seniority list. Scheduling and availability of hours are some of the most contentious issues in unionized establishments. All of my interviewees spoke about the importance of seniority, and many complained that managers sometimes try to avoid seniority rules in order to schedule more hours to a favoured employee.

Of all the issues in grocery retail, seniority provisions are seen as the most critical. For instance, when availability-sheets that inform managers as to when a part-time employee is available for work were discontinued at Loblaws stores, and then removed from the collective agreement in 1990, part-time workers perceived this as a significant loss. As this retail food employee commented, "It seems like your manager or department manager will just put it to you. You get shitty shifts, or just giving you the bad jobs, where seniority doesn't play a role in that. If you want the hours you just work when they're available."[27] Management argued that employees were being too selective about their availability hours. Part-time employees often prefer to work weekday shifts, thus avoiding Friday and Saturday evenings when stores are busy and their children are at home. High-seniority part-time workers could opt to work preferred weekday shifts and keep their weekends free. Part-time workers perceived the availability list as offering some input over scheduling for part-time employees. By eliminating availability-sheets, management had much greater control over scheduling.

Seniority systems vary by supermarket chain, which has implications for job promotion and access to labour hours. Loblaws has separate seniority lists for each department (e.g., frontend, deli, meat). If a Loblaws employee wishes to transfer to another department, he or she is placed at the bottom of the seniority list, because the company and the union assume that employee has acquired "specialized skills" within his or her department.[28] Such a policy discourages transfers within stores, and thereby avoids the need for retraining, and recognizes that part-time workers, just like full-time employees, have learned specific tasks. This is important because part-time employees are paid equal wages irrespective of the duties they perform, while pay differentials for full-time workers are based on job title. Other chains, like Miracle Food Mart, have store-wide seniority within the bargaining-units. Part-time workers carry seniority across departments within a store, as this part-time meat clerk explains:

> Basically, seniority is the name of the game in a store like that. People can take your hours from other departments if they want to. Let's say I only have one day a week, five hours. I got another guy in another department and he's only getting, say, three days a week but he wants four. And he's higher in seniority than me, maybe hired one day before me. He can tell his manager and he can, theoretically, take my day if he wants to, and I can't say anything about it. [29]

At Miracle Food Mart, part-time workers can lose hours to other part-time and full-time employees who "start[ed] switching departments, and taking hours from other departments — like full-timers who need the money, because they have more seniority."[30] Because full-time employees are guaranteed 37 hours of work per week, the full-time workforce has priority over labour hours available in the store.

Profit over People: The Profit-Hour Ratio

Companies use a mechanism referred to as the "profit-hour ratio" to determine the number of labour hours allocated to stores.

This formula maximizes the labour time available at the lowest cost possible. Head office informs managers of the total number of labour hours available in a week as per dollar of sales for all departments at their supermarket. For example, a company may expect a store with weekly sales of approximately $120,000 to make a minimum return of $100 per person-hour for all hours worked. Therefore, the total number of hours allocated to the store would be calculated as $100 per person-hour divided into $120,000 (weekly sales), thus assigning the store 1,200 hours. In other words, the number of labour hours that can be scheduled at a store is dependent on sales volume, specifically sales per person-hour. The higher the sales at a store, the more labour hours are available to the manager to operate the supermarket. Conversely, the more labour hours a manager can save, the higher the profit level at the store.

It must be stressed here that managers are offered incentives to limit labour hours to improve profitability. As a stock clerk explained to me, "The more you save labour hours, the more money you can save. If the profits go up substantially from one manager to the next, he is entitled to a pretty good bonus .... managers worry about the bonus."[31] There is, then, a built-in incentive for store managers to distribute labour hours in the most judicious way possible.

Typically, the distribution of labour hours is discussed at department head meetings where managers, including head cashier and deli, negotiate how many hours are allocated to departments. The work performed in production departments (including meat, grocery and produce) is seen to be essential to running the store, and a core number of hours are assigned to do production work such as cutting meat or displaying produce. With the exception of head cashier, department managers must meet a profit margin. Hence, the issue of labour hours becomes especially important because their profit level depends on the labour time spent on production work. Service departments, or non-productive departments, are viewed as less important for generating profit and are the first to experience cut backs in their hours during slow periods. For instance, cashiers at the frontend and meat wrappers and deli workers who service customers are more likely to see a reduction of their hours compared with workers in other departments.

Loss of hours was a key issue at a union meeting I attended in 1992. A typical comment came from a cashier. "Over the past six months I've only received sixteen hours. I'm not entitled to benefits. I'll never get a [wage] increase."[32] At this workplace, part-time employees must work a total of 400 hours and have one years' service in order to receive benefits. Female-predominant departments often bear a disproportionate burden from lost sales. Of my interviewees, the meat wrappers were most likely to complain of cutbacks in their department. For instance, a woman with six years seniority as a clerk in the meat department was receiving no hours at the time of the interview. Her male co-worker with less seniority was receiving hours because, as she explained, "part-time males do heavier work; they clean the machines: the grinder, the chopper and the meat cooler."[33] Here, the gender division of labour within the meat department worked against this employee.

The profit-hour ratio operates as a company strategy to minimize labour hours and wage costs in stores. Although head office determines the number of labour hours per sales volume, it is the store manager who must find ways to save on labour costs. In this sense, the manager is given a certain amount of autonomy in running a store, and the methods used to improve profitability vary from store manager to store manager. However, in general, managers tend to use three approaches to achieving labour flexibility.

One approach is to pressure full-time employees to work above the usual 37 hours per week without overtime pay. My interviews with retail employees indicate that this strategy is more likely to occur in non-unionized stores; however, it can also occur in unionized establishments. One food retail worker explained to me that during a time of staff reductions, many full-time employees at his store were working as much as 50 hours per week. "They were working crazy hours, right around the time of layoff. Everybody was so concerned ... that they would do anything and everything for the management. It was just sickening."[34] As in most workplaces, full-time workers believed that if they worked overtime they were less likely to be laid off and more likely to be promoted within the company. Unfortunately, for part-time workers the more labour hours worked by full-time employees, the fewer hours available for part-timers.

Most part-timers are unaware of the implications of full-timers working longer hours. "The part-time people just look at the full-time people as nuts to be giving away their labour, rather than seeing it as 'you're taking my hours away.' No one really makes the connection."[35] Some part-time workers may find themselves with reduced work hours or no scheduled hours at all. As such, the core workforce absorbs the labour hours of the part-time or peripheral workers. While this certainly does not eliminate the part-time workforce, it reduces the amount of labour hours available to them in the store.

A second approach is to ask full-time workers (and sometimes part-time workers) to do work in other departments. For instance, stock clerks may work on cash during busy times of the shopping day, thereby reducing the number of cashiers required at the frontend. One food retail worker remarked, "Everybody knows how to use the registers — all the full-time employees. You find that happening every lunch hour now."[36] Similarly, cashiers may be asked to put items rejected by customers on shelves. "I'm not just scanning, I'm putting groceries away, I'm stocking shelves, I'm facing up the shelves, I do everything."[37] Managers themselves may also engage in bargaining unit work in order to reduce the amount of scheduled labour hours in their store. Although this violates collective agreement language, managers may work on restocking shelves as a way to save on labour hours. All of these tactics intensify the work process for food retail employees and reduce the availability of labour hours for part-time workers.

The third approach used to meet the profit-hour ratio is to give part-time employees full-time hours but pay them the part-time wage rate, which contradicts the first approach that intensifies the work of full-timers; however, by scheduling part-timers 37 hours per week, the store manager saves on wage costs. Typically, store managers choose favoured part-time employees to work full-time hours. As one stock clerk explains: "I was still classified a part-time employee. It was just that every week I would work thirty-seven hours. I worked for a stretch there, six months straight, and you might as well count me full-time but I wasn't — technically. Of course, there's a dollar difference."[38] The more managers rely on part-time workers to perform work in supermarkets, the higher their profits. In general, managers find it cost effective to schedule part-time workers because of their lower wages and reduced benefits, and because their shorter shifts require fewer breaks. Full-time employees are entitled to several breaks in an 8-hour shift, whereas part-time employees usually receive only one break. The difference in scheduled breaks is perceived by a part-time cashier as a definite advantage for full-time employees:

> Full-timers [cashiers] have it better than us [part-time cashiers]. They have to be scheduled eight or nine hours. That entitles them to two breaks and a one hour lunch. On average, part-time girls at this store are scheduled five or six hours; this entitles us to one fifteen minute break. A fifteen-minute break for someone standing on their feet for over five hours just isn't enough![39]

There is absolutely no question that the part-time workforce in food stores has been increasing at an alarming rate. When we consider the position of part-timers in grocery retail historically, it is obvious that the demand for flexible labour has increased significantly. For example, as pointed out in chapter 5, in 1967 in Canada the ratio of part-time to full-time employees was low, ranging anywhere from one to one to around one to three.[40] In 1987, only 25 percent of the Miracle Food Mart workforce was full-time in Ontario. One reason for the declining ratio was that companies were not replacing full-time employees who quit, retired or went on disability pension with full-time positions.[41] Rather, companies were increasingly relying on part-time workers to perform most of the labour in stores. Protections concerning the ratio of part-time to full-time employees in food stores also were eroded (see chapter 5).

At the present time, departments are increasingly being staffed by part-time workers, as a Loblaws employee observes:

When I first was at the store we used to have eight full-time people on nights, steady midnights, now we're down to three or four; this is in a matter of three years ... It's happening in other departments. We used to have two full-time head checkers plus two full-time cashiers. Now, all we have are two full-time head checkers. That's total — this is the frontend ... It's in every department. We're losing full-time staff.[42]

In many stores, it is not uncommon for there to be two full-time workers in the frontend, usually the head cashier and assistant head cashier, while the remaining cashiers (sometimes as many as twenty-five or thirty) are in the part-time classification. Similarly, the meat and deli departments may be staffed by one or two full-time employees while the remainder work part-time.

The trend in food retailing is a shrinking full-time workforce. Yet full-time employees are experiencing an intensification of their workday because they are expected to take on more and more work. Management is pressuring full-timers to engage in multi-tasking as a way to reduce the percentage of part-time labour hours. Meanwhile, part-timers are increasingly displacing the number of full-time employees in stores. This is being achieved through a process of attrition in which full-time positions are simply not being replaced with full-time employees, and by concessions in collective bargaining. The high percentage of part-time workers in stores indicates the extent to which companies rely on their part-time workforce to perform an overwhelming share of labour in supermarkets.

The increase in part-timers contributes to the feminization of the retail labour force and promotes labour flexibility. The profit-hour ratio operates as a corporate strategy to encourage store managers to maximize labour flexibility in their stores. Functional flexibility, (e.g., multi-tasking) and numerical flexibility (use of part-time workers) are important managerial tactics to control labour costs in the supermarket. Flexible specialization has a negative impact on women food retail workers who are concentrated in service departments that have low margins. Not only are women the majority of part-timers in food retail, but as the bulk of the grocery service workforce they are also much more likely to experience a decline in their hours during slack times in the business cycle.

*

Retail food companies have responded to increased competition by maximizing labour flexibility at the store level. Corporate policies, such as the profit-hour ratio, were instituted to encourage store managers to distribute labour hours in the most efficient manner possible. The effect of this policy has been to limit hours of work in service departments where women predominate. During times of industry reorganizing, companies have tended to view employees in service departments, as well as the part-time labour force, as the most expendable segments of the retail workforce. Part-time workers, the majority of whom are women, are also extensively used as a flexible labour supply and have been subject to wage reductions in the form of two-tiered or multi-tiered wage grids, and reduced work hours. None of these measures are gender-neutral in their effects; rather, they systematically disadvantage women whose work has been historically devalued in the supermarket. In the current context of industry reorganization and economic adjustment, women continue to absorb an unequal share of the costs of restructuring.

In the following chapter, pay equity negotiations in the supermarket are discussed, and show that the part-time female labour force was detrimentally effected by the corporate drive to maintain a low-wage, flexible workforce.

NOTES

1. See David Broad, *Hollow Work, Hollow Society: Globalization and the Casual Labour Problem in Canada* (Halifax: Fernwood Publishing, 2000); Linda McDowell, "Gender divisions in a Post-Fordist Era: New Contradictions or the Same Old Story?" in L. McDowell and R. Pringle, eds., *Defining Women: Social Institutions and Gender Divisions* (Cambridge: Polity Press, 1992); Steven Wood, ed., *The Transformation of Work* (London: Unwin Hyman, 1989).
2. See, for example, Ann Eyerman, *Women in the Office: Transitions in a Global*

Economy (Toronto: Sumach Press, 2000); Torry Dickinson and Robert Schaeffer, *Fast Forward: Work, Gender, and Protest in a Changing World* (New York: Rowman and Littlefield Publishers, 2001); Leah Vosko, *Temporary Work: The Gendered Rise of a Precarious Employment Relationship* (Toronto: University of Toronto Press, 2000); Christa Wichterich, *The Globalized Woman* (London: Zed Books, 2000).

3. Isik Urla Zeytinoglu (principal researcher) and Mikaela Crook, *Women Workers and Working Conditions in Retailing: A Comparative Study of the Situation in a Foreign-Controlled Retail Enterprise and a Nationally Owned Retailer in Canada* (Geneva: International Labour Office, Working Paper No. 79, 1997), 54–55.

4. The figures on women in the service economy are from Statistics Canada, *Women in Canada, 2000: A gender-based statistical report,* 4th ed. (Ottawa: Statistics Canada, Housing, Family and Social Statistics Division, 2000, Cat. No. 89-503-XPE), 106, 156.

5. Until 1974, part-time work in Canada was defined as working less than 35 hours per week. Since 1975, part-time workers are those who work less than 30 hours per week. In 1996, Statistics Canada identified part-timers as those workers who work less than 30 hours per week at their main job. See Broad, *Hollow Work, Hollow Society,* 13, 15.

6. Broad, *Hollow Work, Hollow Society,* 15; *Women in Canada,* 2000, 123.

7. Karen Hadley, *"And We Still Ain't Satisfied": Gender Inequality in Canada, A Status Report for 2001* (Toronto: National Action Committee on the Status of Women and the CSJ Foundation for Research and Education, June 2001), 18. Non-standard employment refers to various precarious types of employment including jobs that are part-time, seasonal, temporary or contractual, as well as self-employment and work at home such as telecommuting and industrial homework.

8. Ibid., 18.

9. Pat and Hugh Armstrong, "Taking Women into Account: Redefining and Intensifying Employment in Canada," in Jane Jenson, Elisabeth Hagen and Ceallaigh Reddy, eds., *The Feminization of the Labor Force* (New York: Oxford Press, 1988), 81. Several other authors remark that an advantage for employers hiring part-timers is higher productivity when compared with the full-time work-force. See Craig McKie, "Part-Time Work in the North American Triangle: The United States, the United Kingdom, and Canada," in Barbara Warme, Katherina Lundy and Larry Lundy, eds., *Working Part-Time: Risks and Opportunities* (New York: Praeger, 1992), 22, and Ann Duffy and Norene Pupo, *Part-Time Paradox: Connecting Gender, Work and Family* (Toronto: McClelland and Stewart, 1992) , 154. See also Chris Tilly, "Two Faces of Part-Time Work: Good and Part-time Jobs in U.S. Services Industries," in Warme et. al., eds., *Working Part-Time.*

10. See, for example, Rosemary Crompton, "Gender Meanings and Discourses in Employment" in *Women and Work in Modern Britain* (Oxford: Oxford University Press, 1997), which examines the way in which discourse defines femininity in work organizations, and Vosko, *Temporary Work.*

11. On emotional work performed by supermarket clerks, see Martin Tolich, "Alienating and Liberating Emotions at Work: Supermarkets Performance of Customer Work," *Journal of Contemporary Ethnography* 22, no. 3 (1993), 361–81.

12. The gender distribution of workers in the retail labour force in Ontario is from the Labour Market Activity Survey (LMAS) for the year 2001. These data are drawn from a special unpublished tabulation.

13. Zeytinoglu and Crook, *Women Workers and Working Conditions in Retailing,* 54.

14. *Creating the Future: Human Resources Study of the Canadian Food Retail and Wholesale Sector* (CLMPC Consulting Services, 1998), 29. The data are for 1994.

15. *Creating the Future,* 27. See table 3.5.

16. See Zeytinoglu and Crook, *Women Workers and Working Conditions in Retailing,* 54.

17. *Creating the Future,* 28.

18. The categories used in the 1996 census are retail salesperson and sales clerks in the food, beverage and drug industry; cashiers in the food, beverage and drug industry. Statistics Canada, 1996 Census. *Dimensions Series: Labour Force and Unpaid Work of Canadians,* 94F0006XCB.

19. The only data on wage differentials in the retail sector is from an early study by George Radwanski who reports that in 1983 women in retail earned, on average, $5, 410 compared with an average of $10, 254 for men employed in retail. See George Radwanski, *The Ontario Study of the Service Sector, Government of Ontario* (Toronto: Ministry of Treasury and Economics, 1986), 10–11.

20. Statistics Canada, 1996 *Census. Dimensions Series: Labour Force and Unpaid Work of Canadians,* 94F0006XCB. The data are for Canada.

21. Nona Glazer, *Women's Paid and Unpaid Labor: The Work Transfer in Health Care and Retailing* (Philadelphia: Temple University Press, 1993), 68.

22. Gordon Bloom and Marion Fletcher, *The Negro in the Supermarket Industry* (Philadelphia: University of Pennsylvania Press, 1972), 56.

23. Interview, Retail Food Manager, June 27, 1992.

24. Pay Equity Commission, *Pay Equity in Predominantly Female Establishments: Retail Sector,* table 4 (Toronto: Pay Equity Commission, 1988). The data are for 1985 and are drawn from Labour Ontario, Labour Canada.

25. Affadavit of Sarah Shartal, Supreme Court of Ontario and The Oshawa Group Limited (Applicant) and The Regional Municipality of Peel and the Attorney General of Ontario (Respondents) Court File No. RE2799/89. The figure of 28,000 employees probably includes warehouse employees, whereas the number employed in food stores would be much smaller.

26. Interview with union representative, Local 175/633 Miracle Food Mart, November 29, 1993.

27. Interview, Part-time Stock Clerk, January 20, 1992.

28. The rationale as to why part-time employees lose seniority when they transfer to another department was explained by a union official at a General Members Meeting, May 24, 1992, Local 1000A.

29. Interview, Part-time Meat Clerk, July 27, 1992.

30. Interview, Part-time Meat Clerk, September 2, 1992.

31. Interview, Part-time Stock Clerk, January 20, 1992.

32. Union meeting, UFCW Local 1000A, May 24, 1992.

33. Interview, Part-time Meat Clerk, September 17, 1992.

34. Interview, Grocery Clerk, June 27, 1992.

35. Ibid.

36. Interview, Stock Clerk, January 20, 1992.

37. Interview, Part-time Cashier, July 17, 1992.

38. Ibid.

39. Interview Part-time Cashier, March 1995.

40. The employment data are taken from eleven supermarkets at various locations in Ontario with a sample of 236 full-time and 397 part-time workers. See Department of Labour, Economics and Research Branch and the Women's Bureau, *Part-Time Employment in Retail Trade* (Ottawa: Queen's Printer, 1969), 39.

41. In the early 1990s, A&P (Miracle Food Mart, Dominion Stores) and Loblaws implemented a company policy in which full-time positions were not replaced with full-time workers. The trend towards hiring part-time was still in practice a decade later. See Zeytinoglu and Crook, *Women Workers and Working Conditions in Retailing*, 55.

42. Interview, Stock Clerk, January 20, 1992.

Chapter Seven

NEGOTIATING PAY EQUITY
AT THE SUPERMARKET

The main dilemma for any feminist engagement with the law
is the certain knowledge that once enacted, legislation is in the
hands of individuals and agencies far removed from the values
of the women's movement.

— Carol Smart, *Feminism and the Power of Law*

THE OUTCOME of pay equity negotiations in Ontario was not all
that advocates for women might have wished, and the monetary
results were certainly disappointing for many women workers in the
food retail industry. As Carol Smart understood, the *Pay Equity Act*
was subject to interpretation by those who were unlikely to support
wage increases for their female employees, and disappointingly, by
the very unions women workers might have expected to forcefully
represent their interests. Predictably perhaps, supermarket chains
interpreted the Act to suit their managerial prerogatives, and to limit
changes in compensation to the bulk of the grocery workforce, the
female part-time employees. The retail unions shared management's
view of part-time workers as being less important to the operation
of the supermarket than the numerically much smaller, mostly male,
full-time employee group. Unfortunately, the pay equity agreements

that were reached across Ontario illustrated the complicity of the unions with management's view and deprived most women workers in the sector of the potential benefits of pay equity legislation.

In compliance with the legislation, pay equity plans were established at three major supermarket chains in Ontario: Loblaws, Miracle Food Mart and A&P/Dominion. Together, these stores employed approximately 20,000 unionized employees as cashiers, stock clerks, meat wrappers and department managers. An assessment of each case highlights different aspects of the equal pay process. Negotiations at Loblaws elucidate the United Food and Commercial Workers (UFCW) position on part-timers, while the discussion of the pay equity exercise at Miracle Food Mart uncovers the method of job comparison among full-time workers. The A&P/Dominion and Retail Wholesale Department Store Union's (RWDSU) agreement explains why sex-based wage inequities were sustained in the industry. Despite some differences in approach, the final outcome to each set of negotiations is similar and results from the framework of the legislation, the bargaining stance of the unions, the organization of the food retail workforce and the structure of the grocery industry.

Loblaws: Operating "Coolly and Rationally"

At the time of pay equity negotiations in 1990, Loblaws cashiers, meat wrappers, stock clerks and other workers made up about 6,000 of the 10,000 UFCW Local 1000A members, with approximately 2,500 full-time and 3,500 part-time employees. According to the terms of the union contract, full-time and part-time workers had separate seniority systems. Part-time workers accrued seniority within their department; moving to another department (or store) resulted in loss of seniority. In contrast, full-timers accumulated seniority at the store level, so a full-time employee did not lose seniority when transferred to another store.

Full-time employees received higher wage rates and a better benefits package than part-timers. Departmental and assistant store managers received an hourly wage rate depending on sales volume. Included in this category were produce, meat, deli, bakery, service and floral managers, and head checkers. All other employees were subject to a wage progression system based on length of service. Full-time employees received the full rate after a maximum of 24 months of service, while part-time employees reached the top rate after 48 months. The wages of full-time employees varied according to job category, so a produce clerk working full-time with 12 months service received a different wage rate than a full-time baker with the same seniority. However, all part-time employees *received the same rate of pay at equal levels of seniority.*

The composition and structure of the bargaining unit had a direct bearing on the outcome of pay equity. Particularly significant were the separation between full- and part-time employees and a wage structure that not only distinguished full-time wage rates from part-time but also established different wage grids for separate job categories.

DEFINING ESTABLISHMENT

One of the first steps in the pay equity exercise was to identify the "establishment" in order to determine job classes available for comparison. Under the Act, "establishment" was defined as all of the employees of an employer in a geographic division. The union was concerned that Loblaws might wish to determine equity evaluation by region rather than for the entire province. According to a union official, the equity evaluation would then reflect differences in job classifications in the northern and southern districts and disrupt the uniformity of province-wide bargaining.[1] However, the employer also had a vested interest in maintaining common wage rates rather than "going division by division [to] produce a series of different results in different areas of the province."[2] Given the concern by both parties to retain provincial rates, they agreed that "establishment" would be defined as the supermarket chain.

Union officials also wanted to reach an agreement swiftly to prevent fragmentation in pattern bargaining. Under a system of pattern bargaining, the union targets one employer to open negotiations with the intention that the negotiated agreement will set the pattern for the industry. Union officials worried that different evaluation systems could potentially produce wage inconsistencies among locals. By reaching an agreement quickly, they hoped that a standard for pay equity would be achieved for UFCW locals as well as for grocery workers represented by RWDSU. As one union representative put it, "RWDSU has a few people working for A&P. They will get what we get."[3]

Determining Job Class

Two components of "job class" were relevant to the pay equity process. The first dealt with job content or the description of job categories. In other words, a job class was a cluster of jobs or positions with a similar job title, job description and level of compensation. For example, except for the jobs of head checker and assistant head checker, the position of cashier represented a job class using the criteria established in the Act because the job content, recruitment and compensation schedule were similar.

The second component determining job class referred to gender predominance. Under the law, a female job class had 60 percent or more females while a male job class contained 70 percent or more males. Irrespective of percentage cut-offs, the definition of a male or female job class was open to negotiation provided arguments were made concerning historical incumbency or which sex traditionally had performed the work.

The UFCW considered a historical incumbency argument for part-time workers, recognizing the possibility that part-time employees could be declared as one female job class based on the historical pattern of females performing the work, as pointed out by a union representative:

> We attempted to argue that the whole part-time wage historically emerged as a result of its being perceived as female labour. But when we look[ed] at the numbers, the numbers weren't as high as we thought they were. We have always had a lot of part-time workers, many of whom are young men. It's true that of the non-students *the majority were probably women, for many years. Still are women.* But among the students the numbers are not so clear-cut. (Emphasis added.)[4]

Because the workforce data did not show that women dominated in the student category, the union abandoned the position that part-time workers historically constituted a female job class. Certainly a gender stereotyping argument could have been made regardless of workforce data, in view of the long history of feminized part-time labour in the food retail industry. Yet no attempt was made to bring the argument of a female part-time job class to the bargaining table. Instead, the union decided to divide the bargaining unit into part-time and full-time categories, meaning that full-time female job classes were compared with full-time male job classes, and female part-time job classes were compared with male part-time job classes. Consequently, the 3,500 part-time jobs could not be compared to the full-time job categories, thereby undercutting the positive impact of pay equity.

JOB EVALUATION: THE NEUTRALIZER

Once job classes were determined, the next phase of the pay equity negotiation was to evaluate worth by applying a gender-neutral job comparison system. The UFCW Pay Equity Task Force developed its own computerized point-factor scheme adapted specifically to the requirements of supermarket retailing and called it the Neutralizer.

According to the union's newsletter, the computer software package allowed "the computer to compare jobs coolly and rationally" without the interference of the "human factor":

> For each job, the programme leads the user through a series of twenty job evaluation criteria, and each is given a rating between zero and twenty points. On screen "notepads" give basic descriptions to assist in this evaluation process, and these can be altered to suit any specific job and rating ... the computer automatically calculates and generates a report on pay inequities, and even shows exactly how the employer can make pay adjustments under current [Ontario] law.[5]

Following this procedure, job evaluation criteria were assigned to one of the four major elements of skill, effort, responsibility and working conditions required by legislation to measure the value of a job class. The software placed an upper limit of 20 points on 5 "labels" within each of the four major factors, for a possible maximum score of 100 points for each subfactor. A general weighting was assigned to the factors, with skill and responsibility weighted at 35 percent each, while effort and working conditions each received 15 percent of the overall score. (See Appendix C, Table C.1.)

An equal weighting scheme, in which the four major components would receive a weighting of 25 percent, was rejected because the Task Force found that it would upset the wage hierarchy. A member of the Task Force put it this way:

> We knew that to go with a balanced position of 25 percent would obviously do two things. One, it would throw off [the balance], in our view, and we found this out through regression analysis later, it would probably create a reverse problem where it would put too much emphasis in some jobs; those with a great deal of effort but very little skill, and you could wind up where high skill and high responsible jobs were, in fact, worth less than low skill and labour intensive jobs...on a flat weighting you tend to take away from the job of those who are responsible, our assistant meat cutter, our meat managers, our deli, service clerk managers, all of those people.[6]

Following an equal weighting scheme meant that those in managerial positions earned fewer points than the people they were managing.

Given this contradictory outcome, the Task Force experimented with different weights until they arrived at a system that "fit best in the real world" — a subjective one reflecting the Task Force's view of a valuable job in the supermarket. The weighting scheme also had to be acceptable to employers, a fact not lost on union officials who designed the Neutralizer. As a Task Force member said, the UFCW did not want to "squeeze every nickel out of [the company]." So they created a job evaluation system that accommodated employer concerns — one that valued skill and responsibility over effort and working conditions.

Pay Equity Committees consisting of union and management

representatives were then formed at union locals to gather the information required to determine female and male job classes, evaluate the jobs using the Neutralizer, and decide on the appropriate male comparators within the bargaining unit. At Local 1000A, job content questionnaires were not distributed. As a local official explained, "Women tend to undervalue their jobs on the questionnaires ... whereas the men tended to overrate themselves ... so we decided the data wasn't going to help us very much."[7]

Rather than relying on detailed job descriptions from employees, the Pay Equity Committee made the evaluations based on the opinions of union representatives who worked in the various job classes. Despite the perception that the Neutralizer operated "coolly and rationally" to compare jobs, in practice the committee subjectively determined a great deal of the exercise.

DETERMINING JOB RATE:
PERMISSIBLE DIFFERENCE IN COMPENSATION

Establishing the job rate was probably the most contentious aspect of the pay equity exercise with Loblaws. Both the structure of the bargaining unit, especially the division between full- and part-time employees, and exclusions in the Act complicated the process of achieving wage adjustments for workers in female-predominant job classes. The purpose of establishing a job rate was to determine the male comparables or male job rate available for comparison. Ontario's *Pay Equity Act* defined the term "job rate" as the "highest rate of compensation for a job class." However, the employer could make arguments, on the basis of skills shortage, a merit compensation plan, or a temporary employee-training program, as to why the highest rate of compensation should not be considered the job rate. Particularly important in the Loblaws case was section 8, which allowed differences in compensation between female and male job classes if they resulted from a "formal *seniority system* that does not discriminate on the basis of gender."

Because full- and part-time employees in the bargaining unit operated under separate seniority systems and part-time were paid according to a single wage progression grid, the employer interpreted section 8 to mean that part-time employees could be excluded from pay equity adjustments. A union official explained it this way:

> Part-time workers are paid less than full-time in retail. In our situation all part-timers are under a separate seniority system paid the same rate either male or female for whatever the job. Under the terms of the legislation they were excluded, at least the employer argued they should be excluded, and we accepted that ... because of the law itself.[8]

However, section 8 merely offered the parties (typically the employer) the ability to make a case for exempting a high wage rate based on certain permissible differences in compensation. Excluding the part-time job class from the comparison process was unnecessary.

COMPARING JOB CLASSES: FROM "HIGHEST OF THE LOW" TO "LOWEST OF THE LOW"

Another difficulty arising from the legislation was the method of comparing job classes. Under section 6, an employer was mandated to adjust the wage of the female job class up to the rate of the male job class of comparable value, but with the lowest job rate. For example, cashiers could not be compared to assistant managers even if they scored equivalent points in the job evaluation if other male comparators of the same value but with a lower job rate were available for comparison. A female job class that scored equivalent points to several male job classes received a pay equity adjustment based on the highest level of compensation, but the lowest job rate, within the group of possible male comparators, or "the highest of the low."

In Loblaws, a straightforward job-to-job comparison was seen to be complicated by the presence of the part-time job rate in the bargaining unit. Because the employer argued permissible difference in compensation between male and female job classes based on the presence of a formal seniority system, the highest level of compensation was not used as the standard of comparison. The union agreed to exclude the part-time classification in the pay equity comparison because the part-time rate, they believed, would have eliminated wage equity for full-time female job classes. The parties interpreted the Act to mean that a comparison based on the highest level of compensation as per section 6 was reduced to a male comparable based on the lowest level of compensation when section 8 was applied. In effect, sections 6 ("highest of the low") and 8 (permissible difference based on seniority) were seen to converge, to *shift the level of wage equity downward from "highest of the low" to "lowest of the low."* For example, the female job class of meat wrapper who worked full-time nights did not receive an adjustment because the wage rate of this job class ($14.91) was higher than the lowest paid comparable male job class, the part-time produce clerk who worked nights ($12.21). The "highest of the low" male comparator — the full-time night produce clerk ($15.49) — was excluded from the comparison.

Although the parties *assumed* that the part-time rate had to be excluded from the comparison to render a wage adjustment for the full-time female job class, no logical or legal reason for conflating sections 6 and 8 of the Act existed. Contrary to the interpretation applied by Local 1000A and Loblaws, section 6 did not imply that the comparison must be based on the *lowest* job rate. Rather, it provided the employer and bargaining agent an opportunity to negotiate a job rate lower than the highest rate of compensation. The "true job rate" would reflect what a worker permanently employed in the job and performing expected job requirements was to be paid.[9] Had the part-time category been declared female-predominant and a "true job rate" been negotiated for the full-time job class, wage increases could probably have been found for the part-timers. However, the erroneous interpretation meant that only 500 full-time workers or about 8 percent of the bargaining unit received a wage adjustment.

The complexity of Ontario's legislation was undoubtedly a factor in UFCW's decision not to advance the "true job rate" strategy. Still, the union accepted the rationale that all part-timers earned the same wages regardless of gender, so that equity already existed. Their pre-set views of the structure of the retail workforce influenced the pay equity outcome.

The lower paid male job classes used in the pay comparison were the most important factor effecting the insignificant level of pay equity adjustments, which ranged from 19 to 81 cents per hour for the full-time categories (see Appendix C, Table C.2). At Local 1000A and throughout the entire supermarket sector, full-time cashiers (service clerks) were compared with stock clerks, which removed a long-standing wage inequity between female and male job classes. However, comparing female-predominant jobs to stock workers, instead of male job classes in other departments such as meat, meant pay adjustments were lower.

The explanation provided as to why cashiers and meat workers were not compared came out of a classic male-dominant union mentality. "The time it takes to learn how to operate a computerized cash register is about six weeks, as compared with a three-and-a-half-year apprenticeship for a certified butcher," one union representative said.[10] Yet technology and centralized packaging systems had already deskilled the meat department — the traditional "butcher" no longer existed — invalidating the argument that meat cutter and cashier could not be compared.

An additional reason that cashiers and other female job classes could not be compared to higher paying, male-predominant job classes was the Neutralizer's skewed weighting system. Although cashiers received high scores in the effort and working conditions categories, these two factors represented only 30 percent of the total score. By assigning greater weight to the skill factor in the job evaluation system, the most demanding aspect of grocey retail work is undervalued. For instance, the work of cashiers requires strength and physical dexterity. Lifting, hand-to-eye co-ordination, key-boarding and scanning are strenuous activities, as a member of the Pay Equity Task Force explains:

> ... a woman who works as a cashier has a thirty-degree lean picking up bags, say six bottles of pop, so that thirty pounds may equal eighty pounds when you take that [angle] into consideration ... cashiers have to listen to the tone of the scanners, to enter the weight, look at the scale and product, all of these things going on at once ...[11]

In spite of recognizing the intense physical effort involved for cashiers the skill and responsibility factors considerably outweighed the other two measures, resulting in an overall lower score for cashiers compared to meat cutters who generated high points for skill. Had a different weighting been used, payouts might well have been higher.

RESULTS OF THE PAY EQUITY EXERCISE

Angered by the results of the pay equity implementation (see Appendix C, Table C.2), a group of ten head cashiers met to discuss the Loblaws pay equity plan. They argued that they were not adequately informed about the process by the union. Union leaders had hand-picked representatives for the pay equity committee, and very little attempt was made to gain input from the members at large, as this head cashier explains:

> It [pay equity committee] had one head checker, who at the time, had been head checker for six months or something. No one came around to the stores and actually talked to us. It was put that we have representation from our peers, but nobody knew about it. It wasn't brought forth beforehand or while it was done.[12]

Of greatest concern was the selection of their male comparator. The job evaluation showed the male job class of garden centre manager as having equal value to head cashiers. They were angry that this male comparator represented only a few people in Ontario. The head cashier complained:

> At that time at Loblaws there were three garden centres ... so [at] every store [with] two head cashiers [they] were compared to three garden centre managers ... And that was our male comparison.[13]

Because so few garden centre managers existed, the head cashiers believed the comparison was unfair and illogical. A more reasonable approach, they argued, would use one of the male-dominant departmental manager positions in produce, grocery, meat or deli as a comparator. As was pointed out, head cashiers are "basically the only position at Loblaws which is female-dominated in a managerial position."

Like department managers, head cashiers were responsible for running their department. They scheduled staff, trained new cashiers and deposited and balanced cash. However, cashiers did not generate a profit margin. Being a profitable manager was simply not part of the head cashier's position, so the job was not seen as comparable to male managers of departments.

The head cashiers who complained saw the equal pay exercise as a perfect opportunity to challenge the traditional view that their job was not managerial. They asserted that their work was of equal worth to that performed by male managers. Based on the pay equity information made available to them, they argued that the deli manager classification was their best male comparator. However, developments in the pay equity implementation prevented this comparison.

One issue was whether deli manager constituted a male job class. From the head checkers point of view, the deli manager classification had historically been gender-defined a male job class despite data showing it was female predominant. Gendered perceptions of jobs in the supermarket had become fixed in the minds of workers, and shaped ideologies about how work should be valued. Despite the head checkers argument, union and management refused to designate historical incumbency or gender stereotyping to the deli manager position.

Another complaint was that the pay equity evaluation resulted in the elimination of wage rates based on volume of sales. According to a union official, wage rates based on sales volume created an inequity within the head cashier classification, as this head cashier explains:

> They [union leaders] tell me, it doesn't matter that I'm in a small store, every head checker picks up money regardless of how much. This head checker may pick up $10,000 a day, and this one $50,000, and this one $100,000 but it doesn't really matter. A head checker may schedule for ten part-timers, I schedule forty, someone may schedule a hundred; it doesn't matter because it's all the same job. Whereas all other departments, it is based on their sales. But we lost our volume.[14]

She was informed that all head cashiers performed the same work and therefore should be paid according to the same wage rate regardless of volume sales. Losing "volume" eliminated a wage benefit for one of the few female job classes where it applied; but volume was retained for department managers in male job classifications.

Eliminating the wage differential based on sales volume was a flagrant violation of Ontario's *Pay Equity Act,* which prohibited pay reductions to achieve pay equity. Perhaps the company deliberately used pay equity to drive down wages of female-predominant job classes. The union was either unfamiliar with the Act or was complicit with the company position. Economic and industry restructuring may have also influenced UFCW's stance on pay equity and made it vulnerable to arguments put forward by the retail food corporation. Whatever the reason, the outcome was unfair to the cashiers, and a complaint should have been filed with the Pay Equity Commission.

Miracle Food Mart: *"There was absolutely no difference in the job"*

THE UNION LOCAL

UFCW Locals 175/633, which represented Miracle Food Mart employees, actually consisted of approximately 8,500 members in three separate locals. All part-time employees were members of Local 175 Part-time; all full-time employees in cash/service, grocery, produce or bakery departments were Local 175 Full-time. Of the 7,000 members in Local 175, approximately 25 percent were full-time. An additional 1,500 full-time employees working in deli or meat departments belonged to Local 633. Under this structure, part-time employees accrued seniority within the store and could move from one department to another without losing seniority.

Full-time employees accrued seniority within their local. While moving to another local did not effect full-time employees' wage rates or pension contributions, seniority was lost. Hence, transferring outside the local (for example, from meat to grocery) affected bumping rights. During periods of layoffs or store closures, bumping or displacement of full-time employees operated according to seniority by job classification.

The wage rates of full-time employees varied according to job classification. According to the 1988–90 collective agreement, male production clerks earned a higher end rate than female service clerks. In general, male job categories received a higher wage than female ones. For example, the end rate for the bookkeeper or head cashier position was $546 per week, but it was $609 for the assistant meat manager. In comparison, the wage grid for part-timers applied to all employees irrespective of job assignment, as at Loblaws.

The final results of the equal pay exercise at Miracle Food Mart were very similar to that at Loblaws. Because they belonged to a separate union local, the part-time classification could have been declared a single female job class as a union representative explained:

> We have one part-time job class that covers everybody that works part-time hours. It doesn't matter if you are a cashier, a stock receiver or whatever, you have one seniority list, so we were in the best shape to take on the comparison between part-time and full-time under pay equity by declaring that part-time is a female-predominate job class ... and then we could compare it to full-time men.[14]

Unfortunately, this comparison was not achieved because union leaders believed the "structure of the law" prevented it, as the representative goes on to say:

> Our initial attempt was to get the part-time declared a female job class ... *And we knew it would outscore the full-time men.* But it became clear after a while ... that was not about to happen because of the way the structure of the Act was written.[15]

As in the Loblaws' case, the local representing workers at Miracle Food Mart accepted the company's interpretation that sections 6 and 8 of the Act precluded payouts to full-time employees if lower paying, part-time male job classes were included in the pay comparison. Locals 175/633 implemented pay equity in exactly the same way as Local 1000A, comparing full-time female job classes to full-time male job classes while excluding part-time employees.

Because UFCW's Pay Equity Task Force guided the pay equity process at both chains, the outcomes were similar. According to the pay equity plan posted, of 2,065 full-time employees, only 621 in female-predominant job classes received pay adjustments, or about 7 percent of bargaining unit employees in Ontario. (See Appendix C, Table C.2.)

COMPARING FULL-TIME JOB CLASSES

A pay equity bench committee consisting of six bargaining unit members from a variety of job categories, evenly split between female and male, plus company and union representatives evaluated the job classifications. As at Loblaws, union officials selected bargaining unit members they believed were qualified to participate in the job evaluation. Additional input was gathered from selected employee evaluation questionnaires. The committee used the Neutralizer, which produced similar results to Loblaws, because of the same weighting scheme and the locals' similar orientation to pay equity. For instance, in both pay equity exercises full-time cashiers (service clerks) were compared to production (stock) clerks.

At Miracle Food Mart two other female job classes — meat-wrapper attendants and decorator — were also compared with production clerks. This set of comparisons was regarded as a significant gain for women because it removed inequities that had been in place for at least twenty years. Prior to pay equity, women meat-wrapper attendants were performing the same work as male production clerks but earning as much as $50 less per week. A meat manager explained:

> What we had in the meat department was meat-wrapper attendants, and they were female traditionally. Part of the job would be filling meat, frozen food. And we would have a male clerk working in grocery filling frozen food. But there was absolutely no difference in the job.[16]

Similarly, male production clerks worked part of the time on cash, yet previous to pay equity adjustments they earned considerably more than cashiers did. The pay equity implementation was thus perceived to bring about equality in pay because it corrected a problem of equal pay for equal work between women and men.

Although there was a willingness, largely prompted by the legislation, to correct an inequity based on the equal pay for equal work principle, the committee would not contemplate comparisons based on higher paying male classifications. The point-factor scheme that placed greater weight on responsibility and skill probably ruled out such comparisons.

THE DELI MANAGER JOB COMPARISON

The deli manager has traditionally been a female-predominant job at this retail food chain. If we look at the allocation of points for this position, the reasons for the male comparison become clearer. Like the head cashiers at Loblaws, deli managers performed managerial functions, yet the job class was not compared with a department manager classification. Although the pay equity process was supposed to be free of gender-bias, job evaluation once again reflected the view that the traditionally female-predominant position of deli manager should not be equated with (male) managerial jobs. Instead, this female job class was compared with the male-predominant position of night production foreman.

The main role of the night foreman was to supervise the night shift. The position was generally not considered equal to the department manager classification, as the meat manager explains:

> He's just like a foreman in a factory. He's responsible for getting x amount of work done. He gets paid for that. He's an overseer ... If there's a loss or a problem, it comes back to the grocery manager.[17]

Because the job responsibilities were qualitatively different for the night production foreman and managers, why was the position of deli manager compared to this male job classification?

The deli head performed the same functions as any other department manager. Every manager was responsible for scheduling staff, ordering and inventorying products, accounting for spoiled or out-of-date products, plus handling, unpacking and shelving items for sale and providing customer service. Most importantly, all department managers were responsible for achieving a profit margin. The profit margin, which varied by department, was calculated by factoring in wages, overhead costs, supplies and so on. A manager who failed to reach the assigned profit margin would be removed.

Despite the overall similarity of department manager duties, the job evaluation showed various scores, with deli manager ranked lowest and meat manager highest. A close examination of the points assigned to the various subfactors revealed certain inconsistencies. For instance, tasks required of *all* department managers were not evenly weighted (see Appendix C, Table C.1). The deli manager received 5 points for decision-making while all other positions received 10 points. But nothing indicated that the deli manager position was more routine in skill level than the other manager jobs. Exactly the same decisions had to be made by the deli manager concerning budget decisions, scheduling of employees and product quality.

However, the pay equity bench committee was committed to a preconceived notion of the deli manager as having less worth than male department managers. Common gender stereotypes such as women's work not being as responsible or demanding as men's work likely influenced the assessment of this female-dominant job.

In contrast to the situation at Loblaws, at Miracle Food Mart, head cashiers were equivalent to deli managers. The main difference was that the deli manager position at Miracle Food Mart had historically been stereotyped a female job. In the pay evaluation, head cashiers earned slightly more points (122) than the deli manager (119). Scoring indicated that these classifications were roughly equivalent across supermarket chains, and confirmed that both these female-predominant job classes had been unjustly evaluated. Neither union nor management could conceive of these female jobs as being equivalent to male department managers.

REINFORCING GENDER

Overall, scoring laid bare the conventional view that women's work was of less value to the operation of a supermarket than men's work.

A male department manager (Local 175/633), commented on why the deli manager and head cashier positions were not compared to manager classifications:

> I don't think they [pay equity committee] wanted to upset grocery, meat and produce managers by saying this woman is going to be making the same money as you. Because they would turn around and say she shouldn't be making the same money.[18]

Unfortunately, reproducing conceptions of the "proper" ordering of masculine and feminine job hierarchies can be a critical dimension of job evaluation.

Pay equity evaluations typically operate to reproduce gender hierarchies rather than challenge them. Joan Acker argues that comparable worth evaluations contribute to the process of gendering work. In her study of pay equity in Oregon, she found that men resisted definitions of women's jobs that bestowed attributes of complexity and knowledge on female clerical work.[19] Similarly, in supermarkets we find opposition to valuing aspects of women's' work that involve a high degree of financial responsibility, independence and manual skills associated with masculine characteristics. The deli manager and head cashier examples illustrate that the pay equity committees did not confront gender stereotypes and allowed sex-typing into the evaluation process.

Gender-bias may have intruded into the job evaluation exercise because insufficient training was provided to committee members about job analysis. Whenever evaluation teams are used, training in job content analysis is necessary to ensure point assignment is consistent and unbiased.[20] The deli manager scoring indicates halo bias. As Ronnie Steinberg and Lois Haignere explain:

> By halo effects, we mean that global impressions, or halos, of the value of the work are formed by an individual group, and spread to other assessments ... They make valued jobs seem even more valuable, and less valuable jobs seem even less valuable.[21]

The authors point out that the most troubling form of halo effect is "gender halo," which gives greater job worth to jobs performed by men because *evaluators assume that men's work is more important and encompasses greater skill and responsibility.* Women's work is devalued because job related skills are associated with "qualities intrinsic to being a woman."[22] Certainly, the fact that certain aspects of the deli manager position such as financial responsibility were neglected or devalued indicates that gender halo entered the job evaluation. Similarly, the refusal of the rating team to accept that the head cashier and deli manager are equivalent in value may indicate another instance of gender halo effects. Without proper training on gender-bias, value judgements made by committees may uphold rather than challenge existing gender-wage inequities.

A&P/Dominion:
"Pay equity is all negotiations"

Six locals of RWDSU represented supermarket employees at the new Dominion and A&P stores. All of the bargaining unit workers across Ontario were covered by one collective agreement. In 1990, when pay equity was negotiated, 6,651 members worked for A&P/Dominion. Seventy percent worked part-time while the remainder were classified full-time. Of the part-time members, 62 percent were female; of the full-time membership, 35 percent were female.[23]

As at Loblaws and Miracle Food Mart, full-time and part-time employees operated under separate seniority lists. Like Miracle Food Mart, A&P/Dominion part-time employees functioned under a store-wide seniority system. Part-timers could transfer in order of seniority to a different department if they had the necessary training or skills. Full-time employees could bump a co-worker in another classification only if they had demonstrated the ability to do the job. Classification meant both job and wage classification, so that a higher paid employee could displace a worker who earned a lower wage. At the time of pay equity negotiations, almost no full-time workers earned less than the maximum because the company had not hired full-time employees for years. In effect, a kind of phantom grid existed. Nonetheless, in principle, bumping operated according to wage classification, and if hiring were to resume, junior employees would be affected by the existing wage differentials. Pay equity also affected the traditional gender-wage hierarchy, because wage increases to female-predominant jobs had implications on bumping rights.

Wages of full-time employees were comparable to those at Loblaws and Miracle Food Mart. Department managers, head cashiers, bookkeepers and other positions were paid a wage according to volume of sales. Full-time (female) service clerks, referred to as Clerk A, and (male) stock clerks, called Clerk B, were paid on a uniform scale. According to the collective agreement, Clerk A and Clerk B performed distinct functions, but management could assign work from either job classification to an A or B clerk. Each clerk was paid according to his or her classification.

Unlike Loblaws or Miracle Food Mart, two grids governed part-time wages, one for students, the other for non-students. The major difference in pay rates between the two classifications was the start rate. No pay differences existed among part-timers according to particular job function, and they were regarded as one job classification.

A Challenge to their Maleness

The Pay Equity Committee consisted of four union representatives, eight bargaining unit members with equal gender representation, and management personnel. The company and union agreed to use a software package that closely resembled the Neutralizer, with similar weightings for the major components. Pay equity questionnaires were distributed to eight stores representing each geographical division in the province to obtain a representative sampling of job descriptions. The union also held information sessions to explain the purpose of the job content questionnaires. Despite their efforts, the response was limited, as reported by this union representative:

> At A&P we had a moderate response level. Probably 30 percent or 40 percent at the most actually filled out the questionnaires. We've had other retail stores where we've distributed questionnaires and not one was turned back in.[24]

One reason for the low response was that males often refused to complete the questionnaires. Believing that pay equity would not benefit men, they were reluctant to co-operate. A union representative recalled encounters with male retail employees concerning pay equity questionnaires:

> I went to the store in Don Mills. I arrived at 7 a.m. to get the night shift. But the guys didn't fill out the questionnaire. They said, "We don't give a shit about women."
>
> Some meat cutters filled out the questionnaires just the opposite to what should have been filled in. We had to throw those out. There are similar horror stories from other stores. The guys took it as a challenge to their maleness. They were afraid women were going to take over.[25]

Men were anxious about equal pay because they feared diminished male privilege in the workplace.

Women, on the other hand, were cautious and tended to underrate their job worth on the evaluation questionnaires. They left sections of the questionnaire incomplete, rated themselves lower than was considered reasonable by the committee, or provided insufficient detail for an adequate job analysis. The union representative heard women support the family wage ideology:

> Some women believed that they earned good money, and they felt that the men should be earning more. They also thought that men should have bumping rights over women. Basically, the women felt that men have to provide for families. There was some discussion about the need for pay equity.[26]

Despite the occasional remark from women concerning the need for a male breadwinner, in general women approved equal value in pay.

Because the factor evaluation depended on the quality of the responses to the pay equity survey, the lack of detailed answers from women affected the job assessment. The committee sometimes had to second-guess what a job entailed in order to assign a score to a point factor. In this process, company and union decided upon the job point values.

We fill in the blanks by advocating a position that the female job may be doing something theoretically, but in reality the practice may not be doing that. So, there is give and take at the bargaining table. The company may take the position that theoretically okay that may be happening, so we'll say instead of a "D" response, we'll say an "E" response.[27]

Accepting that point factor evaluation was largely a best guess scenario, the union took the position that establishing job scores was a negotiations exercise.

Five female predominant job classes received wage adjustments. Unfortunately, data on the number of employees receiving payouts was unavailable, but likely very similar to Loblaws and Miracle Food Mart. In fact, the numbers at A&P/Dominion might even have been lower than the other two chains because wage adjustments applied only to the top rate, not to each step of the grid. Only employees earning the maximum received a wage increase. According to a union official, this decision was made because Ontario's *Pay Equity Act* said that the job rate, defined as the highest rate of compensation, must be equal between male and female job classes. The union representative who participated in pay equity negotiations summarized the shared company-union interpretation of the Act:

> It was our understanding that pay equity applies only to the highest rate of compensation payable to a job class. Therefore, within the structure of the pay equity document, only the end rates were applicable. There is also provision within the *Pay Equity Act* that says that based on a formal seniority system pay equity is not required. So, in that context there was not a requirement legislatively to have the same rates between male and female dominated positions, in the case of A&P between the Class A and Class B group throughout the entire grid. That was our understanding of the Act.[28]

Here again a permissible exemption under section 8 of the Act was *incorrectly* interpreted by company and union. Ontario's *Pay Equity Act* requires adjustments to *all* steps in a wage progression grid.

The peculiar reading of the legislation diminished the level of equity achievable. In the collective agreement subsequent to pay equity, the wage grid of Clerk A at A&P/Dominion showed a lower rate compared to Clerk B at every step of the grid except the maximum rate. Curiously, the Class A and B wage grids were not equalized for the sake of principle, even though cost was not a factor because no incumbents were in the lower steps of the grid. On the positive side, the pay equity adjustment enabled most Clerk A employees (those at the top rate) to bump Clerk B workers, similar to the pay equity outcome at Miracle Food Mart.

JOB COMPARISONS

The job class comparisons resembled those found in the pay equity plans at Loblaws and Miracle Food Mart. Again, part-time employees were untouched by pay adjustments. No consideration was given to the argument that part-timers represented a single job class. The same union representative who participated in pay equity negotiations suggested that part-time employees were exempt from comparison because they scored lower than full-time employees did in the job evaluation:

> Where a part-timer may on examination receive the same point value as a full-timer in the area of skill, they can earn significantly less in the area of responsibility and quite certainly less in respect to working conditions because of the hours of work in question.

However, when pressed further on the issue of point comparison between part-time Clerk A and Clerk B, he said:

> Well, they [Clerk A] may have rated in the end, higher, in terms of points. But you have to understand something. I mean, pay equity is all negotiations.[29]

Although the union representative wavered considerably on the matter of point equivalency between female Clerk A and male Clerk B, he still argued that the part-time classification could not be compared with full-time. The evaluation at A&P/Dominion contradicted the assessment by Miracle Food Mart and UFCW that the job worth of part-timers was equal to full-time employees. In addition, the distinction between the student and non-student part-time wage category was not considered, and the structure of wage rates remained unchanged for part-timers following implementation of equal pay. Presumably all part-time employees perform exactly the same work, yet a wage differential continued to exist between the student and nonstudent categories.

Neither the deli manager nor the head cashiers received a wage adjustment. According to two union representatives, several women in these two job classes filed a complaint with the Pay Equity Commission. Details of the complaint were not available, but the issue was selection of male comparators. Significantly, as at Loblaws and Miracle Food Mart, the value of deli manager and head cashier positions was at issue. These female-predominant positions must have been perceived by the complainants to have been improperly assessed or undervalued, resulting in a comparison with a lower paying male job class that did not yield a pay adjustment.

Maintaining the Status Quo

What conclusions can be drawn about pay equity implementation? From a strictly monetary perspective, wage equity gains were not significant. In part, the low wage adjustments were attributable to the job evaluation weighting scheme that favoured male jobs and operated to minimize payouts to eligible female job classes. Of particular importance was the fact that service clerks were not compared to workers in the higher-paying meat categories. Similarly, the female-predominant job classes demanding higher levels of responsibility, such as head cashier and deli manager, were compared to non-managerial, lower-paying male job classes. In both instances, the male comparator was generally perceived by these women as an illogical outcome of pay equity. In addition, the fact that at Loblaws the head cashiers "lost their volume" and at A&P/Dominion the deli managers did not receive a wage adjustment, while only the highest rate of compensation in the Clerk A category was equalized to Clerk B, all contributed to a lower standard of wage equity.[30] With the exception of full-time service clerks receiving a wage adjustment equivalent to the wages of male production clerks, pay equity implementation did not provide meaningful wage increases. Most damaging was the exclusion of part-time employees from the pay equity comparison. Bypassing part-timers was a strategic decision to contain the benefits of pay equity reform.[31] In a strictly economic sense, a very small percentage of workers benefited from pay equity, but those few who did receive adjustments were not necessarily satisfied with the results. In short, pay evaluation did not challenge the status quo.

Why did bargaining agents not pursue the argument that part-time workers constituted a separate female job class? At Loblaws the majority of part-timers were women. Even if the percentage cut-off for gender predominance did not apply, the Act permitted parties to negotiate the definition of a female job class in reference to historical incumbency. At Miracle Food Mart, where part-timers occupied a separate bargaining unit, the case for a predominant female job class was made easier since the part-time classification could seek a male comparator outside their bargaining unit. In all three grocery chains the employer, in practice, treated part-time employees as one job class. However, had part-timers been declared a female job class, comparison could have been made to a full-time male job class of comparable value.

The open-ended nature of the *Pay Equity Act* provided opportunities to press for a particular interpretation of wage equity. No matter how complex or vague the specific meaning of particular sections of the legislation, the unions and retail employers negotiated pay equity within a framework that accepted the part-time workforce as a distinct and secondary group. A typical response from union representatives concerning part-time workers was that "part-time got compared to part-time, and since they already had equity there were no adjustments." Union officials expressed a great deal of enthusiasm about the wage adjustments for full-time employees, but were often reluctant to explore the issue of part-timers and pay equity. In general, part-time workers were not viewed as the core labour force; they did not meet the criteria of the "abstract worker." [32] The primary workforce was perceived to be full-time, permanent, and typically male, while part-time workers were seen to be women and students with less commitment to the workplace. Retail unions did not protect the part-time workforce to the same extent as the full-time employees, so part-timers, who overwhelmingly represented union membership, were not safe-guarded by strong collective agreements.

Even though part-time employees comprised a majority of the total workforce in the retail food sector, unions did not exploit the potential presented by pay equity to raise wages for this group. For instance, a further option for achieving wage increases for part-timers would combine full and part-time categories. Given that full and part-time employees were doing the same work, job evaluation should have produced equal points for the two groups and remedied an equal pay for equal work inequity. Applying pay equity in this way would have produced significant wage increases for the contingent labour force. Unfortunately, pay equity committees did not fully explore this option. Instead, pay equity plans maintained the division between a large, lower-paid and flexible female part-time category and a dwindling full-time but higher-paid permanent workforce.

NOTES

1. Interview, UFCW representative Local 1000A, July 9, 1990.
2. Interview, UFCW official Local 1000A, September 28, 1990.
3. Interview, UFCW representative Local 1000A, July 9, 1990.
4. Ibid.
5. "Computers Revolutionize Pay Equity," UFCW Canada Action (1989), 13.
6. Interview, Pay Equity Task Force member, UFCW Local 1000A, September 28, 1990.
7. Interview, UFCW official, September 28, 1990.
8. Ibid.
9. Patricia McDermott, "Pay Equity in Ontario: A Critical Legal Analysis," *Osgoode Hall Law Journal* 28, no. 2 (1990), 402.

10. Interview, UFCW representative, July 9,1990.

11. Interview, UFCW representative, September 28, 1990.

12. Interview, Head Cashier, Local 1000A, March 23, 1992.

13. Ibid.

14. Interview, UFCW representative, July 9, 1990.

15. Ibid.

16. Interview, Meat Manager, Local 633, August 24, 1993.

17. Ibid.

18. Ibid.

19. Joan Acker, *Doing Comparable Worth: Gender, Class and Pay Equity* (Philadelphia: Temple University Press, 1989).

20. The Ontario Pay Equity Hearings Tribunal states that training is crucial to job evaluation. "Where there is a job evaluation committee, it is essential that there be adequate training in bias-free evaluation and that members develop a conscious awareness of the attitudes and biases people bring to point valuing." See Haldimand-Norfolk (No. 6) 2 P.E.R. 105 at 136.

21. Ronnie Steinberg and Lois Haignere, "Equitable Compensation: Methodological Criteria for Comparable Worth," in Christine Bose and Glenna Spitze, eds., *Ingredients for Women's Employment Policy* (New York: State University of New York Press, 1987), 171.

22. Ibid., 165.

23. Interview, RWDSU representative, December 11, 1991.

24. Interview, RWDSU representative, February 19, 1992.

25. Interview, RWDSU representative, December 11, 1991

26. Ibid.

27. Interview, RWDSU representative, February 19, 1992.

28. Ibid.

29. Ibid.

30. McDermott, "Pay Equity in Ontario."

31. Ronnie Steinberg, "Job Evaluation and Managerial Control: The Politics of Technique and the Techniques of Politics," in Patricia McDermott and Judy Fudge, eds., *Just Wages: A Feminist Assessment* (Toronto: University of Toronto Press, 1991).

32. Joan Acker, "Hierarchies, Jobs, Bodies: A Theory of Gender Organizations," *Gender and Society* 4, no. 2 (1990), 139–58.

Chapter Eight

RESTRUCTURING:
THE PAY EQUITY AFTERMATH

SO FAR THIS ANALYSIS has focused on the results of the pay equity exercise prior to the intense period of restructuring in the retail food industry. An investigation of what occurred after pay equity implementation provides a broader picture of the changes in the gender-wage structures and of women's position in the grocery retail workforce. Chapter 5 discussed the development of concession bargaining — a process that began in the 1980s. In this chapter, I discuss the shift to concessions in Ontario in the 1990s that had serious implications for women retail workers. Major job cuts in the full-time classification singled out women and negated gains made under pay equity. There was also a ratcheting down of part-time wage rates and the expansion of part-time employment. All of these developments worsened the position of women and other flexible workers in the supermarkets.

Loblaws

UFCW and Loblaws were the first to negotiate a collective agreement in Ontario that altered the conventional wage structure in food retailing. In 1990, the part-time wage progression grid was changed so that workers could progress through the grid based on the number of hours worked annually. Previously, workers automatically moved through the wage progression scale in six-month intervals. Today, workers move through each step of the grid after 500 hours are accumulated. On the face of it, this change may appear to be minor. However, during a period of reductions in store hours, part-time employees moved through the grid at a glacial pace. If a retail employee worked, on average, 10 hours per week under the collective agreement, then, as this assistant meat manager explains,

> It would take ten years to reach top rate. They still have to schedule on seniority, so there are some weeks you would only get six hours, and then you get vacation and things like that. If you average six hours a week over fifty-two weeks a year, that would be a good average, some weeks you get twelve other weeks you get six.[1]

This retail worker estimated that after ten years, an employee would only have worked a total of 3,120 hours, much less than the 5,501 hours required to reach top rate as stipulated in the wage structure in the 1990 collective agreement. Since the first wage grid was negotiated, two other part-time wage tiers have been added to the collective agreement. Under the second tier, 7,651 hours must be accumulated to reach the top rate of $16.50 while the third tier requires 8,751 hours to reach a top rate of $14.00 per hour (effective 2005) as stipulated in the most recent contract expiring July 1, 2006.[2] The start rate for the first two tiers is minimum wage while the third tier start rate is slightly above the Ontario minimum wage. This kind of wage structure lowers the wage bill because management continuously hires new employees who take longer to reach top rate than longer service employees, a strategy that works to contain wage rates for part-timers.

Job Loss at Miracle Food Mart

In 1993–94, a province-wide strike at sixty-three Miracle Food Mart stores in Ontario ensued over concessions demanded by the employer. Lasting over three months, from November 18, 1993 to February 21, 1994, the strike was one of the longest in the history of retail in Canada. A total of 6,500 workers (1,700 full-time and 4,800 part-time) represented by UFCW Locals 175/633 went out across the province.[3]

The strike itself was not well organized or co-ordinated. Strikers complained about a lack of direction from the union concerning picketing. Part-timers (Local 175) voted against two tentative contract offers, despite full-timers agreeing to both of the tentative agreements and the union executive's endorsement of them. The results from the contract votes divided full-time and part-time employees and created a great deal of confusion over the legality of the collective agreement. A group of disgruntled workers eventually took the union to the Labour Board under a complaint of unfair representation.[4] Shortly after going to the Labour Board, the NDP government appointed a special mediator, Vic Pathe, to resolve the dispute, and two and one-half weeks later the strike was over.

The results of the negotiated agreement are typical of the reorganization and restructuring in food retail. Although the strike was meant to resist concessions and maintain industry standards, the outcome of negotiations reinforced segmentation between full- and part-time workers, depressed wage rates, deteriorated conditions of work and eroded the power of the union. There were three major items negotiated in the contract: (1) wage concessions; (2) a buy-out program for full- and part-time employees; and (3) the introduction of a new part-time wage categories, including the courtesy clerk.

The UFCW and A&P negotiated $1.75 wage cuts across the board for all full-time and part-time employees. A buy-out policy effecting both full-time and part-time employees was also negotiated. As in the situation at Safeway in Alberta, discussed in chapter 5, the aim of the buy-out program was to reduce the full-time workforce. A&P wanted to eliminate 700 full-time positions at Miracle Food Mart. The volunteer buy-out program offered $1,500 for every year of service for full-time employees, up to a maximum of $35,000. Under the terms of the buy-out agreement, a full-timer could accept the cash settlement, and then return to Miracle Food Mart as a "new" part-time employee at minimum wage without benefits. The buy-out program for part-time employees was similar to that of full-time, but offered less money. Part-timers could accept $500 for every year worked, up to a maximum of $5,000. Again, if a part-timer accepted the buy-out, they could return to work as a "new hire" with no seniority. Another critical dimension of the buy-out program was that 60 percent of the "hours" freed up by the elimination of 700 full-time jobs were available to the "new hire" part-time classification. The remainder 40 percent of the 25,900 hours were relegated to the "old" part-time category, thereby saving the company on labour costs. (See table 1.)

TABLE I

Miracle Food Mart Part-time Wage Schedules,
Effective June 22, 1993 – November 17, 1996

Title	Start Rate	Time to Reach Top Rate	Top Rate	Maximum Weekly Hours
"Old" Part-Time*	$6.70	48 months	$11.95	22.4
New Hires	$6.70	42 months	$9.60	16.0
Courtesy Clerk	$6.70	36 months	$8.50	12.0

* Part-time employees hired prior to the date of ratification.

The terms of the new contract were quite complex. In fact, workers at the ratification vote did not fully understand the implications of the changes. As a cashier explained, "You don't sit down with your calculator figuring everything out while he is reading the contract." In addition, the final ratification vote occurred at twenty-eight locations, which further divided workers. "They [the union] split us up so much, so that if there were any rabble-rousers or anybody who would question anything, they were so divided that our meetings seemed tame. Nobody asked anything, ... I kept thinking, I don't know if the union is in cahoots."[5] Although the consequences of the new agreement were not immediately evident to the rank and file at the time of ratification, the outcome of the agreement was immediately felt upon their return to the stores.

Following the strike, there was considerable disruption caused by reorganization and displacement of staff. The company had violated twenty-six articles of the collective agreement and at least 1,500 grievances were filed, many concerning seniority rights.[6] Many people felt the company was selective concerning promotions, and that the terms of the collective agreement were simply ignored. Full-time workers had been assured a job guarantee. However, lay-offs occurred anyway. In the period following the strike, full-time employees had their weekly hours reduced to 24 from 37, causing incredible resentment towards the company and generating over 500 grievances.[7] A survey conducted in 1994 of Miracle Food Mart employees following the strike found that of 310 people interviewed 115 were unemployed. "For those still employed, the average number of hours per week dropped from 37 to 25, the average hourly rate of pay went from $17.34 to $9.79, and the average weekly salary dropped from $641.69 to $251.48."[8]

A&P eliminated female predominant full-time positions. The company assumed full-time workers would voluntarily accept the buy-out offer. However, only 500 employees opted for the pay-out within the first month of its being offered, with the result that head office terminated all full-time meat-wrapper, cashier and deli attendant positions. Essentially, the company eliminated full-time jobs in the service departments where women predominated. Because these job classifications were eliminated across the entire province, under seniority provisions in the collective agreement, cashiers, deli attendants and meat wrappers could not move to another store because they "had no one to bump." Most employees within their job classification were eliminated, thus removing the job guarantee. This fact did not go unnoticed by workers or the union. Five women complained to the Ontario Human Rights Commission that the elimination of these job classifications constituted systemic sex discrimination in employment.[9] The union complained to the Human Rights Commission on the same grounds.[10]

The elimination of these jobs created hardship for women retail workers. In one instance, a full-time cashier with twenty-two years of service with Miracle Food Mart lost her job in the frontend and had to accept a job on the night crew. At 43 years of age, and with no training for the new job, she had to work the graveyard shift in a job that requires very heavy lifting, as she describes:

> The groceries arrive in big skids, they're about fifteen feet
> high. When you go in at night there might be eight big skids.
> What you do is unload them, and take them to where the item
> is. It's called spreading the load ... Mainly you're lifting, sort of,
> over your head ... I just let it fall on me, from there I lift it
> onto the truck.[11]

At this cashier's store, full-time employees were downsized from a
total of twenty-two prior to the strike to nine full-time following the
strike. Basically, the only full-time positions remaining in the store
were departmental managers and most were occupied by men. The
company assumed stores could remain profitable by employing
part-time staff, and by intensifying the work of full-time workers.

Ironically, however, neither assumption necessarily held true.
First, a new hire had to produce at a high dollar ratio, and second,
full-timers had to be willing to work harder. As this meat manager
explains:

> A lot of people thought that with the lower wages there would
> be more help. But as of today, we were told we are going to
> pre-strike productivity. So, they're going to use the same
> amount of hours per dollar as they were using pre-strike, but
> it's going to cost them less. It just means the people who are
> there who are experienced will be expected to work that much
> harder. And they're not going to. You don't come off a three-
> month strike like this and work hard for a company.[12]

In addition to full-time workers having to intensify their labour at
the store, they were asked to train new hires. This struck workers as
an especially painful task to perform and undermined their respect
for the company. "So, you're back at $6.70, taking a roll-back from
$16 to $17 an hour, to train someone to replace you."[13] Meanwhile,
long-time service employees felt that the majority of new hires were
simply unable to perform their jobs in a competent or satisfactory
manner. The entire management strategy of A&P was viewed by
workers as contradictory and wrong-headed, since, in their view,
customer service was inadequate and production work poorly
performed.

There was also a perception by some retail employees that part-timers had been differentially effected by concessions. As this retail worker explained, "Work conditions are not as good for part-timers, most of them are relatively new and are getting paid close to minimum wage ... these new employees are expected to do a lot. In the last two months, I've seen fourteen come and go ... It seems that over the last few years, the union has been making all the concessions for the sake of full-timers job security."[14] Although the majority of retail food employees were part-time, the union protected the wages and job security of its full-time (mostly male) members. In fact, a provision was negotiated in the Local 633 contract to prevent full-time, mainly male meat cutters, from being laid off.[15] Had a similar provision been negotiated for other job classifications, such as meatwrappers and cashiers, they too would not have experienced job displacement.

Buy-Outs at A&P and Dominion Stores

A similar collective agreement was negotiated with A&P and Dominion stores in 1994 and 1995.[16] Both the RWDSU (Steel) and UFCW represented workers at these stores. Again, a buy-out package was offered to full- and part-time employees, with the option of returning to work as a part-time employee for lower wages. The payouts at these stores were slightly higher than at Miracle Food — full-time were offered $1,500 for each year of service and part-time $750. By February of 1995, the corporation began converting stores to franchises as well as selling A&P and Dominion stores. At Dominion, the stores being sold were the smaller, unprofitable stores known as "Group II" stores. Both full- and part-time employees were paid lower wages than larger "Group I" type stores. As a result of store closings, employees began to transfer to other supermarkets, creating a great deal of confusion concerning seniority rights, and a large number of grievances arose over "bumping." In 1995, the UFCW negotiated a lower rate contract for fifteen stores that had been converted from A&P to Super Fresh franchises; workers earned $4 less per hour at the franchises as compared with the corporate wage earned under the old A&P contract.[17] The arrangements of this negotiated settlement also allowed full-time and part-time workers to accept a buy-out, including the option of moving to a Super Fresh store.[18]

Since 1995, the collective agreements that govern those unionized workers represented by the UFCW at the A&P, Miracle Food Mart and Super Fresh stores have merged. Group I has a separate collective agreement and covers workers in the larger corporate stores. These workers earn higher wage rates and have better seniority protection than in the smaller Group II stores, but both groups have suffered major losses in terms of wage levels. For instance, in Group I stores part-timers hired after August 1997 are required to work 8,751 hours to reach the top wage rate of $12.50, those hired before 1997 reach a top rate of $16.00 after 48 months. In Group II stores, wages are even lower in both the part-time and full-time categories with multi-wage-tiers paying different wage rates. For instance, part-timers hired after January 2000 must work 6,501 hours to reach a top rate of $10.75.[19] As in the case of Loblaws, most part-time workers will never reach the top rate, or even the mid-range rate, because it is very unlikely they will ever accumulate the number of hours required to merit a wage increase. The obvious implication of these changes is the lowering of wage-levels for new entrants to the supermarket, and the lowering of the wage bill for employers who depend on employee turnover in the part-time classification to keep wage costs low.[20]

Oshawa Foods and Safeway

Concessions were also experienced at other major food retailers in Ontario. In 1994, Oshawa Foods reduced wage rates for its 2,500 part-time workforce by 23 per cent. The company also introduced a new wage grid, similar to those discussed above, that had a lower top rate for new part-time hires as compared with the rate applied to more senior part-time workers. Like A&P, Oshawa Foods offered part-time employees a voluntary leaving package of $750 for every year worked, with no limits. The 1,000 non-union full-time workers had their wages frozen, their COLA removed and benefits reduced.[21]

By the end of the 1990s, then, all of the major food retailers in Ontario had slashed wages and achieved major concessions in their collective agreements — a trend that continued to be followed well into 2002. Canada Safeway recently demanded wage rollbacks from its unionized workers in Manitoba and in Thunder Bay, Ontario. As noted in chapter 5, Safeway was the first corporate supermarket chain to demand concessions, and the company continues to follow this strategy.

In 1997, 10,000 unionized workers at seventy-three Safeway stores in Alberta went on strike after refusing the company's final offer that demanded greater labour flexibility and other concessions. Following an eleven-week strike by the UFCW, few gains were made by the union while Canada Safeway was successful in implementing a two-tiered wage structure with a majority of workers in the lower tier.[22] In 2002, Safeway threatened to close all of its stores in the province of Manitoba unless the union, UFCW Local 832, agreed to reduce wages for its 3,150 members. To avoid a strike, the union and employer agreed to binding arbitration that resulted in a two-tiered wage system. That the arbitrated settlement did not contain as extensive rollbacks as in the Ontario agreements was disappointing to Safeway, whose spokesperson remarked that "the ruling doesn't go far enough to level the playing field." The company has vowed to demand deeper concessions in the next round of negotiations.[23]

Since the arbitration award, Safeway has introduced counter-ready meat and eliminated 400 meat-cutter positions from its stores. Meat cutters were offered the option of a buy-out or of remaining in the store as meat wrappers and customer service clerks.[24] Men who traditionally occupied the full-time and better paid positions are now experiencing job displacement and wage loss. This has implications for women who may find that traditional female jobs, such as meat wrapper, are being filled by men.

Safeway also demanded major concessions at its Thunder Bay stores, resulting in a lengthy strike which, at the time of writing, had been ongoing for ten months and remains unsettled. As in Manitoba, the company threatened to close its stores unless the union accepted its final offer consisting of major concessions, including a wage freeze and reduced benefits for newly hired workers. The union membership, on the advice of the union local leadership of UFCW Local 175, did not ratify the offer. The Safeway stores in Thunder Bay closed and 450 people are out of work, even though the strike continues.[25]

Pattern Bargaining Breakdown

Another major change in collective bargaining in retail food concerns the dissolution of pattern bargaining. As discussed in chapter 5, historically retail unions in Ontario bargained similar expiration dates of contracts and negotiated similar wages, work conditions and other items in collective agreements. By 1992, the pattern in retail food began to break down when Miracle Food Mart signed a one-year contract and Loblaws a four-year contract.[26] Interestingly, a major issue at the bargaining table with UFCW and A&P during the Miracle Food Mart strike was the expiration date of the collective agreement. The union was keenly aware that they had left the pattern when they negotiated a one-year contract in 1992. The union wanted a three-year agreement that coincided with the expiration dates of most of the other major chains but were unsuccessful. With staggered expiration dates of contracts, locals were in a weak position to co-ordinate bargaining demands. Industry standards that had been well established in Canada until the mid 1980s had been systematically eroded.

Implications of Restructuring

Widespread concessions have redefined the wage standards in the supermarket and introduced new forms of inequality. The wage tiers in the supermarket have divided full- and part-time workers and created wage differentials within the full- and part-time job classifications. Segmentation also exists between the corporate stores and franchises, creating labour disunity and eroding bargaining strength. Common to all of the chains has been the introduction of lower part-time wage rates, often in the form of multi-tiered wage schedules. These wage grids are particularly troublesome because of the built-in inequities they create for the large group of flexible workers. As was discussed in chapter 7, the implementation of pay equity left unquestioned the undervaluation of part-time employment, relative to full-time work. The part-time workforce remained fixed as a separate category, because it was assumed that gender equivalency in pay already existed within this group. A problem that arises from this kind of logic is that part-time workers are essentially performing the same work as the full-time workforce, but receiving lower pay. What is at issue here is a classic case of "equal pay for equal work." Once new part-time wage grids had been introduced at the various supermarket chains in recent rounds of restructuring, not only did the inequity between full-time and part-time persist but obvious wage inequities were also extended within the part-time workforce. The splintering of part-time wage grids into lower-paying tiers constitutes a blatant case of wage inequity for the simple reason that some part-time workers are doing exactly the same work as other part-time workers for less pay. The extent of the wage unfairness is especially apparent when we stop to consider that many workers now performing part-time work were previously full-time, fully trained workers. But because they accepted a buy-out program, they are now paid at minimum wage.

From the perspective of wage equity, paying part-time workers at different rates of pay for performing exactly the same job duties is a clear case of wage discrimination. Since women predominate in the part-time classifications, it is also a case of gender-based wage inequity. If pay equity negotiators had challenged the basis of pay inequality between the full-time and part-time workforce, retail companies may not have been able to implement two-tiered and multi-tiered pay scales quite as easily. As it stands now, however, the exigencies of the market have taken over equity concerns. And the principle of pay equity, which is to remove systemic gender-wage discrimination in pay, has been further undermined as a consequence of restructuring.

INTERNAL OPPOSITION TO CONCESSIONARY BARGAINING

The growing inequities that exist in collective agreements and the losses that have been experienced by food retail workers have led to disasatisfaction on the part of union members. The following discussion focuses on the UFCW, as it is the union which represents the great majority of grocery workers and has sparked the largest amount of systematic opposition.

A reform group called REAP (Research, Education, Advocacy and People) was created in 1989 to try to reform the UFCW. This group charged the UFCW leadership with corruption and accused locals of accepting sweetheart agreements with employers. REAP activists advocate the dismantling of the "top-down business union-ism" structure of the organization and want to take a more militant stand on collective bargaining. They argue that rank-and-file members should have more of a participatory role in decision making in order to promote greater activism and encourage harder bargaining. According to REAP, "The UFCW has presided over the destruction of wages and working conditions in the meat packing, meat processing, and retail industries."[27] The plight of UFCW negotiations is summarized in a REAP newsletter:

> Collective bargaining is in a shambles, with concessions winding through retail, and the same predicted .... for meat packing. The average UFCW member is not receiving a livable wage and has lost tremendous ground in real wages. Low part-time wage earners, which may now be approaching 70% of UFCW's membership, four, five, and six year contracts, permanent multi-tiered wage provisions and extended wage progressions have made the members' economic plight worse.[28]

The response of the union leadership to these criticisms has been inadequate. Concessionary contracts continued to be signed throughout the 1990s and, as was shown above, extend into the present. An indication of the lack of change by the UFCW leadership was shown by their decision to support CASCAR car racing in Canada. At least $100,000 was committed by the union to supporting a stock-car racing driver. One union dissident pointed out that "the venture is another example of how distant UFCW executives have become from members struggling to stay above the poverty line."[29]

My interviews with retail food workers also support the finding that retail unions have a weak presence at the workplace. Numerous retail workers I interviewed did not know the name of the union to which they belonged; were not issued a union card or given a collective agreement; complained that union meetings were not well publicized and the times and place of meetings not easily accessible to members, that union stewards were not elected, and that representatives from the union seldom visited stores.[30]

Women, Youth and Union Representation

The problems of democratic representation within UFCW extend to women and youth. The issue of representation raises questions concerning the special needs of different groups of workers. As was discussed in chapters 1 and 2, achieving substantive equality for differently situated groups within the workplace is difficult because the majority of workers understand equality in terms of a "sameness standard." However, it is evident from the discussion on restructuring and the pay equity implementation outcomes that the economic interests of women and youth workers are being ignored. Women have especially suffered economic loss because they were present in the supermaket workforce prior to the wave of concession bargaining. Why have women's "special needs" not been fully acknowledged in the collective bargaining process?

Historically, women have occupied a marginal place within retail unions. As discussed in chapter 5, the retail unions' roots in the craft tradition helped define the masculine culture of these labour organizations. Men still dominate in leadership positions despite the fact that the majority of the Canadian membership is comprised of women. About 50 percent of UFCW's membership in Canada is female, yet men predominate in leadership roles at both the national and local levels. For instance, in 1995 only one woman in Canada was president of her union local. By 2002, ten women had been elected as presidents at the local level, a significant improvement, but still a small minority given that over 100 locals operate in Canada. Many more women today occupy positions at the union executive level, such as secretary treasurer, than they did a decade ago.[31]

Still, the situation is one in which women are struggling to gain better representation and to obtain improvements in collective agreements that are beneficial to women. As a union official pointed out, "The increase of women as national and regional elected officers [in Canada] has proceeded at a snails pace; women have been more successful in achieving leadership recognition through appointments. The UFCW is fielded with guards who feel change is not needed, especially if it assists women's advancement within the union structure itself."[32] The slow advancement of women in union governance is blamed on the fact that the UFCW still operates as a "boys club."[33]

To break down the traditional attitudes of women and help them gain access to decision-making positions, the UFCW formed the Women's Advisory Committee in 1989 to educate members and promote women's interests within the union. One objective of the committee is to establish a network of UFCW women's committees and conferences through Local Unions and Provincial Councils. The committee works to bring a broad range of social issues — such as the need for childcare, ending violence against women, eradicating sexual harassment at the workplace and promoting employment equity — to their members. In comparison with other unions in Canada, the UFCW was slow to initiate measures to improve the status of women, however, they have made strides since the foudning of the Women's Advisory Committee over a decade ago.[34]

The representation of women in decision making has consequences for collective bargaining. Retail unions have tended to operate in the interests of their full-time, mostly male, workforce. Bargaining issues that pertain directly to part-time workers and women's interests did not appear to receive top priority. In negotiations during the Miracle Food Mart strike, provisions were secured to protect full-time meat cutters from lay-off, while the full-time female predominant job classifications were left unprotected. In the pay equity negotiations, discussed in chapter 7, women felt excluded from the pay equity exercise. The proliferation of multi-tiered wage structures in the part-time classification that offer increasingly lower wage rates is further evidence that the needs of the flexible workforce are not being addressed. The masculine culture, including a predominant male leadership, within supermarket unions gives shape to a gender-specific response to the process of restructuring.

Young workers are another group that have traditionally been underrepresented within retail unions. The position of young workers in the UFCW has been recognized as a problem and there are now concerted efforts to increase the profile and participation of young workers within the union. A youth co-ordinator has been hired by the UFCW National Canadian Office to organize youth initiatives, and UFCW has supported youth programs within the labour movement such as Solidarity Works. These programs are aimed at educating youth about union struggles and increasing their commitment to the labour movement. UFCW stands out as one of most active unions in Canada in supporting these activities. While youth workers benefit enormously from these programs, there remains a need to address their substantive concerns. As was discussed above, the proliferation of multi-tier wage grids undermines the economic position of youth and does nothing to remedy the substantive inequities experienced by them in the supermarket.

RESISTANCE TO CONCESSION BARGAINING?

So far this discussion has emphasized union acceptance of concessions. However, as the union confronts deeper cuts, it is being forced to respond more aggressively to employers. The concessions have deepened to the point where the union is now witnessing the disappearance of men's jobs, as illustrated in the case of Safeway meat cutters in Manitoba. Under concession bargaining, all workers are being negatively affected, despite initial attempts by the union leadership to protect the full-time, male predominant membership. The pattern of concessions has run its course to the point where business unionism is no longer effective and the core constituency of the union — its full-time male membership — is now being threatened. This threat to male jobs has stiffened the resolve of the union. The strike against Safeway in Thunder Bay and the strike vote in Manitoba indicate a greater willingness to refuse concessions by the UFCW leadership — a trend that is also being followed in British

Columbia, where Local 1518 is warning Safeway that it will strongly oppose concessions.[35]

*

Retail food workers were once the most privileged group of workers in the entire retail sector, however, changing economic conditions, corporate restructuring and labour strife have undermined their prominent place in the retail economy. Within a period of ten years, industry-wide labour standards have been significantly eroded. The majority of retail food workers no longer receive high wages. Full-time jobs are rapidly disappearing, multi-tiered part-time wage structures segment workers into "old" and "new" hires and ensure that the majority of workers earn wages not substantially higher than the minimum wage. The process of restructuring that led to the lowering of wage standards had major implications for the implementation of pay equity. While emphasizing the fact that retail food workers as a whole have suffered a severe decline in their wages and work conditions, it is important to highlight the gender-dimensions of restructuring within the industry.

We need to assess pay equity as a policy with the potential to remove gendered inequities in employment. It needs to be determined whether such a policy has had a positive impact in the supermarket industry. To what extent did pay equity policy in Ontario diminish gender wage inequities in grocery retail? Did Ontario's pay equity legislation benefit retail food employees by removing gender disparities in compensation, and more specifically, did pay equity work to lessen retail employers' reliance on a part-time female-predominant flexible workforce? The answers to these questions are taken up in the following chapter.

NOTES

1. Interview, Assistant Meat Manager, April 11, 1994.

2. Collective Agreement between Loblaws Supermarkets Limited and UFCW Local 1000A, Appendix "A" Part-Time Employees, 59–62. The top rates for the first and second tiers are effective June 26, 2004, while the top rate for the third tier is effective June 26, 2005.

3. The strike is important not only because of the large number of people involved, but also because it was the first (and only) major strike to occur under Bill 40; a bill introduced by the NDP government involving a series of amendments to Ontario's labour legislation including banning replacement labour. Two important Ontario Labour Board decisions were made in relation to Bill 40: one rejected the company's request for restricted picketing, and the second prevented the employer from using replacement labour to remove stock from stores. Had these decisions not been made, the strike likely would have been prolonged even further. See *The Toronto Star,* 1 December 1, 1993, A3.

4. At a meeting at the Ontario Labour Board on 2 February, 1994, the rank and file membership argued that the local constitution traditionally required majority vote from both the full-time and part-time members in order for ratification of an agreement to be passed. Since part-timers had voted against the tentative contract, the members felt the agreement had not been ratified. In addition, the union members complained of insecure ballotting (double-voting) at ratification meetings. For these reasons, the membership argued the union should not have negotiated a memorandum of settlement with A&P with respect to the full-time agreement, and by doing so their interests were not properly or fairly represented. The union leadership argued the agreement had been ratified by the full-time workforce. The discussion took place over two days, and finally an agreement was reached, without a formal hearing, in which it was agreed, as per past practice, that ratification required majority acceptance from all three locals (i.e., Local 175 Part-Time, Local 175 Full-time and Local 633). In addition, there were a number of complaints about the running of the strike, for example, picket signs were not provided, coffee and other hot beverages were not offered on the pickets, and poor communication (or complete lack of communication) to picketers about proper procedures created confusion on the picket lines.

5. Interview, Full-time Cashier, March 23, 1994.

6. Interview, Striker (Meat Manager), April 11, 1994.

7. Interview, UFCW Representative, Local 175/633, May 18, 1994.

8. *Needs Assessment for Miracle Food Mart Workers Who Have Lost Jobs or Been Reassigned.* A Report of the Joint Retail Food Adjustment Committee, November 1994. Cited in *Human Resource Study of the Grocery Distribution Industry — Phase I* (Ottawa: Canadian Labour Market and Productivity Centre, 1995), 32.

9. This information was provided to me from an interviewee who was involved in assisting with grievances from the union side, April 11, 1994.

10. Interview, UFCW Representative, Locals 175/633, May 18, 1994.

11. Interview, Full-time Cashier/Night Crew, May 17, 1994.

12. Interview, Meat Manager, April 1994.

13. Interview, Full-time Cashier/Night Crew, May 17, 1994.

14. Interview, Full-Time Bookkeeper, February 1995.

15. Interview, Assistant Meat Manager, April 11, 1994. As explained to me, the agreement stipulates that the company cannot "use a part-time meat cutter as long as a full-time meat cutter is on layoff. If they lay off a full-time meat cutter, they can't hire a part-time meat cutter."

16. In addition to newspaper reports, the results of these negotiated agreements were found in The Memorandum of Agreement of the Renewal of the Collective Agreement Dated the 29th Day of October, 1994 Between New Dominion Stores, and Retail Wholesale Canada, Canadian Service Sector Division of the United Steelworkers of America, Local 414 and CCH Canadian Industrial Relations and Personnel Developments, No. 11, March 17, 1993.

17. *The Globe and Mail,* 28 February 1995, B6 *The Globe and Mail ,* 5 July 1994, B1.

18. *The Toronto Star,* 28 February 1995, C10.

19. Collective Agreeement between The Great Atlantic & Pacific Company of Canada, Limited and United Food and Commercial Workers International Union, Local 175 and Local Union 633, Group I and Group II Stores, Effective January 31, 2000 and September 20, 2003.

20. Employee turnover is much higher among part-time employees than among full-time employees. Almost one-third (28 percent) of employees in food retail quit their jobs within twelve months. See *Creating the Future: Human Resources Study of the Canadian Food Retail and Wholesale Sector* (CLMPC Consulting Services, 1998), 32–33.

21. *The Toronto Star,* 28 October 1994, A6.

22. See Harvey Krahn and Graham Lowe, *Work, Industry and Canadian Society,* 4th ed. (Toronto: Nelson, 2002), 335–36.

23. Leah Janzen and Paul McKie, "Safeway Deal," *Winnipeg Free Press,* 30 April 2002.

24. "No Meat Cutting at Safeway." UFCW. <http://www.ufcw832.mb.ca/safeway.htm>. August 14, 2002.

25. Kris Ketoner, "Safeway Saga Goes On," *Chronicle Journal* 23 July 2002.

26. In April 1992, Loblaws president Richard Currie warned 14,000 unionized Loblaws employees that in upcoming contract negotiations, workers should not expect wage levels commensurate with other domestic unionized chains. He referred to the caterpillar strike in Illinois, USA, in which the United Auto Workers was humbled into accepting a break in industry pattern bargaining. See *Canadian Industrial Relations and Personnel Developments,* CCH Limited, no. 20, May 13, 1992.

27. On the reform movement within UFCW , see "Reformers Adopt Platform for Democracy in Food and Commercial Workers Union," *Labor Notes,* 159 (June 1992), 6.

28. *REAP News and Views,* January/February 1994. In the U.S., many identify the Hormel strike of 1985–86 as particularly symbolic of the UFCW's weak response to economic restructuring. This strike was an attempt by meat packers to halt the cut-backs and concessions assaulting workers in the meatpacking industry. Sadly, the UFCW placed the local under trusteeship and ended the strike by accepting concessions that were unpalatable to many of the rank and file. There is quite a large literature of the Hormel strike that has grown up in recent years. This strike is seen by many as a last gasp effort by rank-and-file members to reverse the trend of economic restructuring and to win back workers control over their place of

work and community. See Hardy Green, *On Strike at Hormel: The Struggle for a Democratic Labor Movement* (Philadelphia: Temple University Press, 1990); Michael Fahey, *Packing It In! The Hormel Strike, 1985–86: A Personal Perspective* (St. Paul, MN: Kirwin and Sons Ltd., 1988); and Neala J. Scheulening, *Women, Community, and the Hormel Strike of 1985–86* (Westport, CT: Greenwood Press, 1994).

29. *The Toronto Star,* 6 August 2002, E11.

30. Stuart Tannock's study of youth grocery workers confirms these findings. He comments that the union is adult-centred and that union representatives are not accessible to young members. See Stuart Tannock, *Youth at Work: The Unionized and Fast-Food and Grocery Workplace* (Philadelphia: Temple University Press, 2001), 131–56.

31. Letter, UFCW National Research Department, August 30, 2002. I would like to thank the research department for providing me with information on the activities of the Women's Advisory Committee.

32. Interview, National Office, February 22, 1995. I am grateful to Debby Da Silva for sharing her interview information with me.

33. That men dominate in decision making was evident at the 1998 UFCW International Union convention where 70 percent of the delegates participating were men. See <http://www.reapinc.org/Briefing%20Papers/Structure%20BP1.htm>. Reviewed on August 14, 2002.

34. On the position of women in Canadian and International unions, see Marina Boehm, *Who Makes the Decisions? Women's Participation in Canadian Unions* (Kingston: Industrial Relations Centre, 1991); Julie White, *Sisters and Solidarity: Women and Unions in Canada* (Toronto: Thompson Educational Press, 1993); and Linda Briskin and Patricia McDermott, eds., *Women Challenging Unions* (Toronto: University of Toronto Press, 1993).

35. At a bargaining conference, the local union president stated, "The only thing I can say to Safeway is this ... if you are coming to British Columbia to pick the same fight you did in Manitoba and Thunder Bay ... you aren't big enough to win a fight with Local 1518 members, and the fight is going to take a whole lot longer than you think." *UFCW.* <http://www.ufcw.1518.com/news/bargaining-2—3/050602-sundin.html>. Reviewed on August 14, 2002.

Chapter Nine

ASSESSING PAY EQUITY AS A LEGAL REFORM STRATEGY

A CENTRAL ARGUMENT made in this book is that pay equity is shaped by a variety of factors — the economy, the law and the social actors involved in equal pay implementation. This chapter investigates the full implications of the pay equity application in the supermarket, taking into account how broader market and social forces influenced the pay equity outcome. It summarizes and expands on specific themes raised in previous chapters beginning with an assessment of how the law affects women's employment situation in a changing economy. Pay equity reform is intended to affect the workplace in economic terms by correcting gender-wage injustices that contribute to gender job segregation and that reinforce labour market segmentation. Did pay equity negotiations earn wage adjustments that challenged the industry or market wages assigned to women? The second theme explored is the ideological struggles over the social definition of women's work, crucial in the fight for equal pay. To what extent did pay equity implementation in the supermarket confront the male norm and gendered images of the "male worker"? A third theme concerns the importance of pay equity implementation in identifying systemic sources of gender-wage discrimination that operate to disadvantage women. Were systemic forms of employment discrimination in the supermarket identified in the pay equity exercise and was redress found to eliminate the source(s) of the gender wage inequity?

A Level Playing Field: The Economy, the Supermarket Industry and Pay Equity Implementation

In the transition from Fordism to post-Fordism, the retail food industry underwent significant changes. While retail expansion, innovation and profitability characterized most of the post-war period up to the 1960s, by the 1970s the supermarket industry experienced increased competitiveness from external retailers, intense internal price competition and decreased consumer demand due to a lower birth rate. By the early 1980s, the emergence of new store formats, competition from fast-food outlets and a major economic recession, urged companies to find new ways of decreasing, or even eliminating, labour in stores. In the 1990s, concession bargaining took hold, with negative results for employees, especially women workers. As we saw, buy-outs at Safeway in Alberta and at Miracle Food Marts in Ontario significantly reduced the percentage of full-time employees at these grocery chains.

Given this background on the economic situation in the food retail trade, we need to consider the importance of the economy and industry dynamics on the pay equity implementation. It scarcely needs to be said that market competition played an important part in how pay equity was applied in Ontario's supermarket sector. When pay equity plans were negotiated in the early 1990s, the competitive structure within food retail in Ontario was well established. The uncertainties that were created in the retail food market raised grave concerns for employers regarding their ability to compete with the independent food retailers, as well as new retail formats such as the warehouse clubs. Companies operating in Ontario were well aware of the need to limit labour costs. Certainly, companies were cognizant of the events that occurred in Alberta with the Safeway chain, and there was concern expressed by supermarkets that wage levels needed to be controlled.

At the time of pay equity negotiations, then, corporate food retail employers were unlikely to be receptive to arguments from retail unions that would lead to an increase in the wage bill. Negotiations concentrated on how pay equity could be implemented within the narrow parameters of Ontario's law that required 1 percent of an employer's total payroll be set aside every year for pay equity purposes. The law was applied to contain the scope and level of pay equity wage adjustments, rather than maximizing its application to improve the wages paid to a greater portion of women. In addition, the tradition of pattern bargaining within the sector established a uniform approach to pay equity — an approach that would not disrupt the competitive business structure within the industry.

Supermarket chains are adamant about maintaining a "level playing field" on which to compete in the marketplace. Once a major food retailer signed-off on a pay equity plan, it was very unlikely that subsequent retailers implementing pay equity would deviate from their approach. In Ontario, retail food employers followed Loblaws' lead when negotiating pay equity. When Loblaws negotiated a plan that excluded pay adjustments to the part-time classification, it was not surprising that other food retailers followed suit. In fact, all of the pay equity plans negotiated by major food retail chains in the province of Ontario did not provide pay adjustments to the part-time workforce, despite provisions in the law that allow job comparison of this group. The rationale for exempting the part-time classification was remarkably uniform across the food retail chains. Both union and non-union supermarket employers argued that gender equivalency in pay was present within the part-time category. A typical explanation concerning the part-time category comes from this manager at the Oshawa Group:

> JK: I am curious about part-timers being one job class. How did you come to that conclusion?

> Manager: We didn't really. We just decided that we wanted to maintain a part-time wage scale that was lower than full-time. And we wanted to keep them all being paid the same so that we had one scale. It was just rationale for administration as well as historically it had just been done that way. And conversations amongst the [Human Resources] group deemed it

would be the most appropriate way to keep equity among part-time employees.[1]

Like the situation at Loblaws, A&P and Miracle Food Mart, retail management at Oshawa also saw the part-time workforce as a separate group in which there "was no possibility of females being paid less than males in any part-time category."[2]

The retail unions also accepted the notion that part-time workers did not require pay adjustments, as a union representative for Loblaws employees explained, "whether you are a meat cutter, a grocery clerk or a cashier you all get the same rate. It was not a problem of a part-time meat cutter getting more than part-time cashier, or a part-time grocery clerk getting more than a part-time cashier."[3] Both management and union perceived the part-time classification as a category unto itself that paid men and women equivalent hourly rates of pay, regardless of job performed. In many instances, there was simply no perception that part-time employees work is undervalued relative to full-time workers, despite the fact that some part-time workers perform exactly the same work as their full-time counterparts. As such, the part-time "issue" centred on pay, not on the value of the work performed. Lower pay for the part-time classification, a well-established industry norm, was not altered as a result of pay equity.

Both the retail unions and the employers understood equity in terms of a formal equality definition. They adopted a "similarly situated" approach in that they explicitly argued that "part-timers can only be compared to part-timers." There was no understanding that the part-time category was a female dominant group that could have been compared with the full-time male dominant category. The logic of union leaders and corporate mangement was that "likes are treated alike." To their way of thinking, all part-timers received the same rate of pay irrespective of gender, and consequently there was no wage inequity. Rather than taking into account the historic systemic discrimination experienced by this feminized group, they understood it strictly in individual terms in which all part-time workers are treated the same — and in their minds, this constituted fairness.

The implementors of pay equity did not understand how part-time women are "differently situated" within the supermarket in comparison with the full-time male dominant workforce. They therefore missed a central dimension of how gender inequality is sustained. An instance of how seemingly neutral work practices can "differently" affect women is the structure of the seniority systems that are especially detrimental to women working part-time. Where seniority operates by department, as at Loblaws, or by separate union local, as at Miracle Food Mart, women in the service classifications are severely restricted from movement and promotion to full-time employment within a supermarket chain (more on this below). While on the surface, the seniority system may appear to function according to neutral principles, the effect of such a system, which serves to segregate men and women onto separate seniority lists, results in unfair treatment of women. The fact that the negotiators in the pay equity implementation accepted the notion that seniority systems are gender-neutral clearly demonstrates an unwillingness or an inability to recognize how seniority operates to disadvantage women in the supermarket.

Further, part-time workers in the supermarket were not viewed as "core members" of the workforce but rather as temporary or irregular participants in the labour market. Their secondary status derives from strongly held ideological views about definitions of the standard employment relationship — a Fordist employment norm that assumes a worker is employed by one employer full-time, full-year over his or her life time. Part-time work does not match commonly held expectations about "normal" standards of job worth — standards based on the notion of the "abstract worker" with its inherent masculine bias.[4] Hence, even though at least 70 percent of grocery workers were employed part-time, the retail unions and management viewed them as somehow separate and marginal to the workplace and the pay equity process.[5]

That employers avoided an enormous cost by arguing that part-timers are paid according to their job worth under the negotiated pay equity plan was another obvious factor. Since corporate stores operate with unionized labour, they must have been concerned about finding ways of containing pay equity in order to be competitive with non-union retailers. From the point of view of the corporate sector, increasing wage rates of part-time employees would have put the corporate stores at a relative disadvantage to retailers paying employees minimum wage. The franchises and independents, which operate with lower wage costs, must have been of particular concern to the corporate chains. It is possible that labour market segmentation within food retail precluded larger employers from establishing equivalency with the full-time category. Even the retail unions may have accepted the employers' position that if part-time workers received wage adjustments, the corporate chains would operate at a competitive disadvantage. A union representative I spoke with argued that pay equity adjustments for part-time employees could produce negative results, such as lay-offs or reduced hours of work. He reasoned that "if part-timers were compared with male-dominated positions, that would, no doubt, in my mind, close a number of retail food stores in the province."[6]

Although this argument may sound compelling, there are important reasons to contradict it. As another union representative pointed out, pay equity did not create "a new monster" within food retail because wage differentials have always existed between the largely unionized corporate and (typically non-union) non-corporate segments within the sector.[7] This union representative acknowledged that industry fragmentation has always existed in food retail, and that employers will use the argument of market segmentation to continue to pay workers a lower wage. As explained in chapter 4, the corporates have been able to devise effective strategies to successfully compete against the independents irrespective of the lower levels of unionization at independent food retailers.

It was incumbent upon retail unions to use pay equity to challenge employers on gender-wage equity. As argued in chapter 7, had the retail unions used the pay equity law to their full advantage, they would have been able to challenge the level of the part-time wage within the industry. For instance, the unions could have negotiated a "true job rate" (see chapter 7) as a means of keeping wage costs down, while still establishing gender-wage equity. It is likely, too, that if one chain successfully negotiated payouts to part-timers, all the major food retail chains would follow, thereby maintaining an "even playing field" within the corporate sector. Despite fragmentation within the industry, it was possible to adjust wages upward for the part-time category. In this way the unions could have established a higher wage standard for the part-time classification and corrected a major source of gender wage inequity within the industry. Because the retail unions were not willing to fight employers on the value of part-time work in the supermarket, pay equity implementation only served to entrench the part-time classification as a low-wage female-predominant category. The unequal position of part-timers in the workforce was reinforced, and segmentation within the industry deepened.

While recognizing that the issue of the part-time classification was problematic in the pay equity implementation, it must also be acknowledged that obtaining adjustments for full-time female-predominant categories was also controversial. Both the job class of head cashier at Loblaws and the position of deli head at the Miracle Food Mart chain were underrated in the job evaluation. Neither one of these positions was seen to be equivalent to the male job class of departmental manager. While the female-predominant job classes performed work with similar duties and responsibilities to those of the classification of male department head, the male comparators used in the pay equity implementation were not in the managerial categories. Ironically, gender stereotypes about the worth of women's work informed the job ratings of the female job classes, thereby reducing the payouts received. In fact, the head cashiers actually lost premium pay based on volume of sales, as a result of the pay equity implementation.

At the Oshawa Group, pay equity implementation in the full-time categories was contentious. A particularly troublesome issue was convincing management of the need to adjust wage rates of full-time cashiers to equal the pay of the full-time grocery clerk, a wage differential of 50 cents per hour. A retail manager, in charge of administering pay equity in a large non-unionized retail division, explains:

... we did percentage banding, and I think it was 7.5 percent up and 7.5 percent down, and [we] grouped the positions within that area and selected the lowest paid male jobs, or the one that we felt was the most appropriate. Cashiers were compared to grocery clerks, while they could have been compared to someone else ... [it] was hell getting a lot of this through because the dinosaurs just didn't understand why a cashier should be paid as much as a grocery clerk. That was the hardest thing with pay equity.[8]

Here we can see that even with banding, which can result in undervaluing of female-predominant jobs (see chapter 3), retail management at Oshawa Foods had difficulty accepting that cashiers perform work of equal value relative to work performed by grocery clerks. Without the persistence and diligence of this particular retail food administrator who pressed management to see the need for gender equivalency in pay between these two job categories, the pay equity adjustments might not have gone through. Like the case of part-time work, we can see how predetermined ideological views about men's and women's work held considerable sway in how pay equity was perceived in the workplace.

In this industry, gender stereotypes of the male and female worker needed to be strenuously challenged in order for pay equity to meet with success. Deli heads and head cashiers had to be seen to be performing managerial labour; part-timers had to be viewed as authentic workers; and cashiers needed to be regarded as performing work of equal value to stock clerks. In effect, the job evaluation process largely failed to critique male standards. Questioning male definitions of work is absolutely critical to the success of the pay equity process. If the evaluators do not accept that women perform work of equal worth to men, then the subjective decision making of the job ratings will remain gender-biased. Alternative perspectives of women's job worth have to be articulated from "below," by the women performing the work, or by feminists advocating pay equity. Proponents of pay equity can use the law to press their demands, for instance by referring to the requirement of gender-neutrality in job comparison, but a feminist viewpoint of the value of women's work must be supported. In this sense, the strategy of equal pay reform is two-dimensional: the goal is economic, but to achieve it, ideological or discursive struggles must be pursued in order to promote economic equality for women. Conversely, if ideological concerns are not central to the struggle, the economic gains will be limited.

Did Pay Equity Work?

Did women in the supermarket "cash in" on pay equity? In this particular instance, pay equity may have actually worked to their detriment. It is very likely that pay equity adjustments urged some retail food corporations, such as Miracle Food Mart, to eliminate the better paying women job classes as a cost-saving measure. Such an outcome raises the issue as to whether gender-specific labour legislation can have uncertain and contradictory effects for women. As discussed in chapter 1, legislation which is intended to "protect" women from discrimination may actually reinforce their subordinate status within the labour market.

When we consider the extent of recent changes in the sector, pay equity reform produced almost meaningless results for a large segment of the retail food workforce. First, it is important to remember that very few employees actually received pay adjustments (e.g., 500 employees out of a bargaining unit of 6,000). Part-time employees received no wage increases, indicating that the market wage was not challenged as a consequence of pay equity policy. This was a serious outcome. If part-time wages had been raised to equal full-time then overall wages could have been lifted; instead, a downward pressure on wage rates followed the pay equity implementation.

Second, not long after the pay equity exercise, a large number of retail workers found themselves working in an entirely new work environment — a work context undergoing restructuring in which wages were reduced, stores were converted to franchises and full-time jobs vanished. In assessing the impact of the pay equity process in the period following implementation, we see contradictory effects of the legislation. Although some women continued to benefit from pay equity adjustments, most notably full-time employees in certain service departments, in particular supermarket chains, other women in supermarkets undergoing restructuring were victim to lay-offs, store closings or suffered reductions in their wages and work conditions. At some supermarket chains, full-time employees who accepted voluntary buy-out packages returned to low-paid part-time jobs. In all of the supermarket chains, part-time workers were subject to lower paying wage scales, and many experienced limitations on the number of hours they were allowed to work. All of these measures obviously affected the level of earnings received by part-time workers, who were disproportionately effected by restructuring. The question of how many women actually were "better off" after pay equity is difficult to determine, but there is every possibility that more women, like the head cashiers at Loblaws who lost their premium volume pay, experienced a deterioration in their conditions of employment, rather than an improvement.

Another outcome of restructuring in retail food has been the erosion of the male wage — the standard by which women's wage equality is measured. As we have seen, wage rates in the sector are declining, and there are fewer and fewer higher paying male predominant jobs in the sector. Ironically, the deterioration in men's full-time employment can make it appear that women are reaching equality with men, when in actual fact it is a situation in which men are simply worse off than they were before.[9] In a sense, everybody is experiencing "bad jobs" and a decline in their earnings. The expansion of part-time employment is especially indicative of the deterioration in employment conditions and wage levels in retail food. Although women still remain predominant in the part-time category, it is likely that more and more men will find themselves working as part-time employees. Supermarket managers increasingly see men as the more flexible worker because they can work at heavy lifting as well as be trained on cash. In these harsh economic times it is possible that women will find it harder to obtain employment, even on a part-time basis, within this sector.

Lastly, the developments surrounding restructuring in the

1990s in Ontario's supermarket retailing sector demonstrate the enormous difficulties of maintaining pay equity. Ontario's *Pay Equity Act* requires employers "to ensure that job rates of female job classes never fall below the male job classes used in achieving pay equity."[10] However, this provision obviously cannot prevent employers from restructuring and eliminating female job classes, creating new jobs with new responsibilities and employment duties or imposing wage reductions on employees. For instance, both the case of Miracle Food Mart, in which female-predominant job classes were eliminated and Dominion stores, which were converted to a discount format and in which a new lower wage schedule for Category II stores was negotiated, do not violate the provision to maintain pay equity in Ontario's legislation.

For pay equity reform to be lasting and produce meaningful results, workers require job security and access to permanent jobs in which pay adjustments will be applied consistently and over a long period of time. Achieving gender-wage fairness can only be accomplished in favourable economic conditions. When employers are reorganizing their operations, downsizing, laying off workers and demanding employees accept wage cut-backs, it is almost impossible to establish gender-wage equity at the workplace.

If substantive equality is to be realized for women and other vulnerable groups, then we have to pay attention to the implications of global economic restructuring on equity policies. Even though male wages continue to be higher than female wages, and male norms of permanent year-round employment continue to prevail, there is evidence that with restructuring, male earnings are declining and contingent work is on the rise.[11] How relevant is a "male standard" when the economy is exerting a downward pressure on male wages and the masculine normative model of employment is disappearing? How can a high standard of equity be measured when more and more jobs are non-standard?

The problem of establishing equity norms is complicated by the fact that under conditions of restructuring we are facing a "moving target" where work sites, jobs (and the people who fill them), corporate structures and state policy are constantly changing. In this economic situation, legislated pay equity is becoming far more difficult to apply as the "traditional model" of pay equity assumes an identifiable and stable employer, a permanent employment relationship and a male breadwinner wage as the basis for job comparison. In the supermarket case there was a historic opportunity in the early 1990s to negotiate pay equity with meaningful results. Now in the twenty-first century, it is questionable whether pay equity could be successful in the new economic conditions where only a handful of full-time permanent male wage jobs exist in supermarkets, the vast majority of workers are in feminized, casualized low-paid employment, and where stores are subject to closure or conversion to new formats. A more comprehensive challenge to the market under neoliberal globalization is needed — an approach that confronts the systemic nature of gender discrimination at the workplace and within the wider society.

Systemic Discrimination: Pay Equity and Employment Equity

While the conditions for confronting gender-based discriminatory wage-setting practices has become more difficult to address under economic restructuring, so too has it become more difficult to confront systemic barriers to equal opportunities in employment. This is the situation in the supermarket concerning women's advancement to full-time employment — the most desirable form of work in the post-Fordist economy.

Policies aimed at removing discriminatory barriers to promotion is referred to in Canada as employment equity, and in the U.S. as affirmative action. Pay equity and employment equity are usually seen as complementary employment policies that promote greater economic equality for women. Pay equity is designed to redress gender-based wage differentials for women as a group; employment equity is an attempt to remove employment barriers that work against equal opportunity for individuals prone to discrimination at the workplace. Although pay and employment equity are often understood to be integrally connected gender employment policies, they have become wrenched apart in the political process of implementing and formulating legislation and other initiatives. As Patricia McDermott explains:

> The tendency [of policy makers] to see unequal pay and discriminatory employment practices as two separate problems, operates to blur the reality of what is occurring and makes solutions fragmented and less effective.[12]

That employment barriers and gender-based wage differentials operate together to produce discriminatory pay for women is evident in the supermarket. The problem of pay discrimination in supermarkets functions on two levels. Women receive unequal pay for work of equal value, as witnessed in the head cashier job classes and the part-time classification (discussed in chapter 7). In addition, women are channelled into low-paying jobs, mostly as cashiers and service clerks, and do not receive training required to advance in a company. The interweaving of these two sources of gender discrimination in pay is clearly illustrated in two well-known cases of sex discrimination in employment: one launched by deli manager Diane Gale in Ontario and the other by cashier Barbara Hall Nuttall in Saskatchewan.

The Struggle for Equal Treatment

In 1985, Diane Gale, an employee of Miracle Food Mart and a member of UFCW Locals 175/633, filed a complaint of sex discrimination in employment at the Ontario Human Rights Commission. Gale alleged that unequal treatment in employment, based on sex, occurs in the chain because of discriminatory hiring, promotion and pay practices at the company. On one level, Gale's case was about streaming women into low-wage occupations and not providing women with equal opportunities to move into better paying positions. On another level, Gale's complaint was about the devaluation of the deli manager position, which she occupied at the chain. The effect of these employment practices at Miracle Food Mart created, and perpetuated, a female job ghetto, in which the lowest paying jobs were held by women.

Discrimination in employment starts the moment women enter a supermarket, and continues for the entire length of time they are employed at a store. The informal work and hiring practices operating in the supermarket makes it extremely difficult for women to enter male-predominant jobs, once they have been hired into service work, as Diane Gale explains:

> What happens, is, if you're female, unless you state otherwise, probably 99 percent of the time they [the company] will train you on cash, if there's an opening. Or, you may get on deli, if you have deli or meat-wrapper experience. Doesn't make any difference, those are the two main departments where all the women work. Cash, or the meat department/deli area. Okay, fine, as long as you're part-time you're doing those jobs. But as soon as you want a full-time job, that's where the discrimination comes in. Because, say, a male has walked in the same time as you, and he's been trained. But he may or may not have been trained on cash, and if he has been trained on cash it's a secondary thing for him. Because he will train on cash until he knows it well enough, but then they put him out on the floor. Brawn, they want muscle, and they don't think women have any muscle, so they will put the guys there. And they will be out on the floor, and they will stock shelves, or work in produce, or in the dairy case ... Of course, once you move to full-time there is this huge wage difference between a simple grocery clerk and head cashier.[13]

Diane Gale's explanation highlights several problems for women seeking better pay in the supermarket. On women's first entry to the store, they are initially hired part-time into female predominant job classifications, making promotion to male predominant job classes very difficult. While all retail food workers must first work in the part-time classification before they are promoted to full-time work, the fact that women are streamed into service clerk jobs, sets up barriers for women who want to enter higher-paying full-time male production jobs. In particular, women are usually denied the opportunity to learn "production skills" required for managerial and other jobs in production departments.

Another problem facing women is the seniority system

within the structure of the bargaining units that segregates part- and full-time employees into separate union locals. Within this particular work setting, there are three separate bargaining units: one local services workers employed full-time in the meat and deli departments (Local 633); another local represents full-time employees in the cash, grocery, produce, dairy and so on (Local 175 Full-Time); while all part-time employees are in a third local (Local 175 Part-Time). When an employee is transferred to a job outside their local, they lose seniority. For instance, a women employed as a full-time cashier (Local 175 FT), who wishes to become trained as a meat cutter, would lose all of her seniority because she would become a member of Local 633. Because of the structure of the union locals and the seniority system, women are systematically disadvantaged in seeking promotion. A concrete solution to the problem of gender disadvantage in relation to seniority, in this particular case, is to amalgamate locals, thereby allowing bargaining unit wide seniority. As Diane Gale explains, "Locals 175/633 should be amalgamated into one local and there's no reason it can't be done. It's just lack of political will. It keeps the union's purpose to keep it that way, and it suits the company."[14]

In 1987, the Ontario Human Rights Commission filed a complaint against the UFCW on Diane Gale's behalf, in part, because of the role of the union and its local structure in preventing women's advancement. But there were other issues. For instance, specific female-predominant jobs such as deli manager and head cashier involve a wide range of skills, but they are paid at low wage rates that do not reflect the level of knowledge and skills required to perform the job. The union did not pursue collective bargaining strategies to remove the historic gender-wage discrimination patterns within the company. As an Ontario Human Rights Commission lawyer points out:

> Joachim said the union was part of the problem because it negotiated a collective agreement that paid women less than men ... Women make up half of its membership yet the union failed to take a leading role in pressing management for an

affirmative action program.[15]

The union was seen to be responsible for negotiating pay differentials that benefit men in production jobs but disadvantage women in service clerk positions. Significantly, pay equity removed the wage differential between full-time production and service clerks, a blatant instance of gender-wage inequality. One can only wonder whether these pay equity adjustments were implemented to avoid disputes at the Human Rights Commission, nor was Diane Gale's complaint the only case filed at the Commission. Between the years 1983 and 1993, around the time of Gale's challenge, a total of seventy-five complaints were opened on behalf of employees at Miracle Food Mart, A&P, Dominion and Loblaws.[16]

Diane Gale's case was ongoing for ten years and was concluded in 1995 by judicial review, without being formally withdrawn. Two unrelated events interrupted the flow of the case. First, Miracle Food Mart, which had been owned by Steinberg Inc., was sold to A&P in 1990. Because Diane Gale had resigned her position as deli manager in 1989, A&P argued that it was not the employer when Gale filed her complaint, and therefore was not responsible for any discrimination that might have taken place. While the Board of Inquiry at the Human Rights Commission concluded that A&P was the proper party before the Board, Gale's case was held up for some time until the issue of liability in the case was determined.[17]

Second, the human rights adjudicator assigned to the case, Constance Backhouse, was ruled by the Ontario Divisional Court as biased because she was one of 120 people who filed a case of sex discrimination with the Commission concerning sexism at Osgoode Hall Law School. As a result of Backhouse's involvement in the Osgoode complaint, "lawyers for the grocery chain and union argued that Backhouse had established herself as an advocate in issues involving sex discrimination and there was reasonable apprehension of bias on her part."[18]

The Divisional Court ruling stopped hearings of Diane Gale's case, and the case was designated inactive by the Commission until it was further reviewed at the level of the Divisional Court. In total there were ten decisions at the Divisional Court regarding the human rights complaint in a period of just two years. This was a very disappointing loss; after ten years of litigation a Board of Inquiry was never appointed to hear her case.

At the same time that Diane Gale's case was proceeding, another important human rights complaint, almost identical to that launched against Miracle Food Mart in Ontario, was filed in Saskatchewan. Unable to make headway at the bargaining table on gender equity, cashier Barbara Hall Nuttall filed a complaint of sex discrimination in employment against her supermarket employer Canada Safeway Limited. With the support of her union, the Retail Wholesale Department Store Union, her class action complaint alleged that cashiers are paid less than stock clerks for work of equal value, and second, that women are given less opportunity for full-time employment than men at the supermarket chain.[19]

This case received considerable media attention, in large part because of the concerted actions of the Pay Equity Coalition of Saskatchewan that was lobbying the government for legislation in the province.[20] Although the case was first filed in 1989, the class action was certified in 1992 and appealed by Safeway 1994. Mr. Justice Kyle ruled that while the complaint of pay equity could proceed as a class complaint, the portion relating to promotion for full-time employment could not.[21] Omitting the employment equity or affirmative action issue was particularly troublesome because the company blocked part-time employees from moving to full-time work by invoking a clause in the collective agreement, as Barbara Nuttall explains:

> Thirty-seven hours [per week] is considered full-time hours. It used to be that you had to work thirteen consecutive weeks at thirty-seven hours. Every week, and you couldn't miss a day. What Safeway would do a lot ... there's two or three girls it's happened a hundred times ... they get up to thirteen weeks, and on the thirteenth week they give thirty-six-and-a-half hours. They never get designated full-time.[22]

Systemic discrimination is evident in employment patterns at Safeway that show very few cashiers working full-time, while a majority of food clerks, deli clerks and managers, who are mostly men, work full-time.[23] Previous efforts by the union to challenge the employer's scheduling practice either through grievance processing or collective bargaining negotiations proved pointless. The union had hoped that by filing a complaint at the Human Rights Commission the problem of promotion to full-time work could be addressed.

Subsequent appeals of the Nuttall case followed with Safeway challenging the authority and the jurisdiction of the the Human Rights Commission to initiate or investigate a pay equity complaint. Canada Safeway Limited further argued that they were being singled out as the only pay equity offender when their competitors in the province paid lower wages to their employees, and the wage disparity between cashiers and food clerks was wider at other chains.[24] In 1999, after ten years of the complaint wending its way through the courts, Mr Justice Wimmer at the Court of Appeal, Queen's Bench, ruled it was within the jurisdiction of the Saskatchewan Human Rights Commission to file a complaint of gender-based pay discrimination and that it had the authority to appoint a Board of Inquiry to investigate it.

At first the Wimmer decision appeared to be a great victory. However, just a few months later (in November 1999) the Human Rights Commission decided, without issuing a statement, that it would not appoint a Board of Inquiry. One reason the Commission chose not to proceed with the complaint was that an agreement had been struck between the union and the company as part of its 1999 contract negotiations. Safeway, along with UFCW, had appealed the Wimmer decision, a decision that would have likely gone to the Supreme Court of Canada. However, at the conclusion of collective bargaining negotiations, Safeway agreed to withdraw their appeal of Wimmer if the RWDSU agreed to petition the Human Rights Commission to end their complaint against Safeway. The union complied with the request because the employer had agreed to close the gender-wage gap between cashiers and food clerks. In June 2000, the remaining 35-cent wage gap was finally closed.

It is puzzling that just at the moment a major legal victory had been won, the union decided to compromise and the Human Rights

Commission stopped legal proceedings. However, it is important to understand the law from a social relations perspective of equality, an approach which emphasizes that legal outcomes are dependent upon the actions of equality seeking groups who are operating within specific socio-economic conditions.

Together, Diane Gale and Barbara Hall Nuttall's human rights complaints represent twenty years of litigation, yet neither case resulted in an investigation of pay equity or affirmative action. These cases illustrate the complexities and contradictions of using the law to promote equality for women and other disadvantaged groups. Although the law recognized that gender-based pay inequities and denial of promotional opportunities for women constitute systemic sex discrimination, the legitimacy of the Human Rights Commissions to investigate the complaints was put into question. The issue of judicial bias arose in the Gale complaint while the question of jurisdiction was raised in the Nuttal complaint. These cases illustrate how employers will use litigation to block or derail the pursuit of gender equity claims. Court appeals seriously prolonged proceedings and required the parties to renew their commitment and mobilize resources to continue litigation. For example, in the Nuttal case the union feared a liability challenge, as the lawyer for the union explains:

> This union, [thought] ... they could be liable ... [they] took that risk throughout this whole thing. To me, that's something that we should be proud of ... that we can defeat the [view] that we're jointly liable. But, the issues were important. They voted constantly to take this forward knowing that risk. Secondly, they fought to make sure that the issue was on behalf of the membership. They refused to let the separation [between men and women] take place.[25]

The Joint Executive Board consistently supported Barbara Hall Nuttall and her claim of sex discrimination and worked diligently to mobilize their membership around the case. It is likely, however, that the the potential costs and commitment associated with a Supreme Court challenge would have heavily taxed union resources had the case moved forward. Similarly, the Saskatchewan Human Rights Commission is seriously under-resourced and may have felt unprepared to undertake a detailed investigation of a large corporation like Canada Safeway.[26] Only the employer was prepared to continue litigating the case up to the Supreme Court of Canada. The willingness of Canada Safeway Limited to pursue legal action is obviously related to its ability to finance the litigation but it also reflects the current business climate in which employers are resisting initiatives aimed at removing sex discrimination in employment. This is particularly evident when low-paid flexible female workers are involved in the legal proceedings as illustrated in recent U.S. cases.

Legal Challenges in the U.S.

The problem of sex discrimination is well known in the American supermarket industry and within retailing generally, and several supermarket chains in the U.S. have been found to discriminate against women and visible minorities in respect of pay and job promotion. For example, an American-based chain located in California, Lucky Stores Inc., was charged with streaming women into lower paying, dead-end jobs, while men were promoted into management positions.[27] Although the company attempted to argue that the gender and racial imbalance in job assignment was due to differences in job interests, the judge did not accept this reasoning, saying "that a company cannot justify different treatment of its male and female workers by claiming that they "wish to be treated differently."[28] The company paid $75 million in damages, effecting 20,000 women employees in 118 stores, while another $380,000 was paid to African-American workers who had charged the company with discrimination against minorities. In addition, Lucky Stores allocated another $20 million in affirmative action programs, as part of the settlement in this class action suit. Following the court action against Lucky Stores, "several similar suits were filed against Safeway, Alberton's and Save Mart."[29]

In 2001, a class action suit was launched against Wal-Mart. Not only is Wal-Mart the world's largest retailer, it is also the largest private sector employer and one of the largest supermarket retailers in the United States.[30] The six women plaintiffs who filed the class action complaint estimate that 700,000 present and former female employees of Wal-Mart represent their "class." They have charged the company with discriminating "against its female employees by advancing male employees more quickly than female employees, by denying female employees equal job assignments, promotions, training and compensation, and by retaliating against those who oppose its unlawful practices."[31]

Over 70 percent of Wal-Mart hourly sales employees are women, but less than 10 percent are store managers and less than 4 percent are district managers. Women are disproportionately assigned to lower-paying positions such as frontend cashier, customer service, health and beauty aids and housewares; men are disproportionately assigned to higher-paying jobs such as stock, sporting goods, guns and hardware. The class action sex discrimination law suit has not concluded but there is growing pressure to settle the complaint as negative media coverage emerges. Since the class action suit was launched, Wal-Mart has paid $140,000 to settle a complaint filed at the Equal Employment Opportunity Commission over its race-based hiring decisions.[32] The United Food and Commercial Workers ongoing national campaign to unionize Wal-Mart stores has also attacted attention to the chain.[33]

Assessing the Litigation Strategy

As these sex discrimination law suits and human rights complaints demonstrate, gender and race discrimination are widespread at the supermarket. These cases also show that wage discrimination is not only confined to pay setting practices alone but also encompasses a wide range of employment practices that operate to keep women's earnings low. Gender divisions and gender-task segregation can mask the practices that produce gender discrimination in employment. This was evident in the seniority system at Miracle Food Mart and in the barriers to women's full-time employment at the Saskatchewan Safeway chain.[34]

Direct forms of discrimination are more apt to be successfully challenged. The fact that the gender-wage gap was closed at Safeway, albeit through collective bargaining, was a tacit recognition by the company that the wage differential was unfair to women and could be successfully litigated at the Human Rights Commission. Similarly, the law suit filed against Lucky Stores is evidence that legal challenges can be won.

However, legal strategies addressing systemic discrimination are often derailed by the tactics of employers who prolong legal proceedings through court challenges. Such tactics wear down and demoralize the plaintiffs who are required under a complaint-based system to file individual complaints:

> Litigation strategies have been widely used by equality agencies and by trade unions, with an emphasis on selecting cases which will have implications for large numbers of women workers and help to clarify points of law ... this strategy is hampered by the absence of collective remedies in the legislation, so that all those wishing to benefit from an equal pay claim have to file separate tribunal applications. For many women, this is a traumatic experience which can cause considerable stress, especially as the complex and cumbersome procedures mean that cases can often take years to resolve.[35]

Although referring to the situation in Europe, the above quotation summarizes the same problems faced by equity advocates in Canada and the U.S. and reinforces the point that confronting gender and racial inequality requires a collective response.

Pay Equity Strategy in a Restructuring Economy

An investigation of pay equity opens a window on the many systemic sources of women's low pay. In the supermarket, we see a workforce rigidly divided by gender where women's work is systematically devalued, a patriarchal union is tied to capital's interests and an intensely competitive industry is undergoing restructuring in which employers are constantly on the search for cheap, flexible female labour. In reviewing the impact of pay equity legislation on the food retail sector, the importance of the economic context is immediately apparent. Struggles around pay equity for women are unlikely to be successful in a declining economy in which companies are undergoing downsizing and restructuring.

The difficulties of implementing pay equity in this economic setting point to the importance of social context in determining the efficacy of equal pay reform. It has become increasingly problematic to rely on a "standard employment relationship" that characterized the Fordist era. In the current transformation to post-Fordism, we face a situation marked by labour market instability. In circumstances of constantly shifting employment conditions, the ability to frame legislation and to carry through on the implementation of pay equity procedures is compromised by an eroding male (wage) standard, by an increasingly tenuous employment relationship and by intensified market competition in which there is a strong emphasis on reducing labour costs.

The problems of implementing pay equity in a restructuring economy are complicated further by the issue of industry fragmentation. In a situation of intensifed competition accompanied by multiplying store formats, the argument by corporate management, such as Safeway, that it is being unfairly targeted by unions demanding pay equity takes on added significance. A legislated approach to pay equity that operates on a worksite-by-worksite basis is wide open to arguments that pay equity adjustments, when applied to some firms but not others, will lead to an "uneven playing field." The issue of applying pay equity across firms or "establishments" to determine an industry-wide standard needs to be further examined and policy recommendations need to be found that can address this limitation.

The problems associated with pay equity implementation at the turn of the twenty-first century have diminished the possibilities that were evident when pay equity legislation was first passed in Ontario. While gender-job segregation and gender-wage differentials continue in the labour market, the ability to confront these realities has changed. The possibilities for pay equity that existed in the supermarket sector even a decade ago no longer hold to the same degree. As mentioned earlier in the chapter, there were real possibilities to achieve gender-wage equity had the unions and corporate management chosen to compare part-time and full-time categories and had the negotiating parties given higher job evaluation scores to key full-time female job classes. In the current environment, the range of possible male comparators has dwindled while the part-time classification has expanded alongside multiple wage tiers. The conditions that would be conducive to successful pay equity outcomes under the legislated pay equity model in Ontario are even more constrained. Moreover, as was amply illustrated in the Barbara Hall Nutall and Wal-Mart cases, corporate management is strongly opposing the advancement of part-time workers into the full-time and better remunerated positions.

The way in which economic restructuring constrains pay and employment equity raises important issues concerning the contradiction between market forces that are creating wage polarization on the one hand, and the goal of greater gender and racial equality in the labour market on the other. This contradiction is happening along two planes: corporations are following discriminatory employment practices that reinforce existing gender and racially based inequalities and the state is pursuing neo-liberal market-driven policies that support labour market flexibility and undermine equity goals.[36] Hence, while corporations have invoked flexible specialization at the level of the workplace, the state has passed labour policies, such as Sunday shopping legislation, that reinforce gender inequities.

To implement pay equity requires a much broader political agenda — one that works in conjunction with a social movement that challenges neo-liberalism and women's disadvantaged position in the labour market and within wider society. In this respect, the need to confront classical liberal notions concerning the market and the individual, which lie at the heart of neo-liberal social policy, is needed more than ever. Just as pay equity advocates identified the market as a key component of the pay equity strategy in the 1980s, so must there continue to be an emphasis on how market forces lead to inequality in the current period of neo-liberalism. The focus by pay equity activists on collective forms of resistance and the systemic sources of inequality must continue to be asserted in the face of the current political orthodoxy that privileges the abstract masculine individual.

In confronting neo-liberalism and its consequences for women, it is imperative that the women's movement continue to oppose the power of capital. There is danger in moving too cautiously, of paying heed to multiple-constituted subjectivities, for instance, while capital marches on exploiting women's low-wage labour in every part of the globe. As a political strategy, it is crucial that women remained united, if political action is to be sustained. The vast majority of women work for pay and their devalued position in the workforce provides the basis for building political identity and political strength.

Pay equity embraces the category of the "woman worker" in order to engage women in political activism. It also relies on women's consciousness of the workplace to challenge male culture. Feminist political mobilizing relies on women having a strong sense of a collective struggle. Pay equity can be a unifying strategy because of its emphasis on how women's work is devalued across a wide range of work places and economic sectors. Any successful pay equity exercise is based on the knowledge and authoritative participation of women workers themselves, and effectively combines the conceptual with the practical. The challenge of pay equity is to build upon the experiences of women and oppose the sanctity of male privilege within the capitalist labour market.

NOTES

1. Interview, Former Pay Equity Administrator at Oshawa Group, June 27, 1992.
2. Ibid.
3. Interview, UFCW Representative, Local 1000A, September 28, 1990.
4. On a discussion of the standard employment relationship, see Leah Vosko, *Temporary Work: The Gendered Rise of a Precarious Employment Relationship* (Toronto: University of Toronto Press, 2000), 24. Vicki Schulz has argued that society views women "as inauthentic workers" because their work patterns deviate from the normative standard. See Vickie Schulz, "Telling Stories About Women

and Work: Judicial Interpretations of Sex Segregation in the Workplace in Title VII Cases Raising the Lack of Interest Argument," in Katharine T. Bartlett and Rosanne Kennedy, eds., *Feminist Legal Theory: Readings in Law and Gender* (Boulder: Westview Press, 1991), 125; Joan Acker, *Doing Comparable Worth: Gender, Class and Pay Equity* (Philadelphia: Temple University Press, 1989), 220–21.

5. For an elaboration on this point , see Jan Kainer, "Pay Equity and Part-Time Work: An Analysis of Pay Equity Negotiations in Ontario Supermarkets," *Canadian Woman Studies* 18, no. 1 (1998), 47–51.

6. Interview, RWDSU Representative, February 19, 1992.

7. Interview, UFCW Representative, Local 1000A, September 28, 1990

8. Interview, Former Manager, Oshawa Foods, June 27, 1992.

9. On the declining male wage see, for example, Judy Fudge, "Fragmentation and Feminization: The Challenge of Equity for Labour-Relations Policy," in Janine Brodie, ed., *Women and Canadian Public Policy* (Toronto: Harcourt Brace, 1996), 64; Barbara Turnbull, "Young Males Losing Ground in Wage Stakes," *The Toronto Star*, 29 July 1998, A2; Margaret Hallock, "Pay Equity: Did It Work?" in Mary King, ed., *Squaring Up: Policy Strategies to Raise Women's Incomes in the United States* (Ann Arbor: University of Michigan Press, 2001), 139.

10. See Pay Equity Commission Newsletter, Vol. 7, No. 1, July 1995.

11. See note 9.

12. Pat McDermott, "Pay and Employment Equity: Why Separate Policies?" in Brodie, ed., Women and Canadian Public Policy, 100.

13. Interview, Diane Gale, June 28, 1993.

14. Ibid., July 2, 1993. On the problem of seniority for women, see Louise Dulude, *Seniority and Employment Equity for Women* (Kingston: Industrial Relations Centre, Queen's University, 1995).

15. The Toronto Star, 22 May 1992, A8.

16. This information was provided to me by the Ontario Human Rights Commission under a Freedom of Information request *(Freedom of Information and Protection of Privacy Act,* FIPPA). The memo was dated November 22, 1993. Of these seventy-five complaints, sixty-three were employment-related complaints, twenty-five cited sex as the grounds for discrimination, and two cited race. Another two cases involved sexual harassment complaints. Except for Diane Gale's case, which has received considerable publicity, the reasons behind the other sex discrimination complaints are not available. It is likely, however, that many involve similar issues concerning access to better paying male-predominant positions or complaints of wage discrimination.

17. Canadian Labour Law Reports, No. 974, August 17, 1992, 6.

18. The Toronto Star, 9 June 1993, A2.

19. The class action complaint represented all cashiers employed or previously employed at Canada Safeway Limited from July 17,1989, when Hall Nuttall initiated the complaint at the Human Rights Commission. The complaint was certified a class action complaint in 1992. (Canada Safeway Limited v. Saskatchewan Human Rights Commission and Barbara Hall.) According to the union representing Barbara Nuttall, the class action represented approximately 3,000 employees. Interview, Barbara Nuttall, December 7, 1997.

20. The Coalition members personally supported Barbara Hall Nuttall throughout her ten-year battle, accompanying her to all court hearings.

21. The Court of Appeal quashed the orginal class complaint, stating that Barbara Hall Nuttall was not a proper representative of her class because, following the birth of her child, she had become a part-time employee at Safeway. Neither discrimination in pay nor the portion related to employment promotion could proceed unless the union as well as the employer were named in the complaint. In response to this court decision, the Human Rights Commission filed a complaint against the Retail Wholesale Department Store union, the UFCW and Safeway corporation. *(Canada Safeway Limited v. Saskatchewan Human Rights Commission and Barbara Hall.)* Safeway subsequently appealed the Human Rights Commission complaint.

22. Interview, Barbara Hall Nuttall, December 7, 1997.

23. Interview, Larry Kowalchuck, Legal Counsel, RWDSU, May 17, 1999.

24. *Canada, Province of Saskatchewan v. Canada Safeway Limited,* Brief of Law On Behalf of Canada Safeway Limited, Affidavit of Jim Witiuk, July 9, 1998, 4–5.

25. Larry Kowalchuck, Legal Counsel, RWDSU, Regina, Saskatchewan May 17, 1999. Unions can be held liable for discrimination under human rights legislation, see. *Renaud v. Central Okanagan District No. 23,* [1992]; *Gohm v. Domtar Inc.* (1990). Cited in Dulude, *Seniority and Employment Equity,* 77–8.

26. See *Renewing the Vision: Human Rights in Saskatchewan. Report of the Saskatchewan Human Rights Commission* (Regina, Saskatchewan, 1996). The report states that "the chronic underfunding of the Saskatchewan Human Rights Commission has reached crisis proportions," 5. The average length of an investigation in 1995 was 404 days while parties typically wait more than a year before their case comes to the attention of the Commission.

27. Gail Sullivan, "Judge Says Discrimination Was 'Standard' Operating Procedure At Lucky Supermarkets," *Labor Notes* (October 1992), 2; *Canadian Grocer* (April 1994), 11.

28. Ibid., note 25. While not explicitly related to gender, the case of Food Lion supermarket chain in the U.S. is indicative of the kind of labour practices that can exist in food retail. Food Lion Inc. was charged with violating labour laws on minimum wages, overtime work, and child labour. A $16.2 million fine was levied by the U.S. Department of Labor, the largest settlement to date, with the majority of funds ($13.2 million) paid to Food Lion employees, *The Globe & Mail,* 4 August, 1993, B12.

29. See Martin Tolich and Celia Briar, "Just Checking It Out: Exploring the Significance of Informal Gender Divisions Amongst American Supermarket Employees," *Gender, Work and Organization* 6, no. 3 (July 1999), 131-32.

30. "Wal-Mart Eyes Supermarket Sweep." *CNN Money.* <http://money.cnn.com/ 2002/06/06news/supermarkets/index/.htm .>

31. "Nationwide Sex Discrimination Case Against Wal-Mart To Stay in California." <http://walmart.walmartclass.com/clients/walmart/press_releases/ 2001-12-04-43382.html.> December 4, 2001. This class action suit was filed June 19, 2001, under Title VII of the *Civil Rights Act* of 1964. Five of the six plaintiffs requested and received "a right to sue letter" from the Equal Employment Opportunities Commission.

32. "Wal-Mart to Pay $140,000 to Settle Charge of Race-Based Job Assignments in Richmond." <http://www.walmartworkersslv.com/news/2002nationwide/retaliation_race_feb_11_2002.htm>.

33. Wal-Mart Workers National Campaign. <http://www.walmartworkersslv.com/news/2002nationwide_feb_11_2002.htm>.

34. Also see Tolich and Briar, "Just Checking It Out," 133. Jeanne Gregory, Ariane Hegewishch and Rosemary Sales, eds., Women, Work and Inequality: The Challenge of Equal Pay in a Deregulated Market (New York: MacMillan Press, 1999), explain that in the U.K. promotion for Black employees has been problematic where subjective appraisals have come into play, 9–10.

35. Gregory, Hegewisch and Sales, eds., Women, Work and Inequality, 7.

36. Ibid, 1–24.

Appendix A

Table A.1

Average Weekly Earnings of Food Store Employees, Ontario

Year	Food Store Employees Weekly $	Industrial Aggregate
1983	225.62	376.57
1984	226.34	395.72
1985	231.51	414.47
1986	234.79	433.35
1987	236.51	453.80
1988	254.95	477.70
1989	256.26	505.11
1990	261.44	526.81
1991	278.62	553.92
1992	270.71	576.85
1993	282.22	589.55
1994	297.77	604.79
1995	291.21	610.29
1996	286.15	625.71
1997	286.79	638.97
1998	304.52	646.78
1999	312.58	651.55
2000	304.87	669.21

Source: Annual Estimates of Employment, Earnings and Hours, 1971, 1983-2000, Statistics Canada. Cat. No. 72-002 and CANSIM — Series Number V283556. Estimates of Average Weekly Earnings [including overtime] All Employees, Firms of All Sizes, by Industry, Canada, Provinces and Territories.

APPENDIX B

TABLE B.1

Percentage Distribution of Employment in Retail Trade by Age and Sex, Ontario, 2001

Age	Male	Female	Both Sexes
15-24	15.0%	17.0%	32.0%
25-44	17.6%	23.2%	40.8%
45+	12.6%	14.6%	27.2%
ALL AGES	45.2%	54.8%	100.0%

Source: Labour Force Survey Special Tabs, Statistics Canada, Annual Averages Reference Number R87018A

TABLE B.2

Percentage Distribution of Part-Time Employment* in Retail Trade by Age and Sex, Ontario, 2001

Age	Male	Female	Both Sexes
15-24	25.9	33.6	59.5
25-44	3.5	19.2	22.7
45+	3.6	14.1	17.7
ALL AGES	33.1	66.9	100.0

Source: Labour Force Survey Special Tabs, Statistics Canada, Annual Averages Reference Number R87018A

*Part-Time employment is defined as less than 30 hours of work per week.

Table B.3

Percentage Distribution of Part-Time Employment in All Industries by Age and Sex, Ontario, 2001

Age	Male	Female	Both Sexes
15-24	17.4	22.5	39.8
25-44	6.2	26.4	32.6
45+	7.7	19.9	27.6
ALL AGES	31.3	68.7	100.0

Source: Labour Force Survey Special Tabs, Statistics Canada, Annual Averages Reference Number R87018A

Table B.4

Share of Part-Time Employment in Retail Trade* By Age and Sex, Ontario, 2001

Age	Male	Female	Both Sexes
15-24	64.1	73.5	69.1
25-44	7.5	30.7	20.7
45+	10.8	35.8	24.2
ALL AGES	27.2	45.4	37.2

Source: Labour Force Survey Special Tabs, Statistics Canada, Annual Averages Reference Number R87018A

*Part-Time employment is defined as less than 30 hours of work per week.

TABLE B.5

*Share of Part-Time Employment in All Industries
By Age and Sex, Ontario, 2001*

Age	Male	Female	Both Sexes
15-24	41.2	54.2	47.6
25-44	4.0	19.3	11.1
45+	7.5	23.6	14.8
ALL AGES	10.4	26.2	17.9

Source: Labour Force Survey Special Tabs, Statistics Canada,
Annual Averages Reference Number R87018A

TABLE B.6

*Ontario Retail Sector, 2001
Part-Time/Full-Time Employment Status of Women
as Percentage of Total Retail Workforce*

Age	Total	Full-Time	Part-Time
All Ages	54.8	47.7	66.9
15-19	52.0	40.8	53.8
20-24	54.5	47.1	62.9
25-34	53.8	47.5	78.0
35-44	59.4	51.4	89.8
45-54	54.9	46.8	85.9
55-64	52.7	43.4	79.4
64 +	47.9	39.9	54.4

Source: Labour Force Survey Special Tabs, Statistics Canada,
Annual Averages Reference Number R87018A

TABLE B.7

Locals 175/633, Miracle Food Mart Full-Time
Weekly Wage Rates Effective June 22, 1987–June 21, 1988

Classification	Start Rate	End Rate	Gender Predominance
Production Clerk	275.20	506.77	Male
Service Clerk	263.97	478.47	Female
Bookkeeper	487.74	500.34	Female
Deli Manager	272.39	488.12	Female
Grocery/Produce Manager	518.01	553.07	Male
Night Production Foreman	511.85	546.64	Male
Assistant Meat Manager	563.36	563.36	Male
Meat Manager	574.33	591.01	Male
Meat Cutter	286.42	591.07	Male
Bakery Manager	536.48	572.36	Male

Appendix C

Table C.1

Neutralizer's Evaluation System, Grocery Manager Results

Class Name: Grocery Manager   Points: 172.4
General Weights:
Skill: 35   Responsibility: 35
Effort: 15   Working Conditions: 15

Score	Sub Factor Points	Label
		SKILL
5.0	20.0	Pre-employment Education and Training
15.0	20.0	On the Job Experience and Training
15.0	20.0	Interaction with Others
10.0	20.0	Decision-Making
10.0	20.0	Motor Skills
		EFFORT
5.0	20.0	Moving and Concentration
5.0	20.0	Lifting and Carrying
15.0	20.0	Cost of Errors
5.0	20.0	Social Disruption Required by Work Scheduling
10.0	20.0	External Contacts
		RESPONSIBILITIES
12.0	20.0	Manage or Direct Others
10.0	20.0	Information Responsibilities
1.0	20.0	Responsibilities for Machines or Equipment
10.0	20.0	Financial Responsibilities
15.0	20.0	Degree of Independence
		WORKING CONDITIONS
1.0	20.0	Temperature Variation from Comfort Level
1.0	20.0	Noise Conditions
3.0	20.0	Work Interruptions and Distractions
1.0	20.0	Nature of Supervision
1.0	20.0	Hazards

TABLE C.2

Loblaws, Local 1000A Pay Equity Adjustments

Full-Time Female Job Class	$ Hourly Wage Adjustment	$ Yearly Wage Adjustment
Meat Wrapper Nights	.58	1,117
Floral Clerk Designer	.35	674
Bakery Service Clerk	.58	1,117
Bake-off Production Days	.81	1,558
Full-Time Service Clerk	.58	1,117
Full-Time Decorator	.46	886
Meat Wrapper Days	.58	1,117
Full-Time Cashier	.58	1,117
Floral Manager	.19	366
Backup Head Checker	.62	1,212
Head Cashier Vol 1-4	.33	635

GLOSSARY

EQUAL PAY FOR EQUAL WORK: Requires women to be paid at the same rate of pay as men for performing identical or substantially similar work.

EQUAL PAY FOR WORK OF EQUAL VALUE: Requires women to be paid at the same rate of pay as men for performing equivalent work, as determined by a job comparison system. Women do not have to perform the same jobs as men to be compared.

PAY EQUITY: Refers to any process that is based on the principle of equal pay for work of equal value. In the United States, the term comparable worth is synonymous with pay equity.

Terms in the Ontario Pay Equity Act, 1987

ESTABLISHMENT: An establishment is defined as all of the employees of an employer working in a geographic division (or divisions if agreed upon by employer and bargaining agent). A geographic division refers to a county, territorial district or regional municipality. Pay equity plans must be prepared for each employer's establishment. Determining the establishment is therefore important for knowing how many pay equity plans are required.

EMPLOYER: The term employer is not defined in the *Pay Equity Act.* The concept of employer is nevertheless critical to implementing pay equity. The employer definition determines the relevant establishment(s) and any employer relationships with one or more corporate entities (eg. franchises). In addition, knowing who the employer is will determine the size of payroll.

JOB CLASS: Defined as positions, which have similar duties and responsibilities and require similar qualifications, that are filled by similar recruiting procedures and have the same compensation schedule, salary grade or range of salary grades. Jobs or positions must be put into different job classes in order to determine which are female and male job classes.

GROUPS OF JOBS: The employer can unilaterally combine job classes to form a group of jobs, under the following circumstances: (i) there is a series of job classes (for example, there are 3 levels to a secretarial job); (ii) the jobs bear a relationship to one another; (iii) the nature of the work in each job class is similar; (iv) the series is organized in successive levels; (v) the entire series is 60 percent female. Only women's jobs can be combined to form a group of jobs. Also, the level with the largest number of employees becomes the representative job class for purposes of evaluation and comparison.

GENDER PREDOMINANCE: All jobs within an establishment are classified as belonging to (i) a female job class; (ii) a male job class; or (iii) a gender-neutral job class (in which neither males nor females predominate). Gender predominance is determined by percentage cut-off, historical incumbency or gender stereotype.

A job class is a female-predominant job class if 60 percent or more female employees comprise the job class. A job class is a male-predominant job class if 70 percent or more male employees comprise the job class.

A job class can be deemed to be female-predominant or male-predominant if the job class has been historically performed by men or women. If a job class traditionally has been performed by men or women, it may be recognized as stereotypically male or female. The percentage cut-off does not have to be present in the situation of historical incumbency or gender stereotype.

VALUE DETERMINATION: The criterion to be applied in determining the value of work. The compensable factors include skill, effort, responsibility and work conditions.

JOB COMPARISON: A job comparison system is typically referred to as job evaluation. There are a variety of job evaluation systems or methods available to compare the relative worth of jobs including: ranking (simple ranking procedure listing jobs in hierarchical order); point methods (in which jobs are assigned points in reference to compensable elements in a job); bench marks (a typical job in a classification is used as a marker or benchmark and becomes the standard to compare other jobs)

Job classes in a bargaining unit are compared with job classes within that bargaining unit. If a comparable job class cannot be found within the bargaining unit, a comparator can be sought outside the bargaining unit.

In a situation where there are a number of value matches, the employer is required to adjust the female job class up to the male job class of comparable value, but with the lowest job rate.

GENDER-NEUTRAL: Gender neutrality is not defined in the Act. However, job comparison systems used to detemine pay equity must be gender-neutral. Any system currently in place, or used for comparison purposes, must be examined for gender neutrality or gender bias.

JOB RATE: Job rate is defined as the highest rate of compensation for a job class. The Act allows the employer to exclude the highest rate of compensation under the permissable exemptions including (i) the highest job rate is due to the presence of a formal seniority system; (ii) the job class is a temporary training program; (iii) the highest job rate is based on a merit compensation system; (iv) the employer red-circles the job rate; (v) the employer argues there is a skills shortage and the highest job rate is only temporary to attract workers.

RED CIRCLE RATE: A term used to describe a management decision to maintain a higher job wage rate for an employee (or employees) than is normally paid to workers in the position. Red circling can be used to protect workers who can no longer perform a job due to illness or because of deskilling or removal of job responsibilities.

SELECTED BIBLIOGRAPHY

Acker, Joan. *Doing Comparable Worth: Gender, Class and Pay Equity.* Philadelphia: Temple University Press, 1989.

———. "Hierarchies, Jobs, Bodies: A Theory of Gendered Organizations." *Gender and Society* 4, no. 2 (1990): 139–58.

Andrew, Caroline, and Sanda Rodgers. *Women and the Canadian State.* Kingston: McGill-Queen's, 1997.

Armstrong, Pat, and Hugh Armstrong. "Lessons from Pay Equity." *Studies in Political Economy* 32 (1990): 29–55.

———. "Limited Possibilities and Possible Limits for Pay Equity: Within and Beyond the Ontario Legislation." In Judy Fudge and Patricia McDermott, eds. *Just Wages: A Feminist Assessment of Pay Equity.* Toronto: University of Toronto Press, 1991.

Armstrong, Pat. "Pay Equity: Not Just a Matter of Money." In Caroline Andrew and Sanda Rodgers, eds. *Women and the Canadian State.* Kingston: McGill-Queen's, 1997.

Armstrong, Pat, and Mary Cornish. "Restructuring Pay Equity for a Restructuring Work Force: Canadian Perspectives." *Gender, Work and Organization* 4, no. 2 (1997): 67–86.

Bakker, Isabella. "Pay Equity and Economic Restructuring: The Polarization of Policy?" In Patricia McDermott and Judy Fudge., eds. *Just Wages: A Feminist Assessment.* Toronto: University of Toronto Press, 1991.

Baret, Christophe, Steffen Lehndorff, and Leigh Sparks. *Flexible Working in Food Retailing: A Comparison between France, Germany, the United Kingdom and Japan.* London: Routledge, 2000.

Barndt, Deborah, ed. *Women Working the NAFTA Food Chain: Women, Work and Globalization.* Toronto: Second Story Press, 1999; now available from Sumach Press, Toronto.

———. *Tangled Routes: Women, Work and Globalization on the Tomato Trail.* New York: Rowman and Littlefield Publishers, 2002.

Bartlett, Katherine, and Roseanne Kennedy, eds. *Feminist Legal Theory: Readings in Law and Gender.* Boulder: Westview Press, 1991.

Blum, Linda. *Between Feminism and Labor: The Significance of the Comparable Worth Movement.* Berkeley: University of California Press, 1991.

Bose, Christine, and Glenna Spitze, eds. *Ingredients for Women's Employment Policy.* Albany: State University of New York, 1987.

Bottomley, Anne, and Joanne Conaghan, eds. *Feminist Theory and Legal Strategy.* Oxford: Blackwell, 1993.

Boyd, Susan, and Elizabeth Sheehy. "Feminism and the Law in Canada: Overview." In Tullio Caputo et. al., eds. *Law and Society: A Critical Perspective.* Toronto: Harcourt Brace Janovich, 1989.

Brenner, Johanna. "Feminist Political Discourses: Radical Versus Liberal Approaches to the Feminization of Poverty and Comparable Worth." *Gender and Society* 1, no. 4 (1987): 447–65. Also reprinted in Karen Hansen and Ilene Philipson, eds. *Women, Class, and the Feminist Imagination.* Philadelphia: Temple University Press, 1990.

Briskin, Linda. "The Equity Project in Canadian Unions: Confronting the Challenge of Restructuring and Globalisation." In Fiona Colgan and Sue Ledwith, eds. *Gender, Diversity and Trade Unions.* London: Routledge, 2002.

—— and Patricia McDermott. *Women Challenging Unions.* Toronto: University of Toronto Press, 1993.

Brodie, Janine. *Politics on the Margins: Restructuring and the Canadian Women's Movement.* Halifax: Fernwood Publishing, 1995.

——, ed. *Women and Canadian Public Policy.* Toronto: Harcourt Brace, 1996.

Burke, Mike, Colin Mooers, and John Shields, eds. *Restructuring and Resistance: Canadian Public Policy in an Age of Global Capitalism.* Halifax: Fernwood Publishing, 2000.

Burton, Clare. *The Promise and the Price: The Struggle for Equal Opportunity in Women's Employment.* North Sydney, AUS: Allen and Unwin, 1991.

Cain, Patricia. "Feminism and the Limits of Equality," Reprinted in D. Kelly Weisberg, ed. *Feminist Legal Theory: Foundations.* Philadelphia: Temple University Press, 1993. First printed in 24 *Ga. L. Rev.* 803 (1990).

Chaykowski, Richard, and Lisa Powell, eds., *Women and Work.* Montreal: McGill-Queen's University Press, 1999.

Cobble, Dorothy Sue, ed. *Women and Unions: Forging a Partnership.* Ithaca, NY: ILR Press, 1993.

Conaghan, Joanne. "Reassessing the Feminist Theoretical Project in Law." *Journal of Law and Society* 27, no. 3 (September 2000): 351–85.

Cornish, Mary. *Equal Pay, Collective Bargaining and the Law.* Prepared for the Department of Labour. Ottawa: Minister of Supply and Services, 1986.

Cornish, Mary, and Lynn Spink. *Organizing Unions.* Toronto: Second Story Press, 1994.

Creese, Gillian. "Gender Equity or Masculine Privilege? Union Strategies and Economic Restructuring in a White Collar Union." *Canadian Journal of Sociology* 20, no. 2 (1995): 143-66.

———. *Contracting Masculinity: Gender, Class and Race in a White-Collar Union, 1944-1994.* Toronto: Oxford University Press, 1999.

Cuneo, Carl. *Pay Equity: The Labour-Feminist Challenge.* Toronto: Oxford University Press, 1990.

Dua, Enakshi, and Angela Robertson eds., *Scratching the Surface: Canadian Anti-Racist Feminist Thought*. Toronto: Women's Press, 1999.

Drolet, Marie. *The Persistant Gap: New Evidence on the Canadian Gender Wage Gap*. Ottawa: Statistics Canada, Business and Labour Market Analysis Division, January 2001.

Duffy, Ann, and Norene Pupo. *Part-Time Paradox: Connecting Gender, Work and Family*. Toronto: McClelland and Stewart, 1992.

————. "Ambivalence or Apprehension? The Labor Movement and the Part-Time Worker in Canada." In Barbara Warme, Katharina Lundy and Larry Lundy, eds. *Working Part-Time: Risks and Opportunities*. New York: Praeger, 1992.

Dulude, Louise. *Seniority & Employment Equity for Women*. Kingston: McGill-Queen's University: Industrial Relations Centre, 1995.

Egri, Carolyn, and W. T. Sanbury. "How Pay Equity Legislation Came to Ontario." *Canadian Public Administration/Administration Publique du Canada* 32, no. 2 (1989): 274-303.

Evans, Sara, and Barbara Nelson. *Wage Justice: Comparable Worth and the Paradox of Technocratic Reform*. Chicago: University of Chicago Press, 1989.

Eyraud, Francois et al. *Equal Pay Protection in Industrialised Market Economies: In Search of Greater Effectiveness*. Geneva: International Labour Organisation, 1993.

Forrest, Ann. "Pay Equity: The State of the Debate." In Yonatan Reshef, Colette Bernier, Denis Harrisson and Terry Wagar, eds. *Industrial Relations in a New Millenium: Selected Papers from the XXXVII Annual CIRA Conference*. Laval: ACRI/CIRA, 2001.

Fudge, Judy, and Patricia McDermott, eds. *Just Wages: A Feminist Assessment of Pay Equity*. Toronto: University of Toronto Press, 1991.

————. "Limiting Equity: The Definition of 'Employer' under the Ontario Pay Equity Act." *Canadian Journal of Women and the Law* 4 (1991): 556-63.

————. "Fragmentation and Feminization: The Challenge of Equity for Labour-Relations Policy." In Janine Brodie, ed. *Women and Canadian Public Policy*. Toronto: Harcourt Brace and Company, Canada, 1996.

————. "The Paradoxes of Pay Equity: Reflections on the Law and the Market in Bell Canada and the Public Service Alliance of Canada." *Canadian Journal of Women and the Law* 12 (2000): 313-44.

Gabriel, Christina. "Restructuring at the Margins: Women of Colour and the Changing Economy." In Enakashi Dua and Angela Robertson, eds. *Scratching the Surface: Canadian Anti-Racist Feminist Thought*. Toronto: Women's Press, 1999.

Galabuzi, Grace-Edward. *Canada's Creeping Economic Apartheid: The Economic Segregation and Social Marginalisation of Racialised Groups*. Toronto: Canadian Centre for Social Justice, 2001.

Glazer, Nona. *Women's Paid and Unpaid Labor: The Work Transfer in Health Care and Retailing*. Philadelphia: Temple University Press, 1993.

Gregory, Jeanne, Sales, Rosemary and Ariane Hegewisch, eds. *Women, Work and Inequality*. London: Macmillan Press, 1999.

Hadley, Karen. *"And We Still Ain't Satisfied":Gender Inequality in Canada, A Status Report for 2001*. Toronto: National Action Committee on the Status of Women; CSJ Foundation for Research and Education, June 2001.

Handman, Suzanne, and Karen Jensen. "Pay Equity in Canada: An Overview." *Canadian Labour and Employment Law Journal* 7 (1999), 65–89.

Hallock, Margaret. "Unions and the Gender Wage Gap." In Dorothy Sue Cobble, ed. *Women and Unions: Forging a Partnership*. Ithaca, NY: ILR Press, 1993.

Hinton, Louisette, Josefina Moruz, and Cheryl Mumford. "A Union Perspective on Emerging Trends in the Workplace." In Isik Urla Zeytinoglu, ed. *Changing Work Relationships in Industrialized Economies*. Philadelphia: John Benjamins Publishing Co., 1999.

Jhappan, Radha. "The Equality Pit or the Rehabilitation of Justice." *Canadian Journal of Women and the Law* 10 (1998), 60–107.

Kainer, Jan. "Pay Equity Strategy and Feminist Legal Theory: Challenging the Bounds of Liberalism." *Canadian Journal of Women and the Law* 8, no. 2 (1995): 440-69.

———. "Gender, Corporate Restructuring and Concession Bargaining in Ontario's Food Retail Sector." *Industrial Relations/Relations Industrielles* 53, no.1, (1998): 183–205.

Kessler-Harris, Alice. *A Woman's Wage: Historical Meanings and Social Consequences*. Lexington: University of Kentucky Press, 1990.

King, Mary, ed. *Squaring Up: Policy Strategies to Raise Women's Incomes in the United States*. Ann Arbor: University of Michigan Press, 2001.

Kline, Marlee. "Race, Racism, and Feminist Legal Theory." Reprinted in D. Kelly Weisberg, ed., *Feminist Legal Theory: Foundations*. Philadelphia: Temple University Press, 1993. First printed 12 *Harv. Women's L.J.* 115 (1989).

Lewis, Debra. *Just Give Us the Money: A Discussion of Wage Discrimination and Pay Equity*. Vancouver: Women's Research Centre, 1988.

MacKinnon, Catharine. "Difference and Dominance: On Sex Discrimination." Reprinted in D. Kelly Weisberg, ed. *Feminist Legal Theory: Foundations*. Philadelphia: Temple University Press, 1993. First printed in *Feminism Unmodified*. Cambridge: Harvard University Press, 1987.

———. *Toward a Feminist Theory of the State*. Cambridge: Harvard University Press, 1989.

Mayo, James. *The American Grocery Store: The Business Evolution of an Architectural Space*. Westport, CT: Greenwood Press, 1993.

McCann, Michael. *Rights at Work: Pay Equity Reform and the Politics of Legal Mobilization*. Chicago: University of Chicago Press, 1994.

McDermott, Patricia. "Pay Equity in Ontario: A Critical Legal Analysis." *Osgoode Hall Law Journal* 28, no. 2 (1990): 381-407.

———. "Pay and Employment Equity: Why Separate Policies?" In Janine Brodie, ed. *Women and Canadian Public Policy*. Toronto: Harcourt Brace and Company, Canada, 1996.

———. "Pay Equity: Lessons from Ontario, Canada." In Jeanne Gregory, Rosemary

Sales, and Ariane Hegewisch, eds. *Women, Work and Inequality.* London: Macmillan Press, 1999.

McDowell, Linda. "Gender Divisions in a Post-Fordist Era: New Contradictions or the Same Old Story?" In Linda McDowell and Rosemary Pringle, eds. *Defining Women: Social Insitutions and Gender Divisions.* Cambridge: Polity Press, 1992.

Morgan, Rosemary. "Pay Equity by Law: Is There a Better Way to Equality of Result for Female Faculty?" In Susan Heald, ed. *Ivory Towers, Feminist Issues: Selected Papers from the WIN Symposia, 2000-01.* Ottawa: Humanities and Social Sciences Federation of Canada, 2002.

Morris, Anne, and Therese O'Donnell. *Feminist Perspectives on Employment Law.* London: Cavendish Publishing, 1999.

Murphy, Marie. "Pay Equity in Quebec." In Caroline Andrew and Sanda Rodgers, *Women and the Canadian State.* Kingston: McGill-Queen's, 1997.

Nelson, Robert, and William Bridges. *Legalizing Gender Inequality: Courts, Markets, and Unequal Pay for Women in America.* Cambridge: Cambridge University Press, 1999.

Pateman, Carol. *The Disorder of Women: Democracy, Women and Political Theory.* Cambridge: Polity Press, 1989.

Quaid, Maeve. *Job Evaluation: The Myth of Equitable Assessment.* Toronto: University of Toronto Press, 1993.

Razack, Sherene. *Canadian Feminism and the Law: The Women's Legal Action Fund and the Pursuit of Equality.* Toronto: Second Story Press, 1991; now available from Sumach Press, Toronto.

Remick, Helen, ed. *Comparable Worth and Wage Discrimination: Technical Possibilities and Political Realities.* Philadelphia: Temple University Press, 1984.

Rhode, Deborah. *Justice and Gender: Sex Discrimination and the Law.* Cambridge: Harvard University Press, 1989.

Schick, Carol. "Keeping the Ivory Tower White: Discourses of Racial Domination." In Sherene Razack, ed. *Race, Space, and the Law: Unmapping a White Settler Society.* Toronto: Between the Lines, 2002.

Seth, Andrew, and Geoffrey Randall. *The Grocers: The Rise and the Rise of the Supermarket Chains.* London: Kogan Page, 1999.

Smart, Carol. *Feminism and the Power of Law.* New York: Routledge Press, 1989.

Steinberg, Ronnie. "Job Evaluation and Managerial Control: The Politics of Technique and the Techniques of Politics." In Patricia McDermott and Judy Fudge, eds. *Just Wages: A Feminist Assessment.* Toronto: University of Toronto Press, 1991.

———. "Gendered Instructions: Cultural Lag and Gender Bias in the Hay System of Job Evaluation." *Work and Occupations* 19, 4 (1992): 387–423.

Sugiman, Pamela. *Labour's Dilemma: The Gender Politics of Auto Workers in Canada, 1937-1979.* Toronto: University of Toronto Press, 1994.

Sullivan, Nancy. "Pay Equity in Manitoba." In Caroline Andrew and Sanda Rodgers, *Women and the Canadian State.* Kingston: McGill-Queen's, 1997.

Tannock, Stuart. *Youth at Work: The Unionized Fast-Food and Grocery Workplace.* Philadelphia: Temple University Press, 2001.

Todres, Elaine. "With Deliberate Care: The Framing of Bill 154." *Manitoba Law Journal* 16, 3 (1987): 221–26.

Vosko, Leah. *Temporary Work: The Gendered Rise of a Precarious Employment Relationship.* Toronto: University of Toronto Press, 2000.

Walsh, John. *Supermarkets Transformed: Understanding Organizational and Technological Innovations.* New Brunswick, NJ: Rutgers University Press, 1993.

Warskett, Rosemary. "Wage Solidarity and Equal Value: Or Gender and Class in the Structuring of Workplace Hierarchies." *Studies in Political Economy* 32 (1990): 55–83.

Warskett, Rosemary. "Political Power, Technical Disputes, and Unequal Pay: A Federal Case." In Judy Fudge and Patricia McDermott, eds. *Just Wages: A Feminist Assessment of Pay Equity.* Toronto: University of Toronto Press, 1991.

Warskett, Rosemary. "Can a Disappearing Pie Be Shared Equally? Unions, Women and Wage Fairness." In Linda Briskin and Patricia McDermott, eds. *Women Challenging Unions: Feminism, Democracy and Militancy.* Toronto: University of Toronto Press, 1993.

Weisberg, Kelly D. *Feminist Legal Theory: Foundations.* Philadelphia: Temple University Press, 1993.

White, Julie. *Trouble in Store? The Impact of Microelectronics in the Retail Trade.* Ottawa: The Women's Bureau, 1998.

White, Julie. *Sisters & Solidarity: Women and Unions in Canada.* Toronto: Thompson Educational Publishing, 1993.

Williams, Patricia. *The Alchemy of Race and Rights.* Cambridge: Harvard University Press, 1991.

Williams, Wendy. "The Equality Crisis: Some Reflections on Culture, Courts, and Feminism." Reprinted in Katherine T. Bartlett and Rosanne Kennedy, eds. *Feminist Legal Theory: Readings in Law and Gender.* Boulder: Westview Press, 1989. First Printed in 7 *Women's Rights L. Rptr.* 175 (1982).

Wood, Stephen, ed. *The Transformation of Work? Skill, Flexibility and the Labour Process.* London: Unwin Hyman, 1989.

Yates, Charlotte. *Making It Your Economy: Unions and Economic Justice.* Toronto: The CSJ Foundation for Research and Education, 2001.

Zeytinoglu, Isik Urla. "Women Workers and Working Conditions in Retailing: A Comparative Study of the Situation in a Foreign-Controlled Retail Enterprise and a Nationally Owned Retailer in Canada." Geneva: International Labour Office, 1997.

———. ed. *Changing Work Relationships in Industrialized Economies.* Philadelphia: John Benjamins Publishing Co., 1999.

INDEX

concession bargaining, 155–59
    resistance to, 225–27, 229–30
convenience stores, 118–19
Cooney, Patricia, 29
Cornish, Mary, 87
Costco, 147
Creese, Gillian, 68
Cuneo, Carl, 89
CUPE. *See* Canadian Union of Public
    Employees

Depression. *See* Great Depression
Direct Product Profitability (DPP), 153
discount stores, 146–49
discrimination. *See* systemic discrimina-
    tion
Dominion Stores, 112. *See also* A&P
    buy-outs at, 221–22
    concession bargaining with, 156
    part-time employment in, 176
    pay equity at, 206–11, 244
    union representation in, 132, 133
    downsizing, 155–56

economy. *See* Fordism; market; post-
    Fordism
    restructuring of, 69–70, 143–46,
        255–58
    and supermarket industry, 235–42
Edwards case, 145
Efficient Consumer Response (ECR),
    153
Employment Standards Act (Ontario),
    82–83, 144–45
Equal Employment Opportunity
    Commission (U.S.), 254
equality
    versus difference, 24–27, 51–52
    legislation about, 25–27, 245–46
    standards for, 80–83
Equal Pay Coalition (Ontario), 87–88,
    90, 96
establishment definition, 91, 96,
    190–91
Europe, 61
Evans, Sara, 52

family allowance, 135
Federated Co-operatives Limited,
    155–56

Federation of Women Teachers'
    Associations of Ontario, 87
Female Employees Equal Pay Act
    (1956), 81
First World War, 78–79, 113–14
Food Basics, 112, 133. *See also* A&P
Food For Less, 156
Foodland, 111. *See also* Sobey's
food retailing, 113–26. *See also* meat
    departments; supermarkets
    deskilling of jobs in, 116–18
    female workers in, 115–16
    feminization of work in, 116–18,
        120
    labour unions in, 134–43
    male workers in, 116–17
    self-service in, 113–16
    technological change in, 114, 116,
        117, 121–25, 141–42
Fordism, 134–43. *See also* economy;
    post-Fordism
Fortinos, 111
Foucault, Michel, 37–39
franchises, 149–52, 221–22
Fudge, Judy, 63–64, 70, 99
full-time employment
    and collective agreements, 157–59,
        248
    at Loblaws, 189–90
    at Miracle Food Mart, 176, 202–4,
        219–20
    for part-time workers, 181–82
    and pay equity, 240–41

Gale, Diane, 18, 246–50
gender bias
    in job definitions, 120, 204–6,
        240–41, 247
    in labour unions, 101, 137, 227–29
    and part-time employment, 220–21
    restructuring and, 166
gender-neutrality, 98–101, 102
gender parity, 58–61
    lack of, 237–38
gender segregation, 81–82, 125–26
    in food retailing, 172–75, 180, 244
    in retail industry, 170–71
gender-wage equity, 170–71, 175,
    239–40, 246
George Weston Limited, 111

men in, 170
at Miracle Food Mart, 176, 182, 217–18
pay equity and, 236–40, 242–43
and scheduling, 177–78
and seniority, 177–78, 194–95, 247–48
women in, 168–69, 256–57
Pateman, Carole, 56
Pathe, Vic, 217
pattern bargaining, 141, 224
pay equity, 77–78, 90
at A&P/Dominion, 206–11
business opposition to, 88–89
in Canada, 61, 64–65, 78–80
challenges over, 64, 253–54
complaints filed about, 18, 68–69
difficulties implementing, 63–69
federal task force on, 14
and full-time employment, 240–41
gender parity in, 58–61
hazards of, 61–66
implementation of, 91–94, 235–42
and labour unions, 14, 67, 137
legislation on, 61, 81, 85–86
litigation over, 13–14, 254–55
at Loblaws, 189–200, 215–16, 269
male workers and, 68, 208
and the market, 64–65, 95–97
at Miracle Food Mart, 200–206, 216–21, 244
in Ontario, 14, 81, 84–90, 236
and part-time employment, 236–40, 242–43
payouts under, 93–94
and race, 61–63
results of, 198–201, 211–13, 242–45
and "sameness" standard, 80–83
strategy for, 255–58
in supermarkets, 15–17, 179–80, 235–42
Pay Equity Act (Ontario) (1988), 16, 85–86
contents of, 90–94
limitations of, 96–97
and male standard, 97–99
and the market, 95–97
systemic discrimination and, 99–101
Pay Equity Coalition of Saskatchewan, 250

pensions, 135, 175
Peterson, David, 84
Phillips, Anne, 40
post-Fordism, 143–46. *See also* economy; Fordism; restructuring
pay equity and, 255–58
service economy in, 167–69
in supermarket industry, 146–59, 235
pregnancy, 27–31
Price Check, 111. *See also* Sobey's
Price Chopper, 111. *See also* Sobey's
Price Costco, 147
profit-hour ratio, 178–84
Progressive Conservative Party (Ontario), 96
Provigo, 111
Public Service Alliance of Canada, 13–14, 66

Quebec, 13

Rae, Bob, 145
Rand formula, 134
Razack, Sherene, 36
Real Canadian Superstores, 156
REAP (Research, Education, Advocacy and People), 226
Reaume, Denise, 30
red-circling, 101
reform. *See also* pay equity
of labour unions, 226–30
of laws, 37–38
repetitive strain injury (RSI), 124–25, 154
restructuring
economic, 69–70, 143–46, 255–58
and gender bias, 166
of the market, 69–70
of supermarkets, 113, 126, 146–59, 166, 224–30, 242–45
Retail Business Holidays Act (Ontario), 145
Retail Clerks International Association (RCIA), 138–39, 142
Retail Clerks International Protective Association (RCIPA), 136, 137–38
Retail Clerks International Union, 132
Retail Clerks National Protective Association (RCNPA), 136, 137

technology
  in food retailing, 114, 116, 117,
    121–25, 141–42, 154–55
  implementation of, 152–53
Todres, Elaine, 86
Toronto Trades and Labour Council, 78
Trades and Labour Congress, 80
trade unions. *See labour* unions
Treaty of Versailles, 79

UFCW Canada, 132–33. *See also*
  United Food and Commercial
    Workers International Union
  and A&P/Dominion Stores, 221,
    222, 224
  and Canada Safeway, 223, 229–30,
    251
  complaints against, 217, 248–49
  and franchises, 151
  gender bias in, 227–29
  and Loblaws, 133, 189–200, 215–16,
    269
  member dissatisfaction in, 226–30
  and Miracle Food Mart, 133, 176,
    200–202, 216–22, 224, 246–50
  in Ontario, 141
  Pay Equity Task Force, 192–93, 202
  reform attempts in, 226
  in Saskatchewan, 155–56
  Women's Advisory Committee, 228
Ultra Mart, 133
unemployment insurance, 135
union dues, 134
unions. *See* business unionism; labour
  unions
United Food and Commercial Workers
  International Union (UFCW), 67,
    132–33, 139, 254. *See also* UFCW
    Canada
United Retail, Wholesale and
  Department Store Employees of
  America. *See* RWDSU
United States
  equality legislation in, 26, 27
  labour legislation in, 26
  labour unions in, 136–38
  pay equity challenges in, 64, 253–54
  women's wages in, 54
United Steelworkers of America, 132,
  148–49

universal product codes (UPC), 121–22,
  153. *See also* scanners
University of Toronto, 13
"Up with Women's Wages" (CUPE), 14
Ursel, Jane, 40

variety stores, 118

wages. *See also* gender segregation; job
    rate
  gender gap in, 170–71, 175, 239–40,
    246
  overtime, 180–81
  reductions in, 155–56
  structures for, 157–59
  in supermarkets, 263
  in United States, 54
Wagner Act, 137
Wal-Mart, 148–49, 253–54
Walsh, John, 120
war. *See* First World War; Second World
    War
warehouse clubs, 146–49
welfare state, 135, 144–45
Westfair Foods Limited, 111, 156
Weston's. See George Weston Limited
White, Julie, 78
Willett Foods Limited, 151
Williams, Patricia, 61
Williams, Wendy, 28–29
Wimmer, Mr. Justice, 251
women. *See also* part-time employment
  as food-store workers, 115–16,
    120–21, 264–67
  job classification and, 96–99, 120,
    167–68, 240–41, 244
  married, 115–16, 137
  neo-liberalism and, 257–58
  in part-time employment, 168–69,
    256–57
  in retail industry, 169–75
  wages of, 54
Women's March Against Poverty, 13
Woolco Stores, 148
Woolworth's, 138
Wrye, William, 84–85

Zehrs, 111
Zeytinoglu, Isik Urla, 166, 169

OTHER TITLES FROM THE
WOMEN'S ISSUES PUBLISHING PROGRAM
AT SUMACH PRESS

Back to the Drawing Board:
African-Canadian Feminisms,
Eds. Njoki Nathani Wane, Katerina Deliovsky
and Erica Lawson

Cracking the Gender Code: Who Rules the Wired World?
Melanie Stewart Millar

Double Jeopardy: Motherwork and the Law,
Lorna A. Turnbull

A Recognition of Being:
Reconstructing Native Womanhood,
Kim Anderson

Redefining Motherhood:
Changing Identities and Patterns,
Eds. Sharon M. Abbey and Andrea O'Reilly

Turbo Chicks: Talking Young Feminisms,
Eds. Allyson Mitchell, Lisa Bryn Rundle and Lara Karaian

Women in the Office:
Transitions in a Global Economy,
Ann Eyerman

Women Working the NAFTA *Food Chain:*
Women, Food and Globalization,
Ed. Deborah Barndt

Women's Bodies/Women's Lives:
Health, Well-Being and Body Image,
Eds. Baukje Miedema, Janet M. Stoppard
and Vivienne Anderson

Women's Changing Landscapes:
Life Stories from Three Generations,
Ed. Greta Hofmann Nemiroff